CANADA'S PLACE NAMES AND HOW TO CHANGE THEM

Canada's Place Names and How to Change Them

Lauren Beck

Concordia University Press
Montreal

Copyright Lauren Beck 2022.
CC BY-NC-ND

Permission granted by the rights holders of logos, coats of arms, and emblems in this book does not in any way constitute an endorsement of the book's contents and arguments.

Every reasonable effort has been made to acquire permission for copyright material used in this publication, and to acknowledge all such indebtedness accurately. Any errors and omissions called to the publisher's attention will be corrected in future printings.

Cover: Sébastien Aubin
Design and typesetting: Garet Markvoort, zijn digital
Proof reading: Saelan Twerdy
Index: Natalie Greenberg

Printed and bound in Canada by Imprimerie Gauvin, Gatineau, Quebec

This book is printed on Forest Stewardship Council certified paper and meets the permanence of paper requirements of ANSI/NISO Z39.48-1992.

Concordia University Press's books are available for free on several digital platforms. Visit www.concordia.ca/press

First English edition published in 2022
10 9 8 7 6 5 4 3 2 1

978-1-988111-39-1 | Paper
978-1-988111-40-7 | E-book

Library and Archives Canada Cataloguing in Publication

Title: Canada's place names and how to change them / Lauren Beck.
Names: Beck, Lauren, author.
Description: Includes bibliographical references and index.
Identifiers: Canadiana (print) 20220399840 | Canadiana (ebook) 20220399867 | ISBN 9781988111391 (softcover) | ISBN 9781988111407 (HTML)
Subjects: LCSH: Names, Geographical—Canada—History. | LCSH: Names, Geographical—Social aspects—Canada. | LCSH: Names, Geographical—Case studies. | LCSH: Emblems—Social aspects—Canada. | LCSH: Canada—History, Local.
Classification: LCC FC36 .B43 2022 | DDC 910/.0140971—dc23

Concordia University Press
1455 de Maisonneuve Blvd. W.
Montreal, Quebec H3G 1M8
CANADA

Concordia University Press gratefully acknowledges the generous support of the Birks Family Foundation, the Estate of Linda Kay, and the Estate of Tanneke De Zwart.

This book has been published with the help of a grant from the Federation for the Humanities and Social Sciences, through the Awards to Scholarly Publications Program, using funds provided by the Social Sciences and Humanities Research Council of Canada.

CONTENTS

Acknowledgements ix

Introduction: Our Place Ecumene 3

1 Knowing in Place 23

2 A Brief History of Settler-Colonial 47
Naming Practices in Canada

3 Gender and Canada's Place Names 77

4 Indigenous Names in a 107
Settler-Colonial Context

5 Marginalized Groups and 141
Canada's Place Names

6 How to Discuss and 171
Change Names

Notes 207

Index 237

vii

ACKNOWLEDGEMENTS

The onset of the COVID-19 pandemic in 2020 is partly responsible for this book's genesis, as my inability to continue research into pan-American naming practices led to the opportunity to focus more intently on my already-completed research for the project. Fellowships for research stays at excellent institutions allowed me to research North American naming practices, particularly a fellowship at the James Ford Bell Library (University of Minnesota) in 2017 and the Kislak Fellowship at the Library of Congress (Washington, DC) in 2018. Other support for this project has come from the Canada History Fund, the Social Sciences and Humanities Research Council, the Canada Research Chair program, and Mount Allison University.

I express gratitude for the conversations I had with my husband Robert LeBlanc, which helped to shape this project, as well as the insightful comments of my editor at Concordia University Press, Ryan Van Huijstee. Many students and former students contributed as research and logistical assistants, including Samantha Ruckenstein and Justin Yoston, and Emily Shaw. I am honoured to see the book adorned by a cover created by Sébastien Aubin, and thankful for the book's beautiful typesetting by Garet Markvoort.

Finally, the basis of this book grew from my article—parts of which have become the foundations for several of the book's chapters—titled "Euro-Settler Place Naming Practices for North America through a Gendered and Racialized Lens" and published in *Terrae Incognitae* 53, no. 1 (2021): 5–25.

CANADA'S PLACE NAMES AND HOW TO CHANGE THEM

INTRODUCTION

Our Place Ecumene

We all come from somewhere. Each somewhere nests into our sense of identity in powerful ways that often evade critical attention. Most of us are powerless to change our place of origin, where our parents or guardians bore or raised us. Switching our somewhere, whether by choice or by force, uniquely complicates the identities and experiences of newcomers who end up in Canada for good. Immigrants, refugees, and permanent residents possess complex place identities. For some, they feel anchored to the place they have left behind while growing new roots of various depths in Canada. Canadians born within the country's borders similarly have a sense of where their ancestors came from before relocating in this settler-colonial milieu.[1] These layers of identity demonstrate how places can both intersect with our sense of who we are and have deep histories of their own that can cross continents. The notion of a "we" or "our place" can be fraught and contested by some people, intersectional and complicated for others, and entirely meaningless to those who instead embrace a more homogenous sense of Canadian identity. Connecting these identities, all our identities, is some attachment to Canada as a place, a political creation, an Indigenous homeland, a point of origin or destination, an object of study, or a former colony that nests into our present place identity.

This book discusses identity—quite likely yours in one way or another—and tries to challenge assumptions about Canada's place names in ways that might be unsettling. I often use the collective noun "we" and the possessive adjective "our" in this book to remind everyone, regardless of their background, that names bear upon everybody, not just the demographic to which they gesture. We, as a Canadian collective, are responsible for the state of our place names. In Canada, where a collective sense of identity has created a sense of "we" and "us," it has become clear that many of us do not necessarily feel a strong connection to Canadian identity. This is understandable given that this book shows how place names in Canada have been primarily an instrument of Euro-settler and masculine identity. For Canadians with different ethnic and racial backgrounds, and for Canadians who are not men, some of these names do not invoke their identities. At the same time, problematizing Canada's place names can alienate others who see themselves more easily reflected in collective Canadian identity. As a result, talking about our place names is difficult because their appearance on the map of Canada reflects a society and its values, which look different in the twenty-first century compared to the eighteenth and nineteenth centuries, when many of our place names were created.

The objective of this book is not necessarily to see names across this country changed or removed or cancelled. By raising awareness about the country's naming practices, this book attempts to underline the ways all of us are represented in one way or another through place nomenclature—women, men, people of colour, Indigenous people, people living with disabilities, newcomers, and so on. It is up to the reader to determine if she or he is satisfied with the status quo or would like to see greater inclusion of the identities reflected in our children, friends, neighbours, and colleagues. Furthermore, in the fullness of time, some of the issues facing Canada's place names will have evolved; racialized and gendered language deemed acceptable today may become problematic fifty years after this book is published. In the balance, this book illuminates the place-naming practices that are responsible for our names. These practices will not change easily in the coming decades without the intervention of Canadians, along with changes to the policies and procedures governing names. This book's readers thus remain custodians of our names in Canada, and as Canadians, they determine whether names stay or go. This

Canada's Place Names and How to Change Them

book's readers, if they so choose, will determine our naming future and its connection to any sense of Canadian collective identity.

Place informs our worldview just as gender, race, and class do. Place shapes what sorts of experiences we have and the people to whom we become exposed. For some of us, place therefore serves as a projection of Canadians' collective identities as a people—the sense of self that we hold in common with each other, based on our shared experiences, values, and worldviews. Shared identities at the intersection of place give rise to a sense of nationalism, of pride to be from a certain city or from having completed one's degree at a particular university. Enthusiasm for projections of that shared place and related identities are exampled by sports teams, logos, and emblems such as a flag or team mascot.

Place knowledge also accumulates through our experiences of the land and its contents. Just as Europeans once believed there to be three continents, people elsewhere understood the world differently. These and other elements constitute our inhabited world, or ecumene, knowledge about which will vary from person to person. In using the term ecumene, I want to recentre our place knowledge from a Eurocentric notion of the inhabited human world that is moored to histories of discovery, exploration, and colonization, and shift to a view which focuses on the presence, movements, knowledge, experiences, and activities of humans. As we will see, many places are named descriptively for their features; names of this nature decentre the human and elevate the non-human world, which at times reflects Indigenous place knowledge and ways of knowing. For our purposes, the Canada–Turtle Island ecumene includes the livingness of all things—plants, animals, geographic features, and human-created objects—and their connections to humanity.

Viewed this way, place knowledge envelops the ecumene, allowing it to be described and characterized, whether in terms of a landscape, an ecosystem, or a built environment such as a city. Place nomenclature comprises a significant element of any ecumene, and like our ecumenes, place names can be layered, contested, and multi- or translingual. Place names can be of the past, present, or future: like everything else in our

Introduction: Our Place Ecumene

ecumene, they live, decay, and perish; they offend, please, and honour; they describe, hide, and destroy; and they empower, disempower, and disrupt. This perspective on place knowledge and the livingness of all things—including place names—is critical to this book's approach to place-name science, particularly as we attempt to value and seek to understand the ecumenes of people whose backgrounds, geographies, or historical moments are different than our own, which is one of this book's overall objectives.

In this sense, there are issues with our place identities from the standpoint of representation and inclusion, and when it comes to the livingness of all things. While laws and policies enacted over the last several decades attempt to ensure that everyone, regardless of their race, gender, class, or disability, can contribute to and benefit from our society without discrimination, the fact is that most of the places from which we originate or to which we migrated were envisioned and created well before these freedoms existed. In Canada, this means that marginalized and less empowered groups have exerted little to no influence on the names and symbols given to our places of origin. Admitting to the harmful legacies of patriarchy and white supremacy on what might be called a Canadian ecumene largely defined by white, Euro-settler men has only emerged in recent times, prompting a contemporary need to deeply question the way we represent our identities. The structures in place to award names and symbols also predate, for the most part, this country's Confederation in 1867, a trend seen elsewhere in the Americas after their colonization by Europeans centuries ago.

This book exposes the ways our identities are mirrored and are not mirrored in Canada's place names to support a critical reflection across this country about our names, whether we want to continue to use them, and what alternatives to the status quo might look like. The topic is an uncomfortable one for some demographics who may feel threatened by the notion of changing a place name with which they identify. For instance, Anglophone settlers whose ancestors relocated from England two centuries ago may see no reason to change a name such as London, Ontario, that reminds them of this linkage to their past, whereas the Anishinaabe, Haudenosaunee, and Wendat people who view this region as their traditional land may disagree. The subject of place names will be uncomfortable for others because in our names they will see the legacies of racism, sexism, and ethnic cleansing. Some of these names continue to harm certain demographics, too. Our identities may also intersect with those of the namers and people who have been commemorated with toponymy, which may result in feeling threatened or guilty when those names are problematized. Recognizing the discomfort occasioned in others while talking about our identities will also help ready ourselves to have a productive discussion about reassessing the identities we have crafted for our places.

To foreground these issues, this introduction will offer an overview of place-name studies and introduce a relatively untouched area of place identity that includes the logos, emblems, coats of arms, and flags, among other material, that serve as visual equivalents to "official" names. These sources for place-name scholarship tend to reinforce the status quo of naming, which is why a careful consideration of how we articulate place identity is urgently needed in Canada.

Place Name Studies, Late 1800s to Today

In the Western academy, place onomastics (place-name studies) began in earnest in the nineteenth century, although they were pre-dated by significant contributions to understanding toponymy in the Americas (a subject explored further in this book's second chapter). Modern place-name studies can be classified into three typical varieties of past scholarly approaches to the subject in Canada (as opposed to other regions of the world, where the topic has been treated differently).[2] First, lexicographical studies attempt to bring an etymological purpose to understanding toponymy by documenting the origin of a name's components and providing this information in a colonial language such as English. These tools are rarely used to learn another language, but rather serve as a reference resource. Many such resources have been published in recent decades and

Introduction: Our Place Ecumene

are usually framed by some geographic or linguistic boundary.[3] Nearly all that I have encountered were prepared by scholars who were not themselves members of the Indigenous communities implicated by the research. Unlike the Jesuit missionaries living among the Wendat in the mid-seventeenth century, few to no toponymists live in the Indigenous communities that they study or have a relationship to the places whose toponymy they explore. To what degree this positionality merits consideration will materialize in due course. Language-based studies often transform into reference resources that may be broadly consulted (and cited) as authoritative sources of knowledge, which means that it is imperative that scholarship of this nature be performed by and with speakers of Indigenous languages, as well as by speakers of the imported languages other than English and French that have considerably shaped Canada's place nomenclature.[4] Making informed connections with non-mainstream languages and their history in this country has the potential to re-orient the objectifying gaze and underlying assumptions exerted by settler scholars and their readerships.

The second variety of earlier place-name studies uses the first variety as a reference work. This scholarship emerges along with the history of cartography and local history as disciplines, particularly throughout the late nineteenth and twentieth centuries. Place names in these interdisciplinary fields of study are looked upon as more than a collective of languages with etymologies. Place names can be viewed as emblems of presence in Canada, particularly European presence, which implies temporal and geographical boundaries once again. Many studies have been published about John Cabot's landing—was it in Cape Breton or in Newfoundland? Understanding this fact, scholars argue, will allow us to trace the man's route, which remains unknown to scholars today. Studies of this second variety tend to be more interested in the movements and experiences of Euro-settler men than those of women, people of colour, and Indigenous peoples. As with language-based studies, the scholar may have no direct connection with the place being studied, the language(s)

Canada's Place Names and How to Change Them

in which its toponym is expressed, or the people for whom the place name serves as a marker of presence. Place names in this context serve as pins on the map that might inform scholars about human movements. In recent decades, new directions for this variety of study have included scrutinizing Indigenous maps and ways of representing place. These directions have demonstrated other values associated with the landscape and its place names, particularly through the concept of "all my relations," and studies devoted to how women and people of colour think about place and identity.[5]

The third, and perhaps most interdisciplinary, variety of place-name studies comes from sources of knowledge expressed when an anthropologist, biologist, historian, or even literary scholar interacts with a particular group of people in Canada. The place stories that emerge from this research comprise more than oral knowledge or field research, and their expression is not necessarily geared toward providing etymologies or a timeline for how the name developed.[6] Often this knowledge is expressed through one or more interviews with the scholar, sometimes in the presence of an interpreter. Toward the end of the twentieth century, some disciplines grew to recognize these stories as legitimate scholarly sources of knowledge for one's research. Place stories entail narratives about a location and can inform us about its character, how it was used or how it supported the people, flora, and fauna that existed there.[7] For Indigenous Canada, place stories can hold significant scientific and historical value in relating the conditions, character, and events of a place's history, including ecological knowledge that can serve as evidence of climate change.

An emerging variety, which I examine in detail throughout this book, is a relatively new form of place-name research called critical toponymy. Critical place-name studies attempt to detach from the anthropological moorings of the early modern period's place onomastics that deeply impacted subsequent nineteenth- and twentieth-century scholarship, the questions scholars have asked, and the way data is collected and interpreted. Critical toponymy as a form of scholarship is more interested in

Introduction: Our Place Ecumene 9

how and why we name, as well as the impacts of naming. It pays scant attention to a name's etymological meaning, and is the methodology undertaken in the present book. Toponyms are undergirded by political agendas, class, and race wars, and in many ways reinforce masculine control over our resources, systems of government, and lives.[8] In the late twentieth century, a critical turn in place-name scholarship occurred in the disciplines of geography, history, and history of cartography. Scholars had grown increasingly concerned with what Robert Fuson assessed was a low geographic and toponymic literacy in the Western world.[9] His observation that Western cultures invest less critical thought into places they are more familiar with than ones they are not as knowledgeable about should unsettle the landscape before us. We are challenged to reconsider the names awarded to our country, provinces and territories, cities, geographic features, as well as commemorative material. The recognition that the Western gaze oscillates more willingly to fall upon the unknown corners of its ecumene, as opposed to the familiar, has pushed scholars to reflect on the quotidian, which includes the building blocks of our identity: gender, race, and class.

Critical toponymy scholarship has been influenced by the development of interdisciplinary fields of study that include Black studies, race studies, women's and gender studies, and Native American and Indigenous studies (NAIS). As Theodore Binnema reminds us in *Common and Contested Ground* (2001), scholars must decentre the period of Indigenous–European interaction so that the Euro-settler is not the powerful actor uniquely endowed with the agency, in this case, to name. Instead, he encourages us to view Indigenous peoples as powerful in their own right and as legitimate agents who impacted their own lives as well as those of the settlers with whom they interacted.[10] The perception that a wave of white men spread out across the continent, moving toward the west, northwest, and southwest from points east and south, contrasts with the reality that much of the American and Canadian mid-west, west, and north remained unpopulated by white people until about two centuries ago. Binnema and others publishing in this period signal a change in how anthropological-ethnohistorical-historical research is designed and executed, and the types of questions and information that would emerge from this recentring of contact and interaction between Indigenous peoples and Euro-settlers. This recentring approach must also occur so that we challenge the white supremacy and heteronormative masculinity inherent in how we think about place, whether in textual or in visual form.

In the last two decades scholars have also been looking at the way names constrain or define how we live and how people perceive us. Toponyms and the policies and laws that govern them can perpetuate social ills and inequalities.[11] Settler-colonial place names, moreover, often differ in qualitative and descriptive ways compared to Indigenous names. Gwilym Lucas Eades argues that the ecological and biological information inscribed in an Indigenous place name provides details about the nature of the landscape and the abundance of its contents, and in ways that can be manifested across cultures. Econyms are names provided by people who know the landscape, how it moves, and which animals feed on which plants; they exhibit a high degree of complexity and inform us about how the land and its climate, as well as the flora and fauna, interacted historically.[12] Eades also observes that names function—much in the same way as a URL—as particles of culture, whose significance cascades into other realms beyond the spatial and geographical.[13]

This overview of place onomastics has confined itself to textual representations of place identity—toponymy—which points to the power that textual culture wields in our society. Throughout this book, references to "official" names are usually paired with the dates of when they were implemented, all of which comprise a record that is imbued with authority. In the case of Canada, this authority lies in the hands of the provinces and territories. Behind this information, which is usually published in gazettes and now in web-based data repositories, are pages of documentation about the place, reasons for the name's implementation or change, and the names of the people bringing this proposal before a

Introduction: Our Place Ecumene   11

provincial or territorial naming authority. Today, expressions of textual toponymy are available online through databases that have supported the research for this book, albeit in a somewhat limited way.

Unlike many countries, Canada has invested some effort into documenting place nomenclature. These efforts have matured into the Geographical Names Board of Canada (GNBC), which offers a place-name database—the Canadian Geographical Names Database.[14] The GNBC has existed since 1897 and parallel institutions can be found in other places in the Western world. The GNBC consists of a committee of individuals helmed by a secretariat, housed within Natural Resources Canada, a federal department, and its output tends to confine itself to classifying and describing places in scientific terms. Its committee and membership extend in some cases to academics, but also to key stakeholders that include other federal departments and Crown corporations, such as the Canada Post Corporation, Fisheries and Oceans Canada, Department of National Defence, Parks Canada, and Indigenous and Northern Affairs Canada. As we will see, the interests represented by these groups might well comprise either a significant hurdle or an advantage when it comes to Canada's naming practices.

Returning to the GNBC database, which is a valuable resource for place-name research in Canada, places can be searched by name or by fragments of a name. Search options include delimiting the search by province or territory, or by the category of geographic feature that is being sought. While the default search parameter is for official names, the user can also select historical or both historical and official names. The search results provide an overview of the name's impact across the country. For example, there are at least seventy places in Canada that contain Windsor in their official or historical name. Each search result leads to a map of the region where the named feature can be found and some basic metadata that includes the location, longitude and latitude, toponymic feature ID, and the decision date when it was embraced or last changed. It provides a link to the place-name authority for the province or territory where the named feature is located. The information for Mount Windsor, Nunavut, for example, appears in the GNBC's database, as well as a link to the territory's Department of Culture and Heritage. Unfortunately, the territory does not provide a database of its own place nomenclature, and no information regarding the naming decision and its history is available in either the territorial or federal websites designated for place-name information. This is the case for most of the country's place nomenclature. While the GNBC receives updates and then uploads certain categories of information to its database, at the moment there is often no contextual information, with some remarkable exceptions.

The provinces and territories have toponym offices housed in a variety of departments with varying sources of support and staffing. As a result, many databases may not have the digital or archival support needed to make them available on the internet or to digitize and provide contextual information. Nonetheless, two provinces have invested considerably in recent years into developing more informative sources for the general public. The first of these is the BC Geographic Names Information System.[15] Users of this database will find the same categories of information offered by the GNBC, however, they will also find, in many cases, contextual information that explains a name's meaning, history, and the dates of when it was implemented or changed—and sometimes even the names of the people involved, as well as the sources for that information. The second of these is the Banque de noms de lieux du Quebéc.[16] This province's database often provides even more detail than that of British Columbia, although fewer of its names are contextualized. It should be noted that both New Brunswick and Nova Scotia offer place-name databases that have limited contextual information. Otherwise, Canadians must consult less reliable resources published online or past scholarship on place names, much of which has limitations, as this overview of place onomastics shows.[17]

Aside from textual expressions of place identity, it is also necessary to address visual descriptions of places. This is a little-treated area with nearly no scholarship bearing on it and makes this parallel, if limited, treatment of place emblems both timely and urgently needed.[18]

Introduction: Our Place Ecumene   13

Place Emblems

Signs or symbols, commemorative statues, and flags and seals collectively perform what a textually expressed place name accomplishes in representing a place, and they should be viewed as visual analogues of textually expressed toponyms. Flags, for example, have recently attracted scholarly attention for how they represent and inform our identities.[19] The visual realm also requires us to consider the complexities of our gaze and our ways of seeing and being seen. We must examine closely how toponyms and their visual counterparts comprise projections of our own identities.[20] Visual representation, particularly when humans are involved, results in the visualization of race and gender in ways that can explicitly exclude certain demographics. People may not see themselves represented in a place name or an emblem that nonetheless informs Canadian collective identity for its citizens and confederates. These issues are compounded by the overwhelmingly colonial symbolism that prevails throughout place emblems, for example, by the flag of Quebec, explored in due course. Scholarship in this vein should be interested in these issues of representation, which arise from the study of visual culture. By connecting these important considerations to visual forms of place name, we will develop a richer analysis of Canada's place nomenclature, one that complicates the quiet ways that it has been racialized and gendered.

This observation makes clear that, despite some interest in understanding the impacts of naming on our identities or how our identities are reflected back at us, textual forms of naming exclude other types of names that are non-verbal in form. In fact, sometimes our visual and material articulation of place disagrees with or sends different messages than a textually expressed toponym. This realization compels us to consider how place is also articulated in visual forms through emblems, as well as through choices in art and architecture designed to embody a place, its history, and its significance. In Canada, many visualizations emerge from their chrysalis nourished by colonization and the country's growing independence from the United Kingdom in the nineteenth century, which was a critical period in the development of place identity throughout the

Americas. It is during this period that most colonies severed or altered their connections to European empires, while colonizers chose to refashion themselves as settlers whose native land was now in the Americas.

Place emblems comprise any visual attempt to represent our location, the origins of Canadians as a people, one's national, territorial, or provincial identity, as well as the history of a place. More than a photograph of a provincial legislature or a national flag, by choosing to view art, symbols, tourist trinkets, and architecture as emblems, we position this material as powerful projections of place and identity. In tandem, we must consider the historical development of these forms of self-representation to understand how expressions such as coats of arms become authorized and manage to gain broad acceptance across the classes, races, and genders. Many emblems also include text, allowing us to simultaneously consider which textual and visual properties seem most representative, and then comprehend the sorts of values associated, historically and today, with this identity-driven form of public programming.

The origins of Canada's place emblems date to the colonial period (c. 1498–1867) in British and French North America, in which many emblematic visualizations represented the Americas as a collective or as regional and national colonial entities. Examples of colonial standards (the flags of Spain and Britain, for instance) associated with European colonies are easily found on early modern maps, such as the ones studied in this book's second chapter.[21] They articulate European presence in an imagined Canadian cartography of the early sixteenth century through the imprint of these countries' standards. Symbols such as these flags comprise some of the earliest place emblems from a settler-colonial perspective and, despite the push for independence over the last two centuries, these colonial visual elements nonetheless persist broadly in our place emblems. For example, every province's coat of arms features some reference to the United Kingdom, whether in the form of the crosses of St. George (England) and St. Andrew (Scotland), or through replications of the United Kingdom's coat of arms, ensign, or flag, and colours associated with that country—white, red, and blue.

Introduction: Our Place Ecumene

We can theorize that colonial symbols do more than remind us of the imperial past that viewed subjugated lands as less developed in the eyes of Europeans. In fact, it seems that settlers in Canada embraced and continue to embrace some of these visual vestiges of colonialism despite the disadvantages that became evident from the extractive relationships between the metropoles in Europe and their colonies, which encouraged Canada to seek independence from British oversight. From a contemporary perspective, European symbols sustain an imagined community connecting settlers today with a romanticized colonial past that looks beyond the evidence and costs of colonial violence.[22]

Emphasizing our connection to Europe also offers a false sense of belonging to a past that existed before Europeans crossed the Atlantic. Many settlers might view the Roman world as a form of historical legacy or heritage that they feel is absent here, yet for which they nonetheless feel some connection. European symbols thus create a sense of belonging and offer roots that settler-colonial peoples struggle to articulate when thinking about their identities. Some settlers may have no explicit ancestral relationship with the United Kingdom or France, while other settlers may view all Anglophone and Francophone peoples as having come from England or France at some stage. In this way, European symbols present in contemporary Canada may have a considerably essentializing function, often in ways that discount the evident presence of Indigenous peoples. European symbols appear in more contexts than just the depiction of the colonial British and French as newcomers. After centuries of immigration, these symbols assert their hereditary pasts by sustaining a connection to the emblems of their motherlands.

Whether on maps, title pages, book illustrations, or on material objects ranging from stationery and flags to jackets and marine vessels, a complex program of heraldry projects this colonial presence in predictable ways. For example, Quebec continues to use France's regal symbol, the fleur-de-lis, on its flag, which was adopted by the province's National Assembly in 1948. First reconnoitered by Jacques Cartier (1492–1557) in 1534–35, and later colonized by the likes of Samuel de Champlain (c. 1567–1635) in the early seventeenth century, by the mid-eighteenth century, New France had fallen to British control. The choices that Quebec took with respect to its flag underline the complexity and powerful messaging that its governments wanted to send to their contemporaries. A fleur-de-lis appears in each quadrant of the flag, separated by a white cross, also inspired by both French regal and Catholic symbolism. The colouring of blue and white (as opposed to France's blue and gold) was meant to honour the Virgin Mary. When this standard was raised on 21 January 1948, the British Union Jack was lowered, and thus this mixture of symbolism comprised a deliberate, even defiant choice on the part of Quebec to reinforce its historical connection with Catholicism and with its first European colonizer, France, while rejecting British symbolism and, more broadly, Anglophone oversight.[23] In light of the province's recent prohibition on religious symbols being worn by public service employees, which unduly impacts women and people of colour, the flag's significance may well shake the province's way of visualizing itself due to the Catholic undertones of its emblems.[24]

A colony's choice to seek independence ushers forward the important moment of determining the would-be-nation's symbolic visualizations as well as its names. Viewing nascent nations as movements informed by principles will allow us to see how they modify European heraldry to suit their own allegorical representations, and how these visualizations become embraced by new nations such as Canada. These principles become emblematized in the country's identity programming in intriguing ways that allow us to see how nations determine which symbols they will use to represent themselves and which colonial symbols will be discarded. For example, the antiquated and much-studied "noble savage" motif embodied in Canadian heraldry transformed following the independence of the United States and Canada into an allegorical figure who represented these countries' core values of liberty, democracy, and equality, among others, but the inclusion of Indigenous bodies also visually differentiated new nations from European metropoles.[25] These choices, like the adoption of the Quebec flag, are deliberate and carefully selected to appeal to a broad

Introduction: Our Place Ecumene   17

public. As will be seen later in this book, the use of neoclassical female figures resembling Lady Liberty furthermore demonstrates the attempt on the part of American and Canadian authorities to develop deep roots between their citizens and the land by maintaining European heraldry.

Place emblems comprise a unique and unstudied field of place identity, one that merits a book in its own right. For our purposes, I will choose emblems at regular intervals within most of the following chapters to explore how critical place-name theory and studies can be brought into dialogue with these visual analogues, because they contain important information and historical references that extend beyond a visual translation of a toponym's meaning. While the focus of this book is primarily textual and verbal forms of representation, I wish to acknowledge the significant ways that visual and material forms of representation also inform our place identities in often silent ways.

In the following chapters, I approach Canada's place-naming history and practices by framing how they intersect with identity. The first chapter explores Indigenous place knowledge, toponymies, and cosmologies cultivated by various groups, spanning the Inuit in Canada's north, the Haudenosaunee in the borderlands of Ontario and Quebec, the Blackfoot in Alberta and Saskatchewan along the border with the United States, the Chipewyan in northern Saskatchewan and Manitoba, and the Tl'azt'en (Dakelhne) in northern British Columbia. Learning about place knowledge and wayfinding practised amongst various Indigenous groups will yield a renewed and deeper sense of how disconnected non-Indigenous Canada's place nomenclature remains from any meaningful relationship with the land. By provoking Canadians to think about Indigenous place knowledge, this book hopes to unsettle any attachment we may have to non-Indigenous place names and knowledge while complicating our own place identities.

The second chapter undertakes an exploration of how settler-colonial place naming took shape in Canada, starting with the dawn of European colonization and sweeping into our present. This discussion will allow

Canada's Place Names and How to Change Them

us to better understand how place-name science developed alongside, and was enabled by, innovations in cartography, navigation, surveying, and book and print making. In tandem, I will offer a general historical and geographical overview of European knowledge about North America and Canada, as the region we today refer to as Canada was subsumed within larger and sometimes contested colonies claimed by Europeans until the nineteenth century.[26] The chapter also traces the development of early place emblems that continue to exert considerable influence in Canada.

After establishing these bases for Indigenous and settler-European place knowledges, three identity-related chapters provide rich insight into the state of place nomenclature today, while focusing on some of the questions with which this book grapples. The first of these questions is, how does gender factor into our place names, both in terms of the namer and his identity, and the context of the toponym itself? Little scholarship has attempted any gendered analysis of Canada's place names, which makes this study urgently needed. Drawing on examples from across our provinces and territories, this chapter shows how systemic barriers may be preventing us from better including women within our place-identity programming.

This book's fourth chapter asks these and other questions about how Indigenous place names and naming practices, as well as the settler-colonial appropriation of Indigenous names, factor into our place names in light of colonization. Performing a qualitative and quantitative assessment of how names originating from Indigenous communities appear (or do not appear) on the map will allow me to point to harmful settler uses of these names. I will also show how Indigenous names and their origins refer to a diverse array of identities and explore how this country's place-naming practices could be better informed by those of Indigenous groups, as well as recommendations about toponyms from international bodies, such as the United Nations and its Declaration of the Rights of Indigenous Peoples (UNDRIP). With the repeated pledges in recent years on the part of Canada's federal government to adopt UNDRIP, this chapter will lay out some

Introduction: Our Place Ecumene 19

pathways for better including and empowering Indigenous place namers, names, and knowledge, while circling back to the richness of Indigenous place knowledge explored in the first chapter.

The fifth chapter performs a similar study of how people from other marginalized groups are represented in our names and emblems. I look to groups who were born in Canada or have settled here, to those who live with disabilities, to racialized and religious minorities, as well as to the class-based factors that may prevent these demographics from contributing to Canada's place nomenclature. Considerations about education and what forces create the authority to name will bring me full circle to ask the reader what they intend to do about our place names.

The final chapter of this book offers the reader tools and case studies that map out how names can be revised and updated. It builds upon the recommendations that conclude each of the preceding chapters to offer solutions that might enable women, Indigenous peoples, and other marginalized groups to both be involved in and reflected by our place names. A description of policies and procedures governing place names, as well as some examples of how name revisions were successful or failed, will provide the reader with a roadmap to facilitate much-needed public discussion and, hopefully, change. By inspiring teachers, community leaders, government workers, and students to get involved in naming, it is hoped that we will one day see all of ourselves in Canada's place nomenclature while fomenting a place ecumene that includes and values everyone.

Note on Orthography, Language, and Capitalization

In Western languages, place names are capitalized, whereas in many Indigenous languages, terms used as or equating to toponyms may not be capitalized. I have respected as much as possible the capitalization practices encountered throughout my research rather than force non-Western names to conform to English- and French-language conventions. When non-English names are given, whether official or unofficial, they are not treated as non-English terminology in that these words will not be italicized; thus, they find themselves in the same peer group as English and French place names. Only non-English words, and not toponyms, will be italicized as per the scholarly conventions otherwise followed in the coming chapters.

Finally, throughout this book, place names with sometimes dated, racist, and sexist meanings and origins will be studied. While the intention is not to reproduce language that may offend readers, it has understandably proven difficult to examine harmful place names without explicating them adequately, particularly for lesser-known slurs whose history and meanings might not be readily apparent. This approach also rests on the notion that harmful names exist across a range of identities and this book, at its core, is attempting to raise awareness about this panorama experienced and shared by all Canadians.

CHAPTER I

Knowing in Place

Today there are more than seventy Indigenous languages spoken in Canada that come from twelve language families. Compare these numbers to the country's two official languages, English and French, which come from two distinct groups (Germanic and Romance, respectively) of one language family (Indo-European). The fact that a place may possess more than one name in more than one language means Indigenous place names far outnumber official settler names. While many of Canada's place names possess Indigenous origins, the vibrancy and complexity of Indigenous place knowledge frequently goes unnoticed among non-Indigenous people.

Knowledge of the landscape and its contents informs Indigenous worldviews and cosmology. How one moves along and interacts with a landscape will impact how she perceives the world around her. Vegetation and other living forms further condition the human viewshed or vista. For instance, dense mature forest inhibits perception by impeding the eye's depth of its observation of the landscape. The land and waterscapes in this country boast an array of vegetation, elements, elevations, in addition to fauna and water-based life. Humans who gain experience of the living landscape thus learn, assimilate, use, and share place knowledge.[1] As the cultural and linguistic anthropologist Keith Basso points out, inter-animation describes the process of meaningfully experiencing a place so that its value and significance resides in and emanates from its observable characteristics.[2]

The intensity of this connection to the land has recently been described by Potawatomi scientist Robin Wall Kimmerer in terms of kinship:

> I too was a stranger at first in this dark dripping forest perched at the edge of the sea, but I sought out an elder, my Sitka Spruce grandmother with a lap wide enough for many grandchildren. I introduced myself, told her my name and why I had come. I offered her tobacco from my pouch and asked if I might visit in her community for a time. She asked me to sit down, and there was a place right between her roots. Her canopy towers above the forest and her swaying foliage is constantly murmuring to her neighbours. I know she'll eventually pass the word and my name on the wind.[3]

These relationships bind the human and other-than-human worlds into a reciprocal state of interanimation whereby one nourishes and cares for the other, making all life personalized, spirited, and corporeal. The individual is entrusted with a responsibility to other life and knows that her livingness is borne by her coexistence with other beings, which results in her protecting and celebrating both the human and non-human worlds.[4]

This worldview also decentres time, as grandmother Sitka Spruce enjoys a centuries-long lifespan during which her roots have deepened and wizened. As Kimmerer recognizes, "The ground where I sit with Sitka Grandmother is deep with needles, soft with centuries of humus; the trees are so old that my lifetime compared to theirs is just a birdsong long."[5] Indigenous place knowledge is therefore difficult to loosen from the environmental science to which it contributes, both in terms of methodology as well as through historical knowledge, and from the cosmology that connects all living things—just as pine needles eventually penetrate and become the soil that nourishes life.

As will be shown, the Indigenous memory storehouse for place knowledge is as impressive as it is vast, particularly among hunters and fishers. Inuvialuit harvester Frank Pokiak, while describing his first caribou hunt in the region of Tuktoyaktuk, Northwest Territories, points to the importance of elders' knowledge about place, in this case for finding migrating caribou, as sometimes the herds disappear and are difficult to locate. Pokiak notes that elders know about seasonal and periodic variations in caribou behaviour: "Mrs. Gruben recalls a time [they had disappeared] before. In the 1930s and 1940s, when she was young, her family stayed in a place called Nalluk, whose name means 'a place where the caribou cross.' She saw the caribou leave that area, and she saw them come back. Now she is seeing them leave once again."[6] His familiarity with Mrs. Gruben's place knowledge, including the meaning of a traditional toponym, demonstrates the sort of intergenerational knowledge transmission that undergirds Indigenous place knowledge as a living body of wisdom and transhistorical experience.

This collective memory storehouse also crosses demographic categories. Women know where and when to harvest traditional medicines and where certain species of shells for making beads can be found. Children learn where and when to hunt deer, how to harvest their hides, how to prepare and to smoke meat. Chiefs represent their people at war and in nation-to-nation meetings that involve journeys. All these activities require knowledge of the living world's patterns, of humans, animals, and plants, and of changes to the landscape throughout the year. But this knowledge is not limited to any particular demographic; it becomes part of the community's knowledge in ways rooted to place.

The following case studies foreground the remainder of this book. More than just place names, many cosmologies and much ecological science weave into beautifully complex place stories that pass from one generation to the next, transforming into vehicles for culture, history, and science. Throughout this chapter, I have attempted to relate place knowledge shared by Indigenous scholars and contributors, as well as Indigenous and non-Indigenous academics with evident connections to the communities under discussion. These case studies—while far from being all-encompassing and in many ways only scratching at the surface of a deeper body of environmental, historical, and cultural practices—seek to

Knowing in Place

illuminate place knowledge among groups from different regions of the land today known as Canada.

Among the Tl'azt'en (Dakelhne)

The Tl'azt'en (Dakelhne, meaning "We Travel by Water")[7] migrated to northern British Columbia from northern Athapaskan regions of present-day Canada ages ago. Their knowledge ecumene crosses time and space. From a young age, children connect their present day with their people's place stories and the histories that weave the past into the present.[8] Athapaskan place names describe the land that they designate, often indicating in tandem the feature's location as well as some notion of direction and distance—for instance, the flow of rivers. This is useful for people traversing through an area and, in effect, reveals Tl'azt'en settlement and lifestyle choices.

Names are often crafted from a human-centred optical perspective. Place names are technologies for wayfinding, with fluvial waterways akin to trails used for trade, travel, and hunting. A traveller understands her orientation through her experience of the place name while being in a place.[9] Rather than prepare paper-based maps, this toponymic and related geographical information is stored in the mind where it can be recalled in a moment's notice for immediate use, comprising a significant, collectively shaped Athapaskan cognitive map containing hundreds of thousands of toponyms used by the map user to make her way.

One localized example demonstrates the complexity of Tl'azt'en names in an area located about 100 kilometers northwest of Prince George, British Columbia. Chuzghun is a lake whose official name is Tezzeron Lake (adopted in 1937), where a legendary Dolly Varden trout is believed to live, and about which stories have been told. The meanings of these Tl'azt'en terms are complex and not easily translated, knitting together a toponymic visualization that embodies cultural knowledge.[10] *Chuz-* describes snowflake and feather, which together share a soft texture and colour palette, and infer another meaning associated with this term—molting waterfowl. Waterfowl typically molt in the late winter and early spring, hence the presence of both feathers and snow, and the appearance of feathers left behind by waterfowl gives the appearance of snow on the water. -*Ghun* is a broad lake located by or along a ridge (in this case, a mountain known as K'azyus whose official name is Pinchi, adopted in 1951—meaning "ghost mountain").[11] It is surrounded by cottonwood trees whose seeds feature cottony hairs that are borne by the wind like summer snowflakes. Chuz tizdli, which has no official name, is the outlet from Chuzghun/Tezzeron Lake to the Kuzkwa River. A person who knows this place name's meaning will understand that *tizdli* indicates where the lake transforms into running water as one travels with the current downstream along with various species of fish, such as kokanee, who leave Chuzghun/Tezzeron Lake to spawn downriver. The term, representing an animated entity, exists as both a verb and as a noun.

People know the region for hunting waterfowl, which nest along the shores of this outlet and whose water does not entirely freeze during the winter, allowing hunters in canoes to follow the current with nets, catching fowl in the outlet. K'uz koh, whose official name is the Kuzkwa River (adopted in 1937), leads out of Chuzghun/Tezzeron Lake and the name seems to come from the village of K'uzche, located at the river's terminus with the Tache River. The meaning of K'uz koh is "downing down," in a sense that implies both motion and direction. Fishers could follow the current downstream and catch sockeye salmon in the fish's journey upstream toward Chuzghun/Tezzeron Lake, and the village's location signals the spawning bed for migrating salmon. Waterfowl nest along its shores, drawing in a second meaning for the place name, from their downing (feathers).

Ecological knowledge about plant life whose presence dovetails with that of the salmon migration also fleshes out this place name's meaning. Tl'azt'en community member Paul Williams relates that "They say the more berry flowers you see in the bush then you know more salmon is going to come. But if you don't see very many white flowers in the bush, like blackberries always got real lots of nice white flowers, you just get a

Knowing in Place   27

few here and there, that means the salmon is not going to be that great of a run."[12] Connecting white flowers with the presence of salmon draws in another soft, white element that further characterizes this place during hunting season.

Each of these elements associated with the place name knit together a pattern that the viewer understands when they find themselves in this place. As evident from their names, the mountain, river, and village all share a relationship and the mountain is imbued with spiritual significance, with some areas of the mountain off-limits or considered taboo, and other areas treated with reverence. Mountains are often thought of as incarnated ancestors or as entities from well-known legends, which makes knowing the place name and experiencing its meaning also a journey of understanding one's culture and history, as well as those of her ancestors. From the perspective of one standing on the mountain looking down toward Chuzghun/Tezzeron Lake and the Kuzkwa River, the region looks flooded with water, hence the meaning of the unofficial name, K'azyus, "water rising." Such is the abundance of water in the spring as snow melts off the mountain that it becomes a spectacle of cascading waterfalls.[13]

These interconnected place names provide cues that a traveller looks for in order to understand where she is and what may be found there; they provide knowledge about the sort of hunting and resources offered by the place and at which time of year. These place names require experiencing the land in order to flesh out their meanings. Without these experiences, the references to feathers, down, snowflakes, and flowers will have little meaning beyond explications such as the one attempted here.

Among the Chipewyan

Chipewyan (Dene) travellers in today's Northwest Territories and the northern parts of Saskatchewan and Manitoba, traditionally have walked great distances overland, sometimes without the aid of waterways and canoes, and used unmodified natural features as markers. Eskers are long fields of glacially formed ridges made of gravel and sand. In northern Saskatchewan eskers extend for tens, and sometimes hundreds, of kilometers unbroken. Together, they form a series that treks northeast-southwest for nearly 500 kilometers over an area that also reflects the winter migration path of barren-ground caribou in the region.

The Kesyhehot'ine (Poplar House People), Ethen-eldili-dene (Caribou Eaters), and Hoteladi (Northern People) have migrated from the north to the south to hunt caribou each year for months at a time in large groups that could number dozens of families. These hunting grounds comprise a region of 97,000 square kilometers and are connected by a migration route that extends from the forested tundra of the north to northeast of Lake Athabasca, connecting to the full boreal forest that lines the Churchill River, and extending east toward Hudson Bay, abutting traditional Cree territory.[14]

In their transit along this hunting corridor comprised of lakes, rivers, muskeg, and conifer forest, no permanent settlements are encountered even today, yet the residual signs of past human presence are numerous. As Robert Jarvenpa relates of his 1971–72 hunting journey from Cree Lake to Patuanak, both in Saskatchewan, with some Chipewyan friends, "along the route we continually encountered the residues of former encampments, villages, and trading outposts, all testimony to a previous era of human occupation."[15] Some vestiges of past hunting trips transform into pinpoints on the map of individual biographies, as hunters and families habitually traverse this route and regularly encounter their pasts along the way. One of Jarvenpa's companions, Norbert George, pointed to the place where he was born fifty years earlier. "Standing in the remains of one of his former homes, he was flooded with recollections of his father's winter hunts, his mother making caribou hide, their team of whining sled dogs tethered behind the cabin, and boyhood games on the lake ice."[16] His recollection underlines the living world's relationships with unoccupied places where the presence and activities of caribou, ancestors, relatives, created objects, and experiences of all sorts become woven together into a

Knowing in Place 29

tightly knit tapestry that reveals how complex the built landscape is when it is anchored to the social history of all living things, both human and non-human.

Because the Chipewyan historically distrusted and feared the Cree, who they believed possessed superior military, medicinal, and magical knowledge, they developed excellent surveillance practices. Along the crests of ideally situated ridges and elevations, the Chipewyan established lookouts (*na'ini*) or "waiting places" (*k'a*) that would enable them to detect both Cree and caribou presence.[17] These protected locations resemble boulders or outcroppings of rock from below, which would be a marker sought out by other travellers as they made their way along this route. Runners trained to return expeditiously to nearby camps spent hours in this occupation, alertly reconnoitering the landscape for their target. As will be seen with the Blackfoot and Inuit, elevation and means of discerning the human from non-human worlds are fundamental elements for both experiencing and understanding the landscape.

Like eskers, lakes and rivers also comprise pre-existing, unmodified markers upon the landscape that enable wayfinding, particularly over larger distances, for both caribou and humans. Traditional knowledge informs a hunter that caribou prefer flat land, hills, or even eskers, but not rocky, rough, or mucky terrain; she looks for the choice foods preferred by caribou and knows that the herd avoids areas destroyed by fire. Layered together, these facts funnel the caribou in a way that draws a hunter behind them in pursuit.[18] Place names such as edagha describe the hunter's experience as she pursues the herd, meaning "a narrow place or area in the lake where the caribous are accustomed to cross and where people sit a little way above (referring to the current) to wait for them."[19]

Place names that indicate how large a feature is also point to its cultural importance. For instance, descok ("big river") today is officially called the Churchill River (ca. 1686). Its unofficial name communicates both its size and its critical role as a resource for the Chipewyan and the Cree, who have lived along its 1,600-kilometer extension eastward to Hudson Bay.

Events also coloured these names. Ena'ikwazeni'I (meaning "enemy stole the little boy rapids") today is officially known as the Haultain River (1931) in Saskatchewan. Ikwaze, a Chipewyan boy whose name means "warble fly," was abducted there by a Cree man (*ena*), who took him upriver never to be seen again by his people. Place names thus describe experiences that themselves transform into lessons for subsequent generations, as the last place name demonstrates Chipewyan concern about Cree violence against their own people and warns of the importance of minding young children when enemies might be nearby.[20]

The diffusion of toponymy as cultural knowledge might first have begun in smaller groups, as the Chipewyan travelled and wintered as groups of families. Movement between these small Chipewyan communities several times in one's life enabled place stories to spread and become more than local knowledge, benefitting people who had never navigated along ena'ikwazeni'I.[21] These exchanges ensured that even smaller rivers, lakes, forests, and also localized knowledge of their histories, would be archived and utilized throughout Kesyhehot'ine territory.

Among the Blackfoot

Like many Indigenous people, the Blackfoot people's relationship with the landscape is one based on reciprocity, rather than on hierarchy, through the notion that people's relationships with animals, rocks, nature, and geographic features coalesce within a cosmology based on the connectedness of all forms of life, converting the non-human world into relatives. As with people, the land and its resources deserve respect; these relationships are founded on ethical conduct that involves obligations and reciprocity to nurture renewal and the continuing health of everybody, whether human or non-human, and to ensure that the cosmos remains balanced. An annual hunting migration, then, should not be viewed as an economic or subsistence necessity for a people's immediate survival. Rather, the Blackfoot's migration for bison is a journey that is made for

Knowing in Place   31

generations. Steeped in history, this pilgrimage involves rituals performed along the route as the Blackfoot hunters and their relations revisit the same places each year, telling stories about those places, which creates an intergenerational knowledge of the landscape transmitted through stories that can be viewed as sacred archeological sites in both the physical and narratological realms.[22]

Sweetgrass Hills, located in northern Montana near the Alberta provincial boundary, is one of these sacred places frequented for time immemorial by the Blackfoot during their odyssey to hunt bison. Blackfoot traditional territory encompasses a large region of the present-day northwestern United States and southwestern Canada. These hills are the site of several paths crossing the region, each of which have associated narratives that illuminate their traditional place names, making the names themselves sacred. The hills as a landmark, or iniskim ("buffalo calling stones"), were created by the Old Man (Napi) who, like one Blackfoot generation to the next, left stories, songs, sacred objects, and rituals to commemorate these places. As one picture book explains to Blackfoot youth, while creating the world, "Old Man Napi carried rocks with him. He made the Sweet Grass Hills," and when he finished laying his buffalo calling stones, "Old Man Napi turned toward the West, disappearing in the Rocky Mountains."[23]

The journey to hunt bison parallels Napi's passage of creation and transforms into a means of recording the Blackfoot's history while practising—and emulating for the next generation—their responsibilities to the living world and the underlying ethics that would ensure balance. In tandem, the journey itself comprises a process of creation through the quotidian actions taken by humans to shape or create the landscape that they occupy. Paths maintained by generations of travellers imprint Blackfoot presence and history on a place. Sweetgrass Hills serves as a mnemonic device in this larger story of creation and the cosmological balance of all living things, which compels the narrative to be told.[24]

Sweetgrass Hills consists of three buttes, which possess official names registered in the United States as the East Butte, Middle Butte, and West

Butte. Each rises about 2,000 meters above sea level, and about 1,000 meters above the prairie from which they extrude vertically toward the sky, making them visible from southern Alberta. The Blackfoot call them cut to yis, meaning "sweet pine," which is noticeable toward the buttes' respective summits.[25] As Sweetgrass Hills demonstrates, the traditional territory of the Blackfoot cannot be contained by recently conjured borders cleaving the United States away from Canada. Blackfoot territory stretches from Edmonton in its northern reaches, westward toward the Rocky Mountains, and eastward toward Regina, Saskatchewan, before plunging southward into Montana and the northwest corner of North Dakota. Annual sojourns borne along wizened trails have brought the Blackfoot to Sweetgrass Hills from hundreds of kilometers away.

The Blackfoot are not the only people who have traditionally frequented this site. To protect themselves during battles against hostile groups they encountered along their route, the Blackfoot have dug rock-rimmed war lodge pits, a form of circular depression that allowed scouts and warriors to discretely perform their duties with the protection of the land from enemy arrows. One location's physical remnants link to a battle that occurred in 1866 when the Blackfoot dug pits in order to hold off an encroaching enemy who had killed their great chief. The battle that ensued is known as "Retreat Up the Hill." The Gros Ventres, supported by the Crows and Crees, converged on Sweetgrass Hills where they knew the Blackfoot camped in the winter. They killed their chief, Many Horses, and his wife while they collected buffalo skins near East Butte, unaware of the considerable population of the Blackfoot in their midst.[26]

The anthropologist Gerald A. Oetelaar relates what happened next: "In the meantime, a party of Blackfoot warriors visiting The Writings (today known as Writing-on-Stone) read the signs of the impending attack and rode back to warn the occupants of all the lodges."[27] These petroglyphs, according to Patricia Steepee Barry, honour and celebrate the Blackfoot's spiritual entities in the form a shrine, and remain a locus of Blackfoot pilgrimage. They traditionally leave gifts such as cloth,

Knowing in Place   33

tobacco, and moccasins for the ghosts commemorated on the shrines: "One could learn from the images about enemy tribes in the neighbourhood, the location of bison herds and lost horses, or hear one's name pronounced among tomorrow's dead."[28] The Blackfoot decided to go on the offensive and, after locating the Gros Ventres, the latter attempted to flee the Blackfoot by running up the West Butte, hence the battle's name.

The presence of pits along Sweetgrass Hills serve as mnemonic devices that prompt this story, as do cairns and other commemorative additions to the landscape left over the centuries, and which are related and passed intergenerationally while travelling. An example of transforming the landscape for sacred purposes can be found in the planting patterns of cottonwood groves, which the Blackfoot used to protect deceased members of their community whose bodies rested on platforms suspended in trees.[29] Stories about the deceased thus became anchored to a place, which itself became transformed by the presence of that person's body, demonstrating the nature of reciprocity that undergirds the relationship of the human and non-human worlds.

Sweetgrass Hills also attracts annual ritual gatherings, serving as the Sun Dance grounds. Household leaders traditionally gather, along with their families, for this celebration and tell stories, including many about this landmark, being the place where Katoyis (Blood Clot) sleeps. The related story is then rehearsed: a son-in-law refuses to share buffalo meat that he asked his father-in-law to prepare with his in-laws. Only one of the couple's three daughters, all of whom are married to the younger man, provides her parents with food. One day the old man harvests a clot of blood from a dying female bison and from it they make a broth. While preparing the broth, they hear an infant crying from within the vessel, so they retrieve Blood Clot from the container. After four days, Blood Clot asks them to tie him to some tipi poles, from whence he would transform into an adult, and he then kills the son-in-law and the two daughters who refused to give their parents sustenance, before going on to help others like them who had been mistreated.[30]

Several related stories about the succeeding activities of Blood Clot also circulate, and together they teach ethics and model behaviour valued among the Blackfoot that would be useful during the bison hunt at Sweetgrass Hills. Men are reminded to share the choice cuts with their parents-in-law, which reinforces ties between family lines. Furthermore, infrastructure for vision quests initiated during the Sun Dance usually faces landmarks, the majority of them oriented toward Sweetgrass Hills. U-shaped stone structures, where men spend four days during the Sun Dance, are an important component of the Blackfoot's cosmology and also a form of built environment that remains visible for generations. Some supplicants, during their vision quest, document what they learn on their tipi's lining, which is taken with them when they move on, or on the walls of their rock enclosure as petroglyphs, and in that form withstand time, making them part of Blackfoot sacred geography.[31]

Elders and Blackfoot warriors also study petroglyphs and interpret them as messages sent by spirits in their pilgrimage down the Milk River to consult The Writings at Sweetgrass Hills. These images offer ceremonial and biographical information in the form of myths, personal experiences, historical events such as battles, prophecies, and so on. When read against the landscape, they offer directions that inform decision making.[32] For example, Oetelaar relates that "Sometime before the battle of Retreat Up the Hill, the old men of the camp consulted The Writings and advised Many Horses [their chief] to travel down to the Missouri River with a party and to make a big peace dance with the Gros Ventres. Many Horses refused to heed the advice of the old men and paid for his transgression with his life."[33] To the Blackfoot, Many Horses lost his life because he failed to heed the Great Spirit's message inscribed on the cliff facing the Milk River. Reading the landscape and telling the story of what happened there and how it came to exist invests its knowledge into a living archive of traditional knowledge. As the story of Many Horses demonstrates, renewing his story and its implication while moving "across the landscape becomes a journey through history."[34]

Knowing in Place

Among the Inuit

Many Indigenous place names can be read visually, often as seen while one experiences the landscape and narrates its story. This relationship between names, land, and the human experience of it echoes cosmovisions elsewhere in Canada. Such place names serve as economizing markers of space so that the person who utters the name need not relate its story in casual conversation or while giving directions because other members of the community already know it and can wayfind accordingly.[35]

By some accounts, the Inuit came to the region known as western Canada about 1,500 years ago and began to spread across the Arctic, continuing eastward for the next millennium.[36] They travel widely for all sorts of purposes beyond colonization, particularly in the eastern Arctic where plants are scarce and there are greater seasonal changes in the weather and ice, all of which impact the availability of fauna.[37] Inuit geographical knowledge is vast, requiring by some estimates that they recall information about landmarks within an area as large as 300,000 square kilometers. This knowledge is ordered according to the wind felt by a traveller or the cardinal directions shown in the form of a wind compass. Other spatial reference points include shores and the flow of rivers, and the vista described by the traveller usually encompasses all landmarks viewed from her position along the horizon. Wayfinding in this form is a textured, sensorial experience, and narratives associated with places describe how one will perceive her location.[38]

While roads or trails serve in other regions of Canada as enduring markers of a traveller's path, in the north established and traditional routes exist but their physical presence is often obscured by snow and ice. Their presence depends on the season, much as encampments populated by tents vanish when their inhabitants migrate to another location or when snow houses eventually melt. Centuries, and even millennia, of Inuit impact on the north is slight, leaving little to no trace on inhabited landscapes. This makes any indication of past human activity a significant named feature, and visual markers in the form of cairns such as *inuksugait* (inuksuk) comprise prominent marks on the horizon that a traveller will

36   *Canada's Place Names and How to Change Them*

perceive and know are an indication of a trail's change of course, a place offering good hunting or fishing, or a place with a dwelling history.

Inuksuk normally are constructed using two or three boulders stacked in such a way that they would be noticeable from the distance with sky backgrounding them, being raised high enough off the ground to not be obscured by snow. Due to their prominence, they attract perching birds whose guano supports the lichens that give these beacons a crown of green, orange, black, or white that might catch a traveller's eye.[39] Shorter-term markings include blood on the snow where an animal was butchered, or carcasses and broken sleds that also disrupt the landscape and comprise human-created visual aids indicating not just space but also time—blood on the snow will relate to seasonal hunting patterns and the prey sought by hunters.[40]

Topographic markers guide a traveller, and these are known by the entire community, such that wayfinding relies on them. Herve Paniaq, an elder of Igloolik, describes his journey from Igloolik to Imiq (Arctic Bay) in 2005:

> When you reach the sea, you'll notice that there is land ahead of you. This land is called Quurnguq. Once you have reached Quurnguq you'll see [from the snowdrifts] that Kanangnaq [the Northeast wind] now prevails. Snowdrifts [uqalurait] formed by the Uangnaq [Northwest wind] are absent, and you find that the snow here is somewhat smoother. You should now keep close to the land, which will be on your right hand. The further you go from land the rougher the snow conditions will be; so therefore, try to stay close to the land in order to be on smooth snow. You will then reach a very obvious point of land that veers to the right. From this point you cross over some land to Imiq.[41]

Elder Paniaq's directions, written in the present tense, reinforce the understanding that a community has experienced this travel and that

Knowing in Place   37

the places he describes have a human-experienced history. The narrator inhabits a traveller, relating the trail's features so that a traveller can find her way, unfolding the land's character in the chronological order in which a traveller can expect to experience it, as if a map upon the landscape. These narratives also make remembering and recalling place names and information about places easier.

Many Inuit names link space and time to the Inuit experience of both. Meaning "little island," Qikiqtarjuaq, located on Igloolik Island is not a small island but rather a peninsula. Its meaning recalls the legend of Uinigumasuittuq (she who never wants to get married), a woman whose father—frustrated that she would not take a mate—told her to couple with a dog and then to remove themselves to an island. As Inuk author and translator Alexina Kublu relates the story, the woman's mate provided food for her and the pups she bore, but when her husband died, the woman's father assumed this responsibility, although only for a little while. Unable to feed her children, the woman sent them off in groups to fend for themselves. The first group went toward the south and only possessed bows and arrows; they became First Nations. The second group went away in an old boot with promises from their mother that they would return in a boat (becoming white people, *qallunaat*). And, the third group stayed nearby but became the unseen people who show up as caribou (a normally invisible spirit or trickster called *ijirait*).[42] Uinigumasuittuq is eventually tricked into coupling with a fulmar masquerading as a handsome man. They remove to a different island and bear children, but she grew unhappy as her new partner's true self emerges, and her father secretly came to take her away. The fulmar angrily stirred up the wind to cause his boat to capsize, and the father tried to give his daughter a quick death by throwing her in the water. When she attempted to get back in the boat, he chopped off her fingers and they became the sea mammals. She then sank in the ocean and became the dweller of the sea floor. In his grief, the father soon joins her, and her first husband was already there, being the place where people who have not lived well end up.[43] The Inuit believe the woman's island is Puqtuniq, and with the intercession of time, sea levels at Puqtuniq have receded so that it sits as a hill upon the island of Qikiqtarjuaq in Baffin Bay, Nunavut. Today waters have receded further, turning the island into a peninsula connected to the island of Igloolik ("there is a house here"), while delineating traditional Inuit spaces (the little island situated upon another island) that go back for time immemorial, and whose transformation (into a peninsula) demonstrates how names remain the same even though the landscape has changed.[44]

Inuit onomastics and name assignment are multivalent in that names could accumulate and change over time, or even become fossilized in ways that link a person to an event, a particular place, or a social context, becoming "like archeological deposits that were stratified in time."[45] One of the most complex naming systems in the world, Inuit *sauniq* practices commemorate people in ways conceived as a form of reincarnation. In some cases, non-Inuit names entered into Inuit onomastics as a means of making themselves more familiar to foreign traders and diplomats by donning a name that they would recognize and feel some connection to, being itself a form of intercultural communication echoed by wearing objects from the other's culture.[46]

Among the Haudenosaunee

The Rotinonshonni (People of the Longhouse) are known by many names. As a confederacy, they may be called the Haudenosaunee, Iroquois, Five Nations, and Six Nations. Or, they may be known by their constituent nation names: Mohawk (Kenienké:haka, the Flint People and Keepers of the Eastern Door); Oneida (Oneota:haka, People of the Standing Stone), Onondaga (Onontaka:haka, People of the Hills and Keepers of the Fire); Cayuga (Kaokwa:haka, Mucky Lake People); Seneca (Sonontowa:haka, People of the Great Mountain and Keepers of the Western Door); and Tuscarora (Skaroo´ren, Hemp People), who joined the Confederacy in 1714.[47]

Their traditional territory is vast and has long been described through architectural characteristics: the sky is the roof, below which Mother

Knowing in Place   39

Earth is the floor, while the setting and rising sun are doorways to their territory.[48] This cosmology is then projected onto the earth and, in several ways, defines the Haudenosaunee as a confederacy of nations. The Peacemaker, during his attempt to quell warring between Haudenosaunee nations, gathered the nations together and promised in Onondaga that there would be a "longhouse that they will live in [that] will represent an even greater dwelling that will include all the nations who accept the message of peace; it shall run from the nations living in the east to the nations living in the west. It will be shaped like the Sky World with an ever-growing tree in the middle. I will place something on top of the tree to watch over it as was done by Ancient Uncle, the thunder, in the Sky World before the creation of this world."[49] The Peacemaker compels those who join in the peace to build the Longhouse of One Family, situating it on an east-west axis that links it forever with the Haudenosaunee's cosmological origins, whose rafters are the council members that represent their respective peoples.

The Haudenosaunee conceive of their territory as a Longhouse, making the Seneca the guardian of its western door and the Mohawk of the eastern door. The central knowledge keepers, and keepers of the Confederacy's fire, as well as the nation located in the Confederacy's centre, is the Onondaga Nation. The orientation of east to west allows us to visualize the position of the Longhouse relative to the cardinal directions. Longhouses always contain fires, sometimes several of them, so the positioning of the Onondaga in the centre of the alliance also complicates the Longhouse as metaphor for a people, their existence on the earth, and their knowledge ways.[50] The Longhouse's protective walls and roof also offer a metaphor for the Confederacy itself and hints at its collective values, which together inspired American politicians to experiment with a democratic system of governance based on the Haudenosaunee model.

Wampum belts and other representations comprise a significant emblem of geographical knowledge that is steeped in symbolism. Traditionally, women undertake the craft of making beads by selecting and machining quahog shells so that they are smooth and round. They are then

40   *Canada's Place Names and How to Change Them*

drilled through the centre so that they may be incorporated into adornments and, when the wampum were used, into words read aloud primarily by men.[51] Wampum descends from *wampumpeag*, whose origin traces to the Algonquian language family in the area of New England, among the Lenape (Delaware) people, and is the word that describes the white and purple beads made of this variety of shell.[52] Viewed another way, Indigenous women create the shell-based analogues of the plates or blocks used in the printing press. Their contributions enable the historical record to exist in the form of a wampum, which will also become a form of map, making Lenape women the equivalent of historians and cartographers.[53] Their beads crisscross North America, as do wampum-making practices, which stretch across the Algonquian and Haudenosaunee worlds, covering much of Canada, from the Prairies to the Maritimes.

Wampum strings signal authority and authenticate one's identity. According to Tehanetorens (Ray Fadden), "No Iroquois chief would listen to a messenger or pay attention to a report until he received official information through a runner who carried the proper wampum string or belt."[54] Similarly, treaties require wampum as a means of endowing the agreement with authority and inviolability, and they function as a seal of friendship. The Onondaga Nation was selected to be the Keepers of the Wampum, and each year the Wampum Keeper from the nation shared every wampum and their meanings with the Haudenosaunee, passing the belt or string along to each person in attendance. The Six Nations, whose collective wampum is six strings of purple wampum, each have their own wampum, which represent their nation in all business and at council meetings.

The symbol of the Five Nations is known as the Hiawatha Belt (Figure 1.1) and functions as a projection of their traditional territory. Its wampum is dark and consists of thirty-eight rows; in the centre is a tree or white heart, and on either side are two rectangles, all joined by a horizontal line. When viewed with the north oriented toward the top, the rightmost square represents the Mohawk and their territory; the one next to it represents the Oneida and their territory. At the centre, the

Knowing in Place 41

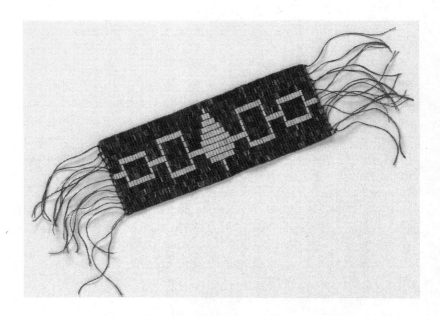

Figure 1.1 A replica of the Hiawatha Belt of the Haudenosaunee, c. 1990–2010. Washington, DC, National Museum of the American Indian, Smithsonian Institution (26/9056). Photo by NMAI Photo Services.

tree or white heart represents the Onondaga and their territory, being the heart of the Iroquois and the place of the Great Peace (Onondaga confederate chiefs), where the Council Fire burns for the Five Nations. The next square on the left represents the Cayuga and their territory, and the fourth represents the Seneca and their territory. Two lines extend from the two exterior squares, signifying that others are welcome to travel the Path of Peace and take shelter within the Iroquois Confederacy.[55] The wampum thus depicts the west (Seneca)–east (Mohawk) axis of the Confederacy, whereas the line connecting each represents both a figurative and physical passage meant to be free of conflict, stretching from the Genesee River in the west to the Schoharie River in the east.[56] This latter signification can be found throughout wampum-belt culture where lines that join symbols of nations signify friendly relations.

Belts can also incite movement because they convey messages that compel or instruct an individual to undertake a journey (such as for the purpose of war), or to serve as a means of recalling individuals who had chosen to live outside of the Five Nations. For this latter purpose, a black Emigration Belt is presented by a messenger to the person living outside of their community as a way of signalling the Council's order that they return to their original home.[57] These visual expressions of place are a means of tying people to the pinpoints of their lives from biographical, cosmological, and geographical perspectives, and echo the multivalent, layered, and complex place stories encountered elsewhere in Indigenous Canada.

Knowing in Place

The case studies contained in this chapter only glimpse at the names and place knowledge of a selected few groups of Indigenous and Inuit people. From them, we see a deliberate, thoughtful, and patterned relationship cultivated between the human and non-human worlds. Returning to the image of a forest that impedes one's perception of a landscape, that mature forest has been maintained and perhaps even cultivated by the humans who live in its midst. Certain trees may be blazed to aid travellers as they traverse the forest, serving as markers on the mental map of the landscape, all of which comprises in and of itself a form of built environment of living things. The technologization of plant life is also evident in how Indigenous groups make use of the living world. For example, in western Canada Sitka spruce is useful for making bows, arrows, ladders, containers, and shelters, whereas white spruce traditionally transforms into canoe frames and paddles, as well as hide stretchers and snowshoe frames.[58] Place knowledge in this way extends to an understanding of how the place is occupied by the non-human world and joins the human experience of that place. In tandem, it decentres the human along the landscape while emphasizing her individualism.

Viewing the landscape as a built environment in which humans live symbiotically offers an environmental philosophy to balance the global climate crisis and its human causes. Indigenous peoples have been and continue to be the human architects of that symbiosis: they remain partners in a relationship that endows non-human beings with the agency to lead us, know more than us, and to address imbalance when it occurs. Philosophy arising from the landscape as a built environment also draws upon spiritual beliefs that describe the creation of the world, its flora, its fauna, and eventually its people, in the hands of a spiritual entity or the spirit world. When divine beings entrust humans to become one of many varieties of custodians on earth, this trust inscribes environmental architecture and protection within worldviews and the very purpose of life.

Finally, this brief study of Indigenous place knowledge will make apparent the superficiality of most non-Indigenous names studied throughout the balance of this book. Indigenous place knowledge is multivocal in that a plurality of voices share, teach, and repeat this knowledge as a means of transmitting it while also authenticating it and its sources. As we embark on this journey through Canada's place nomenclature, the reader must ask himself how he knows a place name, its meaning, and the story of its creation or commemoration. How does the name inform him about the contents of a place and its history? Might the name offer a cautionary tale that could save him from certain harm? And how did this knowledge come to him? Is it through books, or has he or his ancestors experienced places and preserved this information for time immemorial, being a living, multivocal, and intergenerational archive possessed and used by all?

Throughout the remainder of this book, I challenge the reader to know in place—a process of being in a place while experiencing and relating to it—while considering whether place knowledge obtained and shared in this fashion is reflected in the names that adorn Canada's settlements, geographical features, and even streets. What other names and stories might be anchored to a place? How might they enrich being in and knowing that place? What sorts of names and stories might threaten to do quite the opposite by obstructing or perhaps contributing nothing to our place knowledge? By knowing in place, we can also hear the multivocality of place knowledge. This may allow us to think more broadly about how places are named and to become open to complicating our place names by allowing them to exist in more than one state as living, transhistorical emblems of our existence.

CHAPTER 2

A Brief History of Settler-Colonial Naming Practices in Canada

In her poem "The Reincarnation of Captain Cook," Margaret Atwood describes how most of us learn about and experience toponymy. Were Captain Cook to come to Canada today and exercise his profession as an explorer, his acquisitive eye would be displeased by the existence of so many place names signalling that the land had already been explored and claimed: "Earlier than I could learn / the maps had been coloured in. / When I pleaded, the kings told me / nothing was left to explore."[1] Her Captain Cook departs anyway in search of a place with no names, which foreshadows the problematic legacy of Cook in places such as Canada, particularly for Indigenous peoples. Frustrated by his lack of success, the poem continues:

> Burn down
> the atlases, I shout
> to the park benches; and go
>
> past the cenotaph
> waving a blank banner
> across the street, beyond
> the corner
>
> into a new land cleaned of geographies.

The explorer is unwilling to accept that most places in the world are not nameless. His invocation to do away with the instruments that officiate naming emphasizes his belief that geographies can be erased to make space for his names.

My intention in this chapter is to provide an overview of how place naming developed with respect to North America, in general, and Canada, in particular. By focusing on key figures and contributions to place naming, I will establish a useful historiographical and demographic frame for Canada's non-Indigenous place nomenclature in the broader context of the European colonization of the Americas. Doing so will underline the fact that Canada's place names did not develop on their own, but that they emerge from the naming practices, and even from the bestowers of names, found in other regions of the Americas. While examining some of the most studied primary sources used to understand a place name's meaning and development in the Americas, I will raise some fundamental questions about naming, power, and authority that the remainder of this book will address. At the same time, I expose the historical harms occasioned by place names such as Canada and North America in that these names deny the existence of Indigenous names such as Turtle Island, here rendered in the colonial language of English. The intention with this overview of settler-colonial naming practices is to scratch at Captain Cook's erasure of the landscape and ask: what is it about the Western condition that makes a name's bestower feel empowered to assign toponyms and to layer them upon existing ones?

The Earliest Naming and Discovery Practices

The earliest account of European place naming in the Americas was transformed into a long-unquestioned model followed by subsequent British and French settler-colonizers in Canada. Christopher Columbus (c. 1451–1506) affirms in the diary documenting his first journey to the Americas in 1492–93 that the practice of recording names, whether Indigenous or the ones he and his crew developed for the Caribbean islands, intertwined with the need to represent accurately what comprised for him a new geography. The concept of a "new geography" implies a special form of power, one which resembles that of a parent bestowing a name upon her child. This paternalism emphasizes a Western gaze activated by Europeans as they sought to comprehend what they quickly termed a "New World."[2] In the Western world, naming implicitly creates a paternalistic relationship with the named and provides the scaffolding for a dynamic of subjugation with the metropole—in the case of Columbus, with Spain.

The impulse to rename as well as the technology that supported this significant articulation of power requires greater consideration. Each night Columbus would prepare an entry in his diary about what had happened that day and, at the end of the prologue for his journey, Columbus confesses that he intended to make a map so that his sovereign could see the relationship of water to lands, as well as the names of the places he encountered.[3] This "picture," as he called it, was meant to follow scientific practices of the day and would include, he says, longitudes and latitudes so that one could navigate and presumably return to the places that he named and described. The place names on the map Columbus conceives in his prologue serve as moorings, or what we today may call pin drops, which allow the navigator to orient himself and to find his way.

Columbus, along with other Europeans, was aware that places, people, geographic features, and objects already possessed a nomenclature developed by the islands' native inhabitants, but he nonetheless bestowed names upon them. A representative example of this practice is the naming of one of the first islands he encounters, San Salvador (today part of the Bahamas Islands), on 14 October 1492. He notes in tandem that the Taino name, Guanahaní, was told to him by the people with whom he met there, even though this information was articulated absent any cultural intermediary who could provide translation and interpretation.[4] Just like subsequent explorers to Canada, Columbus had no way of understanding if their utterance comprised a place name or referred to some other context. Scholars for the most part have chosen to believe that Columbus could understand which words constituted place names, even

A Brief History of Settler-Colonial Naming Practices in Canada   49

though the man repeatedly describes how he reverted to hand gestures—which do not amount to some universal form of communication—in his exchanges with islanders. These same communication challenges give rise to names such as Canada, which French explorers misunderstood to be a place name, rather than a generic noun referring to a village.

Despite these challenges, Columbus pushes forward with what becomes a place-naming program the likes of which had never before been seen in Europe. All the while, Columbus documented over a hundred Indigenous toponyms, however imperfectly, and we can understand from the outset that the projection of a European name gave a place its substance in Columbus's eyes. Perhaps they signified to him, while signalling to his patrons, Isabella I of Castile (1451–1504) and Ferdinand II of Aragon (1452–1516), the monarchs of Spain whose names quickly appeared on the map, that it was worth returning to these places. We may ask ourselves why Columbus, or any other European, would rename a place that already possessed a toponym of which they were aware. In contrast, when an Osage delegation travelled from French North America to Europe in 1827–30, spending time in Belgium, Germany, Italy, and the Netherlands, they certainly knew or learned the place nomenclature but did not rename the cities and bodies of water that they visited.[5] This comparison demonstrates the Euro-settler use of a form of toponymic colonialism that other cultures felt unnecessary to implement when finding themselves in other lands.

In her monograph on Columbus's naming practices, Evelina Gužauskytė includes an extensive appendix cataloguing both the names he conjured and bestowed, as well as the Indigenous ones that he believed he encountered. She observes that despite the parallel existence of these names, scholars for centuries have chosen to ignore Taino and other Indigenous toponyms, a pattern repeated in Canada and other regions of North America, particularly by the general public.[6] In other words, noncolonial names exist for us to use when we talk about lands invaded by Europeans, but we fail to use them, preferring instead names that seem more familiar, that come from a language we know, or that invoke a history from elsewhere to which we feel rooted. This suggests that many non-Indigenous Canadians, even when they are born in Canada, identify strongly with elsewhere, likely Europe through language and intergenerational history, helping to maintain Canada's toponymic status quo.

For centuries, scholars have demonstrated a preference to use almost exclusively European and settler names, even when presented with a parallel nomenclature (for instance, Guanahaní and San Salvador), or where the Indigenous name is used locally more than a European one. Scholars, when discussing early modern place names, often fail to connect place names through time and, in some cases, through space. Fuson's observation that we today possess less geographic and toponymic literacy is part of the problem because knowledge about the world is temporal—our place ecumenes will be different a century from now, just as they were different a century ago. We struggle to know a place's toponymic history, to link these names together as referring to the same place, and to award some temporal signature that informs us when and by whom it was known by a name. As a result, Guanahaní is detached from San Salvador and relegated to a past that is not represented on maps and digital wayfinding tools such as Google Maps. This scholarly and educational problem exposes for our purposes an element of the identity-driven naming agenda that this book tries to articulate, deconstruct, and confront. At the same time, works such as Columbus's diaries comprise the earliest attempts by Europeans to list names, to occasionally provide a meaning for what they signify, and to specify in which Indigenous or European language they have been rendered. Put another way, lists of place names were not common before 1492 and tended to be confined, in the Western world at least, to notable cities from the Bible or from antiquity.[7] Indigenous names were rarely positioned alongside European names in ways that allowed both groupings of toponyms to take up space on the colonizing tool and document that is the map, not even in a postcolonial context.

Many other Europeans from nations beyond those that served the interests of the Spanish Habsburgs followed in Columbus's wake. The British, French, and Spanish monarchies strictly guarded their knowledge

A Brief History of Settler-Colonial Naming Practices in Canada

of geography abroad, which allowed them to leverage a perception that they had already occupied and colonized broadly in North America. Such imperial anxieties can be found on maps produced in the first two decades of the sixteenth century by the likes of Martin Waldseemüller and Johannes Ruysch. They express the presence of certain nations with names indicating the languages associated with Britain and Spain, as well as with depictions of their national flags.[8] These maps incorporated the latest reports and offer the earliest European place names associated with Canada from the Cabot voyages, including Bonaventure and Cape Breton. The mixture of European languages expressed through these maps' toponymic recordings reflect regional competition for territories and resources, particularly between Britain, France, and Spain, with no nation having a clear sense of if and where the others were establishing themselves.

The authors of many travel accounts reveal anxieties about encountering other European nations. British or French expeditions were concerned about encountering the Spanish, which reflected their uncertainty about how far north Spain's influence extended.[9] This anxiety prompted Francis I of France (1494–1547) to seek out and secure a ruling in 1533 from Pope Clement VII (1478–1534) about whether France too could establish colonies in North America. This decision, for his nation and Canada, changed everything. Italian-born Clement VII determined that the late fifteenth-century Treaty of Tordesillas and the papal bull issued by Spanish-born Alexander VI (1431–1503), which awarded exploration and colonization rights to Spain and Portugal, only applied to then-known lands and not to those later reconnoitred by representatives of other European monarchies.[10] The implication of this judgment reverberated throughout Western Europe. It was widely cited, particularly in the latter half of the sixteenth century, as a justification for undertaking expeditions: if one could not invade a land already occupied by a Christian prince, then it was acceptable to do so if no Christian presence could be detected. This assessment propelled a period of French exploration into North America that commenced immediately following Clement VII's ruling. Place names remained at the centre of hotly contested determinations about

Canada's Place Names and How to Change Them

who occupied which space or who was entitled to use a territory's resources. As we will see, this remains a problem of our own time.

The Treaty of Tordesillas was a precursor to Euro-settler legal and rhetorical rationales for taking lands that were clearly occupied by others, often referred to as the doctrine of discovery.[11] While the treaty and papal bull delineating which lands Spain and Portugal could take relied upon an absence of Christianity, by the nineteenth century these arguments had matured after centuries of refinement. To take lands, a colonizer had to (1) demonstrate that the lands had been discovered for the first time (and as long as the inhabitants, if there were any, did not have permanent settlements or farms), or (2) show that no Christian settlement was there, or (3) convince Indigenous groups to agree to be ruled by the colonizer. Absent Christianity, and following in France's footsteps, entrepreneurial Europeans such as John Dee (1527–c. 1609), Humphrey Gilbert (c. 1539–1583), and Richard Hakluyt (1553–1616) in the 1570s and 1580s also challenged the validity of the papal bulls that favoured other countries' claims and eventually convinced their sovereign to grant them permission and the right to discover, claim, and colonize land in what became New England. They questioned Indigenous entitlement to these lands because they did not use European farming techniques, rendering them vacant and without civilization by ignoring Indigenous forms of land tenure—a status that later becomes known as *terra nullius*, a concept that partly forms the foundation of settler Canada.[12]

The supposition that a land had been "discovered" by Europeans allowed them to construct justifications for claiming it, particularly because one of the two other criteria for justifying a claim—Indigenous submission to the would-be colonizer's rule—was unlikely. The gaze of the discoverer in this sense harnessed what David Matless has termed "the eye of power-as-domination," which became manifested through the map as a tool of colonization.[13] Positioning Canada as a discovered land made way for the cartographic discourses of domination and submission during a period in which British and French map makers attempted to render their sovereigns' territories larger, more consequential, and thus occupied either

A Brief History of Settler-Colonial Naming Practices in Canada   53

textually or physically by Britain and France. We can also understand how these same powerful discourses narrowly defined Indigenous peoples as a homogeneous constituency in need of custodianship and civilization who, in European eyes, could hardly grow their own food. Naming in this sense reinforced the doctrine of discovery and a related epistemological frame called "firsting."

Firsting is the process through which a scholar presents an act, accomplishment, circumstance, or phenomenon generated by man to have occurred for the first time. It necessarily implies seconding and lasting as concomitant processes that help structure historical exchanges. Firsting involves complex issues that trouble our present, including those of race and ethnicity, gender and sexuality, religion and language, and place of origin. This powerful discourse occurs when scholars attempt to determine when and where Europeans travelled for the first time. Not all scholarship or primary accounts arising from expeditions participate in firsting, but this fact does not deter subsequent academics, editors, and translators from using that scholarship and documentation to support firsting. Many place names in Canada celebrate firsts, and this way of thinking should be viewed as one of the greater issues with settler-colonial forms of commemoration. The knowledge created from firsting is constrained by its limited relevance beyond the Western world. In a contemporary context, firsting protects and privileges the eminence of the predominately white, Western world at the expense of those who follow in the wake of its development.[14]

If firsting can be associated with discovery through assertions exampled by the Treaty of Tordesillas, then "lasting" finds its match in extinction, effacement, and *terra nullius*. An evident tension exists between one's ability to discover and to either shroud or render a thing, person, or place as nothing. Lasting has been just as complicit in shaping the spread of European presence in places that they desired to possess by constructing extinctions on lands they would then occupy. The Western gaze has shown little interest in seeing pre-European peoples (ironically called First Nations in Canada). Important works of scholarship expose the fictional disappearance of Indigenous groups—the construction of their extinction in linguistic, spiritual, territorial, and sovereign forms as part of a larger colonial agenda that persists today. As Jean O'Brien has concluded concerning the Indigenous peoples of New England, who have been previously constructed as extinct, the matter can be understood thus: "Driven to understand Indianness through a degeneration narrative about race that insisted on blood purity and coupled with an understanding of Indians reckoned within the temporalities of race, non-Indians failed to accord Indian peoples a legitimate place in modernity."[15] This observation reminds us that civilizing discourses narrowly focused on the project of modernity often arise along with firsting.[16]

In this light, firsting unfirsts the peoples and even countries perceived to be less civilized or modern to Western eyes. Claims to territory compose, as Ashley Glassburn Falzetti determines, "a willful insistence that the most recent conquest defines which people count, resulting in a refusal to acknowledge the histories of those who lived in a place before that moment."[17] Along with firsting, lasting, and Columbus's naming program, which became a model followed by others, the concept of discovery as a form of first is also a product of modernity. Let us consider the language employed by Christopher Columbus in his letter to his royal patrons in Spain about his arrival in the Caribbean region. He often used the Spanish verb *hallar* (to observe one's location or to perceive a place) in the original letter published by Pero de Posa in Barcelona in 1493. He believed that he knew where he was—somewhere in eastern Asia, the precise location to be determined later. This changes when his contemporaries, who later published the letter in other languages, characterized the lands as "nuper inventis" (recently found),[18] which translators and editors subsequently termed "nuper repertis" (recently discovered).[19] Were he in Asia as most believed at the time, the matter of discovery in the sense that it is used today makes no sense, and Columbus's initial expression did not claim any discovery.

A Brief History of Settler-Colonial Naming Practices in Canada   55

Like Canada's toponymy, there are issues with the lexicon used by scholars both today and historically. In recent decades scholars have been careful about discussing discovery, as it has become recognized as a colonial concept. The term has an intriguing history. An examination of early modern dictionaries will demonstrate that the verb "to discover" at the dawn of the sixteenth century was associated with concepts and facts that could be apprehended (and thus acquired).[20] The legal term "discovery" remains in the English lexicon. Places, however, were rather encountered or happened upon through perception. In other words, discovery was not used to describe the encountering of places until after Columbus's report on his initial voyage.

How did Columbus become one of the world's greatest firsters by discovering a known land and by populating it with names for places that were already named? When we examine the terms used initially to describe the European encounter with the Americas, and then reflect on how the verb "to discover" supplanted them, an evolution occurs during the decades following 1493 in several European languages that parallels legal arguments espoused by Europeans such as Dee, Gibson, and Hakluyt. This evolution away from perceiving one's location and toward claiming (acquiring) it through discovery enforced the Spanish and subsequent European firsting of various parts of the world during the much lauded "Age of Discoveries."[21]

This was the climate in which Jacques Cartier (1491–1557) and later Samuel de Champlain (1567–1635) arrived in Canada. Cartier reconnoitered the St. Lawrence region in the 1530s and published his travel account in 1545. This document is likely the first and most significant published account arising from France in which the French staked a claim to a corner of the continent and brandished French-language place names as evidence of their occupation.[22] Using practices similar to Columbus, Cartier named places: (1) for saints, a practice known as hagiotoponymy; (2) with descriptive characterizations of a place, such as the Baie de Chaleurs ("bay of the warm waters") along the eastern coast of present-day New Brunswick; and (3) with Indigenous names that he claims to have

Canada's Place Names and How to Change Them

learned while interacting with the Haudenosaunee, Innu, and Mi'kmaq peoples who occupied the lands along his route, although they did not share a verbal language in common.[23]

This discussion about the earliest names and discovery practices foregrounds the importance of textual culture with respect to power and colonization. The text-based method of documenting names, furthermore, evolves considerably in the sixteenth century with the advent of new technologies, giving rise to greater detail—a way of creating space or filling in *terra nullius*—on maps and in books, and making way for even more place names.

Early Modern Documenting of Names

Early modern scholars, travellers, and cartographers would take accounts such as that of Cartier and read them against other ones to flesh out a more complete picture of a particular area. Maps made based on multiple travel accounts, in addition to information from existing maps, aggregated place names and used them almost as homing devices that over time allowed one to cross-reference the experiences of one explorer against the movements of another. The Americas, and particularly North America, become a quilted invention of cartographic masterminds in Europe who processed historical and new data provided by travellers and then generated the most up-to-date picture of these lands. The desire to view the most recent information propelled not only the publishing industry but also the science of mapping space, which in turn increased the detail a map provided and thus the space available for toponymy.

In tandem, cartographers eventually implemented European scientific practices for surveying and measuring that became standard cartographical practices by the latter half of the sixteenth century.[24] Works by the likes of Flemish humanist Gerardus Mercator (1512–1594) and Brabantian cartographer Abraham Ortelius (1527–1598) reinforced the importance of including the most recently received accounts, utilizing science in ways that accounted for the distortion that might misrepresent scale (and thus

A Brief History of Settler-Colonial Naming Practices in Canada   57

the size of one's empire), and offering the latest place names and measurements. New mapping techniques that improved navigation, such as rhumb lines and loxodromy, developed alongside innovations in map projections that attempted to correct distortions caused by the representation of three-dimensional space on the two-dimensional page. As a result of this compulsion to broaden both the Western ecumene and knowledge about it, a new map was required when either a new travel account materialized or a new cartographic tool emerged. Place names were influential and lucrative mechanisms through which the printing and knowledge industries, as well as imperial authorities, both invented and staked a claim on space.

When considered in this light, map making implicated place naming in its sixteenth-century journey to become a rigorous instrument of scientific knowledge and authority, which in turn made the quality and quantity of place names of paramount importance. The language in which a place name was written often pointed to which nation's representative performed the naming or claimed occupation. It is also during the sixteenth century when humanism gives rise to documented scholarship where sources became increasingly detailed. Maps usually came accompanied by some acknowledgement about the sources of its information. Viewed in this way, the technologizing of the map is in part made possible through the instrument of accurate toponymy, which cartographers accessed through primary sources provided to them sometimes by the travellers themselves or through published travel relations and existing maps. Maps had grown to reflect Roland Barthes's concept of *lexia*, the texts that give rise to, become projected onto, and sometimes become incarnated by the map.[25] Place names as discrete lexia anchor the map to the textual foundations that made the map possible. They have an indexical function that allows the scholar to connect these lexia, which range from published and manuscript texts to a legacy of cartographical production, to the map.

By the seventeenth century, a studious approach to place naming unfolded on the part of European travellers. While continuing to use the diary style initiated by Columbus—and thus we can often trace when a place was named and sometimes why—they also began to compile place names and their meanings into lists and to position them on maps in some cumulative fashion. Champlain spent the last three decades of his life in eastern New France establishing colonies in the name of his sovereign. Of his many written and cartographic works, one ideally models how place names had increased in prominence over the decades following Columbus's inaugural voyage, as well as how they had intermixed with the importance of demonstrating a scientific approach to naming. His map, *Carte geographique de la Nouvelle Franse* (Paris: Chez Jean Berjon, 1613), accompanies Champlain's account of his travels in the region published the same year (Figure 2.1). The subtitle of his book attempts to emphasize the truthfulness (*tres-fidele*) of the account's "description" of the land through its place nomenclature as well as the character of the landscape, its peoples, and its resources.[26]

The map, which spreads across two facing sheets, represents eastern Canada and the northeastern corner of the present-day United States of America, and contains several place names scattered throughout. Many components of the map build one's confidence in its scientific accuracy, including the use of rhumb lines, the compass rose, the illustration of a compass used for measurement, among other elements that describe how the map was prepared. Positioned in its own cartouche and featured prominently along the bottom of the map are Champlain's list of place names, which the map reader can identify using the alphabetic and numerical index contained in the map's legend. These letters and numbers appear

Figure 2.1 (overleaf) Champlain's map of New France, from *Les Voyages du sieur de Champlain Xaintongeois, capitaine ordinaire pour le roy, en la marine, divisez en deux livres: ou Journal tres-fidele des observations faites és descouvertures de la Nouvelle France: tant en la descriptio[n] des terres, costes, rivieres, ports, havres, leurs hauteurs, & plusieurs declinaisons de la guide-aymant; qu'en la crea[n]ce des peuples leur superstition façon de vivre & de guerroyer: enrichi de quantité de figures* (Paris: Chez Jean Berjon, 1613).

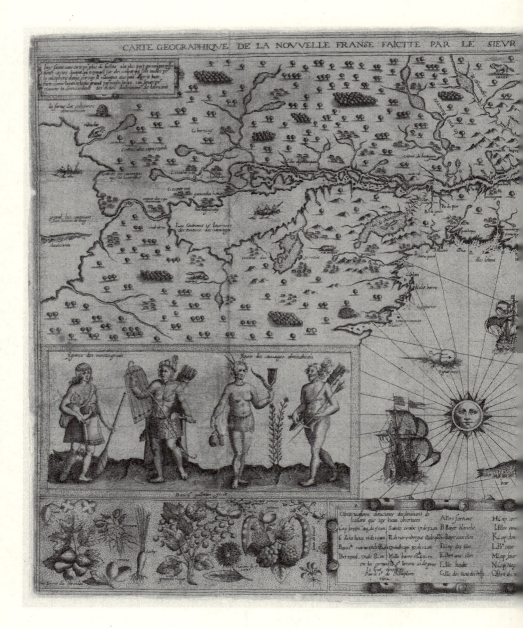

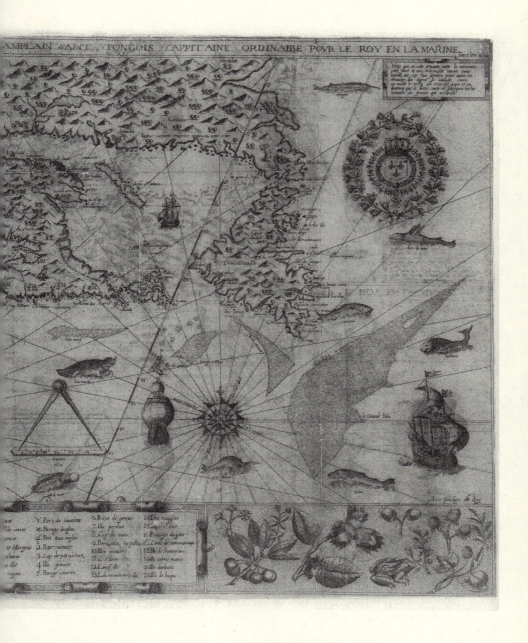

on the map as pin drops referenced in the legend and provide examples of the kinds of naming practices Champlain shared with Columbus. "*3.* Cap de Potrinicourt" is located in present-day Minas Bay, Nova Scotia, and is a commemorative place name for one of Champlain's patrons. "*G.* Ille des mont desertz," today still known as Mount Desert Island in Maine, is a name intended to describe the condition of that particular island. "Rv. de St Jehon," which is still called the Saint John River in New Brunswick, is just one of several hagiotoponyms awarded by Champlain. By positioning these names in a series of orderly columns, Champlain could add more visual detail to show us the shape of the coastlines and, in some places, the character of the landscape without textual toponymy occupying the map's space and possibly obscuring the geographical knowledge on display.

By the end of Champlain's life, he had authored many books and maps about his time in New France. Most of them contained detailed illustrations of the region's flora and fauna. A product of his time, Champlain attempted to catalogue places and the events that took place in them, all of which builds upon the period's trend to create compendia, encyclopedias, and atlases that might offer a complete set of knowledges on any given topic. Having grown up in a mariner's household in Brouage on the west coast of France, Champlain somehow learned to read and write. As of today, we do not know which published works might have motivated his prolific undertaking as an author and a cartographer, in addition to a mariner. Certainly, his approach to amassing place knowledge emulates other compendia projects, such as the atlas, with which he may have become familiar prior to leaving for the area of Canada he referred to as Nouvelle France.

In the hands of Mercator and Ortelius, among other cartographers from France, Germany, and the Netherlands, the atlas had stabilized as a genre by the latter half of the sixteenth century. By the end of the century, the attempt to document the world's shape and contents—including its place names—comingled with an intensifying interest in one's lived experience in the world. These trends resulted in challenges such as running out of space on a map or needing to publish multi-volume compendia to

62   *Canada's Place Names and How to Change Them*

include all the details expected of the genre. Theodore de Bry's *Grands Voyages* (1590–1634) was an attempt to create a complete, illustrated set of travel relations describing European experiences in the Americas. It was illustrated and published in several vernacular languages as well as in Latin.[27] De Bry's Flemish-German printing company paid little to no attention to French colonization efforts in the early seventeenth century, however, which left room for Champlain and his compatriots—among them lawyer Marc Lescarbot (c. 1570–1641)—to document and illustrate French experiences abroad. The overarching project of these two men, who themselves travelled but did not write together, occurred during the very decades in which de Bry's compendium was translated and published in French. It is no accident that their approach to place nomenclature makes use of many of de Bry's strategies for authenticating the quality and authority of their sources. For these reasons, it is difficult not to view Lescarbot and Champlain's written and cartographic contributions within the broader context of similar compendia projects that articulated European empire-building efforts abroad. In this spirit, cartographers were compelled to never leave a place name off the map; maps had to include as much information as possible. Importantly, and in contrast to the Indigenous world, in the Western world, place knowledge is not multivocal. These compendia projects should be viewed as deterministic and rigidly concerned with establishing singularly authoritative knowledge, steeping our place ecumene and ways of knowing in the experiences, perspectives, and desires of white men.

While scholars have traditionally turned to these compendia and the maps contained therein for place-name research, little attention has been paid to how this knowledge was being restructured in the seventeenth century. Both Lescarbot and Champlain experienced challenges in their efforts to create a compendium of knowledge about French North America, and we can see similar difficulties experienced in other European compendia projects. Barriers to their success included the growing expanse of information and space to be documented, as well as the increasingly voluminous textual culture that was inventing the Americas for Western occupation and consumption. To overcome them, they had to seek out new ways of containing and presenting so much information while making it accessible to their target readers. A particular challenge was including more place names than could be legibly displayed on a map itself when even its cartouche ran out of room. In this era, excluding names that ought to be on the map would only diminish the quality of the map in the eyes of scholars and knowledgeable map readers.

The solution was to create secondary resources that supported how the map was read. It is this form of secondary literature that eventually becomes a vehicle for place-name research, an overview of which can be found in this book's introduction. Champlain's "Table pour cognoistre les lieux remarquables en ceste carte" (Table with which to understand this map's remarkable places), which is a chapter in his final relation published in 1632, was meant to accompany a map featured in the same book.[28] This table contained a numbered list of place names, which one could then find through seeking the corresponding number on the map itself. In many ways this map serves as a place where all of Champlain's toponymic knowledge becomes aggregated, and because he possessed so much of this knowledge, he contrived a secondary source that the map reader could use in order to further endow the map with detail.[29] Lescarbot and Champlain decided to create secondary sources that would provide additional context, in the form of a chapter inserted into a book alongside the map. A secondary source could inform how we interpret maps as primary sources (for instance, maps based on their travel experiences to North America) and maps also give rise to secondary sources created for the maps' explication.

While not necessarily the first traveller-cartographer-historians to generate secondary sources for scholarly toponymic inquiry, Lescarbot and Champlain's practice nonetheless leads to a more serious consideration of place-name significance in the latter half of the seventeenth century. This interest in meaning characterizes place nomenclature scholarship well into the twentieth century. While it dovetails with early modern lexicography projects interested in definitions and name history, this preference to understand a name's meaning does not necessarily consider the livingness of names as anchors of human and non-human experience. Pinning names to a landscape therefore narrowed the elements or characteristics of a place in ways that obscured other experiences associated with it. Mount Desert Island (Ille des mont desertz) was defined narrowly in this way because Champlain saw no vegetation on its rocky surfaces from his perspective on his ship, even though this island contains a complex ecosystem comprised of flora, fauna, and marine life, in addition to human settlement going back thousands of years. His choice of toponym reduces the island to one primary characteristic—nothingness—despite the evident presence of inhabitants who are not represented by the name. When included as part a list of place names, with little difference from a vocabulary list or dictionary, the complexity of a place's contents and experiences may have been silenced.

Dictionaries, like maps, as large compendia of language knowledge become commonplace by the eighteenth century and transform into nascent manifestations of nationhood. They exist in various states, depending on the language, before this time—particularly in the form of vocabularies that drew parallels in meaning from one language to another. When toponyms are found in vocabulary books, they are sometimes translated in ways that reveal the name's meaning, unlike other kinds of words where the equivalent term in a second language is typically listed in parallel. For instance, in his seventeenth-century Spanish–Quichua vocabulary, Jesuit Diego González Holguín (c. 1560–c. 1620) gave the Spanish parallel translation for Arequipa as "a city in Peru," which, while helpful if one does not realize the location of this settlement, nonetheless does not provide the etymology of Arequipa or any information about the landscape of Peru.[30] These reductive naming practices, exampled by Champlain's Ille des mont desertz, are common elsewhere, particularly up to the middle of the seventeenth century.

Moving beyond definitions of Indigenous and settler-colonial names, orthographical rules also impact how a word from one language is textually represented in another. During the Recollect expansion into the

A Brief History of Settler-Colonial Naming Practices in Canada   65

Great Lakes region of present-day Canada and the United States, and following trends seen in the Spanish Americas, missionaries quickly concluded that language training would greatly enable them to evangelize to the Indigenous populations. This is partly why so many language resources produced in Europe were authored by religious men. The missionaries went about recording the names of "nations" and rendering them into French, without necessarily concerning themselves with how the name for a people may closely resemble the word that informs their place nomenclature. For instance, in the 1620s French missionary Gabriel Sagard (1590–1640) heard *Aquannaque* (the Wabanaki Confederacy) and rendered it as the French word *Algoumequins* (whose English equivalent is Algonquin, modernized today as Algonquian). He created the French word, *Houndate*, to define the Wendat (meaning the islanders; Wendake being their homeland), which was later replaced by the French word for this people, *Hurons*. In his vocabulary listing Wendat words and their French equivalents, Sagard listed the Wendat word, *Gontara* (lake), as equating to the French word *Lac*, and by the following century, these words became projected onto an important body of water still known as Lake Ontario—a name to which we will return later in this book.[31]

Hidden within the French missionaries' transformations of Wendat place nomenclature is the etymology of Wendat terms. Sagard, like other missionaries, failed to note the meaning of *Houndate* as "the islanders" as well as the broader significance of this name from a Wendat cosmological perspective, which gives the name its significance. Furthermore, his linguistic equivalencies in no way relate to Wendat place-name or knowledge practices, but rather constitute a false toponymy that projects Indigenous names onto places where they do not necessarily belong, or where an Indigenous group would not necessarily use the name. Wendake, which the French called Huronia, thus becomes known to the French by an insulting medieval French word, *huron*, that shares no etymological connection with the Wendat word for their homeland. Lake Huron remains named for the French word assigned to this people in southern Ontario. An explanation given by Sagard in his dictionary, as well as in several contemporaneous works, reveals the reasons for which the French decided to bestow an insulting name, which I explore further in the next chapter. They then projected this name upon both the people and their land. Vocabularies such as Sagard's became a common feature of seventeenth- and eighteenth-century travel relations. They were also published as stand-alone lexicographical works geared toward missionaries. Despite these elements of interest in Indigenous languages, however, scholars made few attempts to understand Indigenous etymologies for Sagard and his colleagues' place names until recent times.

Toward Post-Colonial Names

Following the work of missionaries in the early seventeenth-century, the Enlightenment and what some English-language and settler scholars refer to as the "long eighteenth century" (1660–1830) brought with them a shift in the sorts of questions being asked about place nomenclature.[32] With the Wars of Religion petering out in the second half of the seventeenth century, the establishment of authority over knowledge increasingly found itself in secular hands. New questions for toponymy developed alongside the emergence of a new demographic of individuals asking them. No longer the domain of church or state-sponsored or -approved publications, the Enlightenment brought with it new scientific methods, developments in cartographical practices such as topographical documentation later in the eighteenth century, and a broadening readership comprised of an increasingly consequential and educated middle class on both sides of the Atlantic. New disciplines such as anthropology and biology emerged, and information about the Americas, its flora and fauna, its landscape and place names, was increasingly being provided by scientists, academics, well-to-do and middle-class "explorers," as well as "colonists" (to whom I will refer as settlers) in the name of these new disciplines' objectives. During this period, not only does the size of the map increase or become divided into multiple book pages—which allowed for more information to be included—but Euro-settlers also began to look at Indigenous knowledge as something that they could acquire and utilize. This practice eventually changed how place nomenclature was understood and studied.

Even in the mid-seventeenth century, French and Spanish missionaries in the Americas understood that bestowing names as Columbus had done was not itself sufficient to accomplish all the ambitions of imperialist monarchs and churches. One of their collective goals, which they certainly did not pursue in any collaborative way, was finding a navigable waterway that would allow them—particularly the British and French—to penetrate the continent in order to reach the Pacific Ocean. One passage had been found in South America decades after Columbus's initial voyage and it is still known today as the Strait of Magellan. It was thought that a northwest passage might enable ships to pass from the Atlantic to the Pacific without relying on the southern passage. Hope remained that similar arteries would be found in Canada. When this goal first became more urgent in the early sixteenth century, Indigenous peoples were provided with synthetic, European-generated place names as reference points for questions about how to reach a western ocean, names that may have held no meaning to them. By the dawn of the Enlightenment, however, missionaries had realized that learning Indigenous names would better allow them to acquire and navigate using what they could understand about Indigenous place knowledge. Traders such as Samuel Hearne (1745–1792) commissioned Indigenous knowledge holders familiar with the northern reaches of what becomes Canada to learn how he might reach the Arctic Ocean for resource extraction. Not only did Hearne and his contemporaries attempt to map and record their travels based on what their Chipewyan and Cree guides related to them, but he also then re-enacted their journey in the early 1770s. Chipewyan and Cree knowledge allowed him to arrive at the Coppermine River, whose colonial name informs us about the sort of resource extraction pursued by Hearne. The community located there is now known as Kugluktuk ("the place of the moving water," 1996), and formerly as Coppermine. These interactions demonstrate the quality of Indigenous place knowledge because it was detailed enough for a Euro-settler to map and successfully travel through a region with which they had no prior experience.

Ultimately, journeys such as the one undertaken by Hearne were costly investments—for Hearne, his journey amounted to no copper mine, despite the place's name. Declining investment on the part of colonial authorities in Britain, France, and Spain occurred alongside an increase in conflict among these and other nations in Europe. In tandem, colonies began to want more autonomy, giving way to independence movements that often resulted in toponymic rebranding, such as the Thirteen Colonies becoming the United States of America in the eighteenth century and Upper Canada and Lower Canada (after other former names, as well as additional provinces) becoming Canada in the nineteenth century. These name changes reflect some collective sense of national identity. Place names played a significant role in projecting these national, state, and provincial identities to the world, often while maintaining some connection to the colonial past, as the province of British Columbia demonstrates. As we will see later in this book's fourth chapter, sometimes Indigenous names such as Ontario and Quebec were appropriated in ways that nativized the settler-colonizer, providing them with some sense of belongingness to the land through a name that originated from it and not their own origin cultures.

An important element of this new Canadian identity connects to Hearne and people like him, as well as to Britain, as proponents of the fur trade. Perhaps unsurprisingly, references to trade and resource extraction, among the primary Euro-settler motivations for the colonial project in Canada, figure prominently in our names, and even more so in this country's emblems. The coats of arms for both the Hudson's Bay Company (HBC) and Canada exemplify these attempts to forge a settler identity in this country while maintaining their roots within the European metropole through a medieval form of visualization (Figure 2.2). While the HBC's arms and logo predate that of Canada by over two centuries—coming into being in 1670—it nonetheless offers what might be one of the

A Brief History of Settler-Colonial Naming Practices in Canada　　69

Figure 2.2 The Hudson's Bay Company's coat of arms, last updated in 2013. Courtesy of the HBC Corporate Collection.

first attempts to brand the country using heraldry that did not entirely reproduce British arms and symbols. In the shield's centre is the cross of Saint George, perhaps the only explicit reference to England, between whose arms are four beavers, symbolizing an important and lucrative resource pursued by the company. Supporting the shield are two elk, another symbol of the country's fauna, and perched above it a third animal, the fox. The company's motto, *pro pelle cutem* (a pelt for a skin), layers the ancient language of Latin upon the composition, while implicating the pelt (comprised of skin and fur) and warning about the danger of the fur trade, as Europeans struggled against the climate and environment of Canada while trying to extract its resources. As Rachel Hurst observes, these animals also signify "the signs of fur—as a luxury commodity, as gendered and sexualised, as decadent—[that] cannot be separated from its status as the trade item that brings 'Canada' into being."[33] As demonstrated by the coat of arms of Langley Township, British Columbia, which contains a flag bearing the initials HBC, several places in Canada explicitly refer to the company in their coats of arms.

Figure 2.3 Canada's coat of arms, last updated in 1994. Courtesy of the Government of Canada.

Canada's coat of arms was adopted in 1921 and revised in 1994 (Figure 2.3). Unlike the HBC's arms, Canada's only features animals either from elsewhere in the world (lions) or from the medieval imaginary (the unicorn). Its model is the United Kingdom's coat of arms, with red and white maple leaves added to reflect the symbols and colour choices for the country's flag (adopted in 1965). The lion wearing a crown is taken from the British coat of arms, but it is modified by having the lion hold a red maple leaf. Other symbols for England, France, Ireland, and Scotland can be found on the shield. Two textual components also catch our attention—the ribbon encircling the shield, *desiderantes meliorem patriam* (desiring a better country), adopted in 1987, and the motto, *a mari usque ad mare* (from sea to sea), adopted in 1921. In comparison to the arms

A Brief History of Settler-Colonial Naming Practices in Canada   71

of most provinces and territories, this coat of arms offers the strongest connection to settler Canada's colonial past and surprisingly, with the exception of the maple leaf, displays no uniquely Canadian symbolism. The maple leaf nonetheless comprises a powerful signifier of Canadian identity; among other contexts, it has emblazoned the country's soldiers, passports, and athletes since the nineteenth century.[34]

Canada and the United States continued the colonial project by pushing westward, to reach areas not yet inhabited by settlers while leaving a trail of place names behind them. This expansionism dovetails with modern projects and technologies such as the extension of the railway, which resulted in the creation of railway stations, post offices, and towns, all requiring names. Fort St. James, British Columbia, is an example. Originally created and named by the North West Company in 1806 as a trading post, a national historic site of the same name commemorates its fur trading past as well as the HBC's custodianship of the trading post until its closure in 1952. In 1875, a post office with this name was added to the map, followed by a village incorporated in 1952, attracting the Fort St. James railway station in the 1960s. Fort St. James is now a municipality located in the Range 5 Coast Land District in Dakelhne territory.[35]

This colonial naming project continues into the twenty-first century in the most remote regions of Canada's north, echoing Hearne's naming of the Coppermine River. International mining companies such as Rio Tinto develop and name companies that subsequently assert their presence on the map. The Diavik Diamond Mine in the Northwest Territories near Yellowknife is an example of this practice. Established in 2000, the name itself has not yet been approved by any naming commission, even though this place boasts an airport (Diavik Airport), while its head office is located in Yellowknife. A Dog Rib–English dictionary project includes the place in its list of mining sites, giving it the name ʔek'adıì (Ekaadi, meaning "mine"), while not embracing the name Diavik itself.[36] The word seems to be a Tlicho-English hybrid that could refer to the mine's product, diamonds, mashed up with a common particle found in

Tlicho language. Interestingly, the name existed well before the mine and agreements with local groups were forged, showing how names can compel groups to approve outsider activities in their milieu. It also shows how names exist before the arrival of Western infrastructure—echoing an observation we can make about Columbus's named places, which served as placeholders for European colonization. With each expansion of this nature, whether today or in the past, a new map was crafted, a revised picture in text and image drafted about the fabric of a nation. In some cases—perhaps most famously in the early nineteenth-century Lewis and Clark expedition westward—the processes of mapping the nation also shaped its identity. Place naming comprised one of the justifications for scientific enterprises "in the field" and on the very lands that settlers sought to take from Indigenous inhabitants.

Field studies such as those undertaken by Peter Fidler (1769–1822), along with Meriwether Lewis (1774–1809) and William Clark (1770–1838), into much of Canada's central and western regions and their borderlands might be characterized as a form of science that requires the scholar to leave his or her library, laboratory, or desk and to engage with the environment that is under study. In theory, one might experience the landscape through field study in ways that would allow them to better comprehend Indigenous place knowledge. For many scholars before the Enlightenment, field study was impossible due to the cost and time one had to invest into crossing the Atlantic in order to see colonial development in action. Just as the historian's pilgrimage to an archive constitutes field studies, so too does the toponymist's journey to the region he wishes to study in order to speak with the local populations and record the meaning of their place nomenclature. This was one of Fidler's objectives.[37] As anthropological and ethnographic sources, toponymical studies from the nineteenth century and beyond can offer a rich source of knowledge about a people precisely because the scholar has engaged with a people's language and cultural practices in order to understand how a place name came to be and what it means.

There are complications with this approach to scholarship, particularly involving the power of the gaze to construct and assign identity. From a logistics perspective, the freedom to move about in order to conduct research of this nature had never existed as it did by the conclusion of the Enlightenment. The period witnessed increasing safety to the traveller, expanding networks of roads and later railroads, the development of mass transit, the emergence of well-paid positions for middle- and upper-class scholars at universities that supported their research, and an expanding ability and incentive to publish one's findings. It cannot surprise us that a burgeoning place-name science occurs in the nineteenth century, spilling into the twentieth century, especially in wealthier countries such as Canada, the United States of America, and allied nations. Today, the digital world has placed this massive textual archive at our fingertips, further enabling place onomastics and the study of place-naming practices.

Looking Forward

In this exploration of place-naming practices at the crossroads of scholarship, I have established a scaffolding upon which a critical assessment of Canada's place names can occur. Canada's place names have largely been created by non-specialists in toponymy, such as explorers, missionaries, traders, and corporations, who themselves may have had no experience or direction for developing place nomenclature. Naming commissions such as the Geographical Names Board of Canada have inherited a wealth of names of this variety, in addition to ones of Indigenous origin that may themselves comprise false toponymies, as Lake Huron demonstrates. Naming practices occurred alongside the cultivation of this country's identity, which inscribes explicit references to colonialism within both names and emblems, whether this is through references to Britain and France or to Euro-settler motivations for expanding into the land now known as Canada. Furthermore, technology in the form of cartography, surveying science, knowledge compendia (from the map and atlas to the dictionary and internet), the printing press, railways, among other developments, pushes place nomenclature to the foreground as a means of legitimizing occupation premised on the misconception that the landscape was in need of contents.

Might it be possible to take a different course than Margaret Atwood's Captain Cook, upset to find places that already had names, and demanding that the landscape be cleared of toponymy so that he could perform his job? Could the harms occasioned by problematic and patriarchal names be washed away, and if so, what might be revealed in their wake? In the remaining chapters, devoted to the ways that race, gender, and colonialism inform our place names, I attempt to reveal the historical fissures often violently created through the settler-colonial project that only recently have garnered broader attention. My goal is to arrive at not only an understanding of how place informs the complex contours of "Canadian" identity expressed by Canadian toponymy but also to eventually articulate possible solutions that address the white supremacy and patriarchy that undergird it. In tandem, I will uncover the foundations of place naming and demystify the procedures required to change the way place names represent the people of Canada.

A Brief History of Settler-Colonial Naming Practices in Canada

CHAPTER 3

Gender and Canada's Place Names

When I reflect upon my own place identity—a resident of Sackville, New Brunswick, who hails from St. Thomas, Ontario, and attended schools such as Tom Longboat Elementary in Scarborough, Ontario, and the University of Waterloo—it becomes apparent that the landscape of my identity is masculine, as all but one of these names commemorate the actions and lives of white men. The exception is Cogwagee, or Thomas Longboat (1887–1949), an Onondaga (Haudenosaunee) man from a Six Nations reservation outside of Brantford, Ontario. The Scarborough Board of Education selected his name to commemorate my elementary school when it opened in 1978. He was known for his career as a runner, but his connection with the city of Scarborough remains unclear, as Onondaga territory does not include this area. In a settler context, it is his anglicized and not his Haudenosaunee name by which he is most recognized—a colonizing name that is imposed. To some extent, the imposition of masculine names colonize the identities of women when we talk about our pasts or even show our driver's licences, all in ways that men may not experience.

In looking at our place identity through the lens of how and where groups are privileged or disadvantaged, we can observe foundations of the modern condition. Through the lens of the modern-colonial matrix of power as understood by Walter D. Mignolo and Catherine E. Walsh, identities are anchored to the complex forces of modernity, which encompasses five centuries of colonization in Canada. Certain groups find themselves marginalized and without power, whereas others—white settler-colonial men—until recent times have exercised power over everybody else. When place names and emblems are selected by individuals who hold patriarchal and white supremacist worldviews, those biases will be reflected in a place's identity.[1] The modern era's emergence from the medieval period ushers in the structures that perpetuate white patriarchy and supremacy, as we saw in the last chapter, in various forms of textual culture, including scholarship and the valuation of knowledge. These structures urgently require an analysis focused on gender. The consideration of gendered toponymy that follows will also be informed by an awareness of the harm caused by a gender binary that assumes one is either male or female.

Quite simply, modern place names betray an identity matrix that manifests a systemic architecture of knowledge favouring the experiences and gaze of white men. At least until more recent times, place-name studies were produced by and for this demographic, who have also greatly influenced Canadian place nomenclature and scholarship by serving on place-name commissions or legitimating masculine place names. Confronting the relationship between modernity and coloniality in place names exposes the inherent links between white male privilege and settler-colonialism, which means we must also deal with the inequalities caused by these patriarchal structures. Identity circumscribes how an individual receives and makes meaning from place names, and the experience of uttering names will likely be different for women and people of colour than for white men. Haudenosaunee students of Tom Longboat Elementary may think it strange to have a school commemorated for a man with no connection to the area, but they may also recognize that this name is a rare example of commemorative Indigenous place nomenclature becoming embraced by settler society.

Women of any background rarely come from a place that is overtly characterized as feminine. It is from this perspective that scholarship on place names needs to address the complex socio-cultural impacts of naming and the power dynamics inscribed within naming practices. By studying toponymies in this way, it is possible to problematize the representation of gender in Canada's place nomenclature, both in qualitative and quantitative ways, and expose the white masculinity of this country's names. At the same time, this approach shows how Indigenous place names acknowledge women's presence and experiences more than settler-colonial names. This intersection between gender, race, and naming practices in North America requires further consideration in light of the ongoing project of colonization in Canada.

Commemorative Names

Many non-Indigenous names found in North America belong to the commemorative class of place nomenclature whose purpose is to celebrate the achievements and recognize the failures of individuals deemed worthy of being remembered. When these names are awarded by outsiders, they are categorized as exonyms.[2] As seen in the last chapter, some of Christopher Columbus's first place names included those that reflect both genders and comprised either hagiotoponyms commemorating saints, or ones that celebrated his patrons, the king and queen of Spain. Following this paradigm, more than half of the names bestowed by Jacques Cartier in the 1530s upon modern-day maritime Canada were inspired by important figures in the history of Catholicism. Responsible for updating the name of Canada River, which adorned many sixteenth-century maps, to the still-in-use St. Lawrence River, Samuel de Champlain crafted more than 330 place names for parts of Canada and the United States during the first three decades of the seventeenth century, only 9% of which have Indigenous roots.[3] The naming practices of these European explorers and colonizers impose upon or even erase from the landscape the existing Indigenous names for places and their contents. They also exhibit a gendered character that projects a masculine skein upon today's Canada because they ultimately celebrate the namers and their worldviews rather than those of women and of the region's Indigenous peoples.[4]

The naming practices of Columbus, Cartier, and Champlain must be contextualized from a European perspective. For Europeans, the concept of creating a city or town was not one that they had thought about for a long time, particularly since the Roman invasion of northern Europe and, in the case of Spain, since the Umayyad invasion of the Iberian Peninsula in 711. European names often descended from Roman or Romanized names awarded two millennia ago, demonstrated by Triana, in the province of Seville, named for the emperor Trajan. Others are descriptive in nature, such as Newcastle Upon Tyne, a city named for its late eleventh-century fortification along the River Tyne. Europe already contained named settlements by the time of the growth of Christianity and it is urbanization, rather than the founding of new settlements, which characterizes the post-medieval period.[5] With the Americas, these men activated a naming enterprise never before seen in Europe, and they reached for familiar sources of inspiration in order to populate *terra nullius* with names.

The rendering of North America as an unpossessed land was a significant concept that enabled the expropriation of lands from Indigenous peoples so that they could be claimed and possessed through Western legal means by both colonizers and settlers.[6] Seen in this light, place naming reinforced the arguments sustained by Europeans that they could legitimately claim and occupy lands and their resources in the Americas. These naming acts clearly disenfranchised Indigenous authority and knowledge while elevating masculine voices who not only bestowed toponymy but were also subsequently commemorated with place names, as the country of Colombia and the province of British Columbia demonstrate. This latter name was officially adopted by Queen Victoria (1819–1901) in 1843, inspired by the ship *Columbia Rediviva* (Columbus Revived), whose captain named the Columbia River.[7] As this example signals, British naming authorities, from the queen to the captain of the *Columbia*, appropriated an explorer's fame to characterize the success of British expansion into northwestern North America. This name also evinces the varying types of authority as well as powerful legacies undergirding place nomenclature.

The connection between the namer and the name—for example, between Cartier and Champlain and the settlements they named or created—implicates gender as a characteristic of our toponymy today, a reality that complicates women's ability to see themselves in this country's place names.[8] Naming practices provide the opportunity to normalize new places by making them more familiar through the use of names from the bestower's culture. A similarly normalizing practice can also be accomplished through visualizations of familiar institutions that powerfully operationalize gender.[9] When place names are viewed through a gendered lens we can better apprehend the degree to which national identity and power traditionally reveal patriarchal and masculine control over land and even selfhood.

A Christianized Landscape

During the medieval period throughout Europe, bestowing Christian names inspired by saints upon children grew across all social classes. Their use as place names significantly impacts the toponymy of the Americas, whereas saints' names in Europe served as denominators for churches and their adjacent plazas but were not commonly used for settlements.[10] Hagiotoponyms and gender need to be framed in light of the dominance of men in the Christian religion, as opposed to female figures: with no women among Noah's children or the twelve apostles, with the patriarchy of the priesthood and the papacy, and with Adam's mandate to bestow names upon all creatures on Earth, the Judeo-Christian perspective for naming was and may still be a masculine enterprise. These aspects give us pause to consider how a similar project unfolded in the Americas where both secular and religious namers applied gender to spaces and places.

Statistics regarding the nature of saint-inspired place nomenclature in Canada can easily be studied through regional and national place-name databases (whereas most countries in the Americas have no such resources). Only four of the thirty-five nations of the Americas participate in the United Nations' Commission on Geographic Names and offer a names database that facilitates the granular and big-data approaches to place-name research taken at various points in this book; however, only

Gender and Canada's Place Names

those of Canada, Mexico, and the United States are functioning, with Brazil's database no longer active.[11] Excepting the work of Jean-Yves Dugas, a gendered inquiry does not appear to have been undertaken as yet for the hagiotoponymy of Anglophone and Francophone Canada.[12] Quebec's place-name database registers nearly 2,500 places in the province as containing *Sainte*, denoting female saints (20%), compared to the nearly 10,000 places named for male saints, *Saint* (80%). Indeed, nearly 80% of saints during the early modern period were male, which significantly constrained the pool of female names available to those bestowing names, many of whom themselves were male missionaries. This observation is even more interesting because the data under study reflects names that exist today, even though the gendered dynamics of saints' names has considerably changed over the last two centuries, with a significant cohort of women saints joining the canonized collective. Today about one quarter of saints are women—an increase from the early modern period of only five percent.[13] Nevertheless, it appears that the gender gap in hagiotoponymy reflects the ratio of male to female saint names of the early modern period rather than that of more recent times. Renaming efforts in the eighteenth century resulted in revising some female hagiotoponyms with names such as Fredericton, New Brunswick, which reflected British wishes to see their names reflected on the map and not those of the French (who used the name Pointe-Ste-Anne). There are also considerably more hagiotoponyms in central and eastern Canada than in the west, which reflects not just who determined these names but when. Most of western Canada's official names were assigned by nineteenth- and twentieth-century settlers rather than earlier missionaries. These later naming practices reflect a period when Christianity had grown less influential than it had been in previous centuries.

A map prepared by several Jesuits and attributed to Jean de Brébeuf (1593–1649), named by the Catholic church as Canada's patron saint in 1940, illustrates related issues (Figure 3.1). *Description du pais des Hurons* exemplifies the complexity of missionary naming practices in the area of present-day southern Ontario during their attempts to convert the

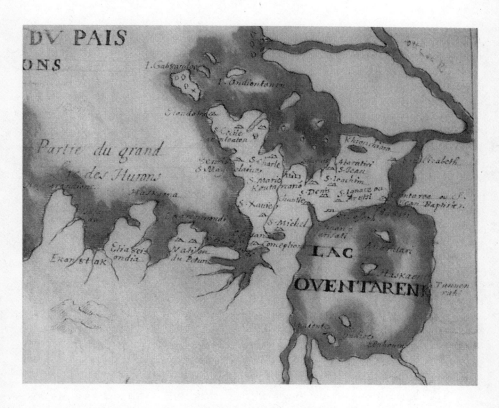

Figure 3.1 Detail from Jean de Brébeuf (attributed), *Description du pais des Hurons*, initiated as early as 1631 and completed in 1651 (detail). Washington, DC, Library of Congress, Geography and Map Division, G3460 1651 D4.

Wendat (Huron) people to Christianity. By the middle of the seventeenth century, Jesuits had lived for a couple of decades among the Wendat, whose settlements migrated to new areas whenever the land and natural resources required renewal. The Wendat bestowed a different name for each settlement that they established. European settlements, however, tended to be fixed in terms of both their locations and names, and even when their settlements moved the same name tended to be used for the new location. Not only did Jesuits award names but they also almost always chose to celebrate their faith rather than create descriptive or politically informed names: their professional dedication inclined them toward framing the landscape of the Americas with toponymy that favoured male hagiotoponyms. Incidentally, there are twenty-nine places in Canada that bear Brébeuf's name, including townships in Ontario and Quebec, and a Quebec municipality.

Brébeuf's map also signals a shift, noted in the last chapter, away from relying on European-derived toponymy and toward embracing Indigenous place knowledge to further the settler-colonial agenda. Brébeuf and his colleagues continued to award Catholic place names, but they paired them with Wendat ones. The Wendat names describe the landscape so that one could orient themselves through it, whereas the European ones celebrated people who had no knowledge of the Americas and remained disconnected from the land in ways that precisely emphasized the Wendat's connection.

Seemingly Indigenous names sometimes exhibit a disconnection between the authentic context of the name, in this case the Wendat people, and how they would use the term, and comprise false toponymies. The names that were given by French missionaries for the Wendat, Huron, and their ancestral homeland, Huronia, can be traced to the missionaries' impression that male Wendat's hair arrangements resembled a boar's bristles, and the French term's second meaning is ruffian. The term *huron* descends from a medieval French word describing these two nouns, which imposes upon this territory a gendered if inauthentic identity that subsumed Wendat and Wendake as the names for the people and their land.

In contrast, the Wendat name for their land, Wendake, continues to be absent from the map. This absence occurs repeatedly throughout North America and in ways that obscures the presence of women and people of colour. Wendake has a gendered component anchored to the origin story of the Wendat people, a version of which is shared by many other Indigenous groups in North America: after a woman fell from the realm of the sky into the realm of water below, animals supported her by creating an island, and Turtle Island is the name for North America.

The Wendat, whose name means islanders, live upon the island, Wendake, and thus descend from Sky Woman.[14] The name embraced by the Wendat infers this story, yet linguistic barriers historically have prevented scholars from performing a gendered reading of the name. In this way, Indigenous peoples can easily be othered and rendered without gender by settler-colonizer naming practices that rely upon normative forms and Western expressions of gender to exert power over lands, peoples, and their resources.[15] Over time, the gendered background of names such as Huron also fades, which in this case demonstrates how Indigenous masculinity can be obscured on the map.

The Brébeuf map furthermore points to a hybrid naming regimen through which the map becomes bilingual yet the toponyms themselves do not possess any common meaning as linguistically distinct appositives, just as Huronia (land of the boar's brush hair men or ruffians) has no conceptual relationship with Wendake (land of the islanders) as signifiers of place. As seen in the first chapter, authoritative Indigenous sources, as opposed to Euro-settler textual sources, feature women more prominently in place nomenclature. They can also depict Indigenous men in positions of power, authority, and as worthy of respect in ways that may not be reflected in Euro-settler nomenclature. As scholars are increasingly concluding, moving away from relying so heavily upon textual sources of information, and divesting them as sources of authoritative knowledge, will better elevate both women's and Indigenous knowledge and voices.[16]

Scholars who, for linguistic or cultural reasons, cannot interpret Indigenous place names will not see Indigenous masculinity and, from a Western perspective, the power implicated by that gender on the map. Rather, Indigenous names remain emasculated in settler-colonial eyes, which points to the underlying signification of women's names that will be explored in due course. Viewing Indigenous names as masculine challenges a significant instrument deployed by the settler-colonizer to claim and occupy space, in that Euro-settlers tend to obviate forms of gendered Indigenous power, which from a Western perspective has traditionally meant patriarchal power. By asserting Indigenous masculinity through

Gender and Canada's Place Names

place nomenclature, Native Americans re-appropriate their spaces precisely through the act of embracing Western perceptions of gendered power, although this tends to come at the cost of not re-subscribing to matrilineal power and forms of authority.[17] This perspective also reminds us that Indigenous men in Wendake and other Indigenous groups held key roles in the creation of settler-colonial societies.

While hagiotoponymic practices on the part of Europeans continued, during the seventeenth and eighteenth centuries naming trends changed once again from a gendered perspective. The novelty of the initial wave of naming initiated by Cartier and Champlain and their successors led to a second one centered on secular names. Claude Bernou (c. 1638–1716) takes up this practice in order to curry favour with the French monarch and his court with his c. 1681 map of North America, created shortly after the newest colony of France, La Louisiane, had been established (Figure 3.2). Bernou, motivated by his desire to be appointed the bishop of France's next colony, Nouvelle Biscaye, created this beautifully coloured manuscript map using the most recent information at his disposal during a period in which the Mississippi River and Great Lakes basin were emerging on European maps. We might even imagine the moment in Versailles when the king and his advisors first encountered this map. Bernou re-baptizes this river the "Riviere Missisipi ou Colbert" after the king's advisor, Jean-Baptiste de Colbert (1619–1683). In the region of the Great Lakes, the names for remarkable features have similarly transformed to regale other men at court, including the Lac des Illinois dit Dauphin (Lake Michigan), after the prince, the Mer douce des Hurons dit d'Orleans (the king's older brother, Phillip; Lake Huron), and Lac de Conty (brother and successor to the king; Lake Erie). Several other place names celebrate prominent individuals at court who were of importance to these men, and unlike hagiotoponyms, these individuals were living at the time that these names were bestowed, comprising a form of vanity place nomenclature. Their presence on this and subsequent maps further whitens, Westernizes, and masculinizes space within the architecture of colonization. Bernou's approach also makes room on the map to celebrate political and colonial authorities beyond the monarchy, which foreshadows another significant change in place-naming practices with respect to the adoption of names belonging to otherwise unremarkable people.

While Bernou's revision of the names awarded to the Great Lakes does not endure, other commemorative names remain, as the example of Moncton, New Brunswick, demonstrates. Robert Monckton (1726–1782) led several incursions into Acadia and other North American lands claimed by France. He helped initiate the Acadian deportation from Atlantic Canada in 1755, which resulted in a catastrophic diaspora of people who had been living for over a century in the region. While the nineteenth-century Acadian Renaissance saw this community return, albeit diminished in numbers and nonetheless governed by British and later Anglophone-Canadian politicians, relations between Anglophones and Francophones remain troubled in the area.[18] The growth of the city in recent years makes it the province's largest urban settlement and remarkable for its socio-economic and cultural diversity that often falls along linguistic lines. Two places in Quebec also celebrate Monckton, and he is not alone: Edward Cornwallis (1713–1776), Monckton's peer in Nova Scotia, beyond being a founder of Anglophone Atlantic Canada, also placed a bounty on the scalps of the Mi'kmaq. In 2017, Halifax-area residents, including local Indigenous communities, lobbied to have a statue commemorating the man removed from a downtown park.[19] There are eight places in five provinces and territories that commemorate Cornwallis. Similarly, John A. Macdonald (1815–1891), a founder of Canada as well as author of the Indian Residential School system responsible for the cultural genocide of Indigenous peoples in the country well into the 1990s, also created the Indian Act. His statue was removed from its site of public memorialization in Victoria, British Columbia, in 2018. There remain 134 places across the country that bear his surname, and these numbers do not include the countless street names inspired by these three men and others like them.

Masculine toponymy dominates the Americas in part because the place namers were men who valued the activities and accomplishments of their peers and cultural icons in ways that link toponyms to identity

Gender and Canada's Place Names

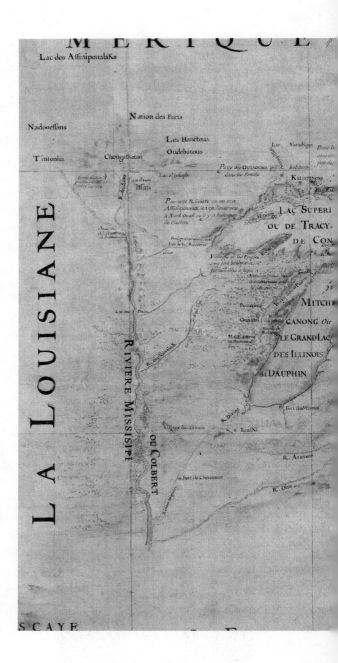

Figure 3.2 Claude Bernou (attributed), *Carte de l'Amérique septentrionale*, c. 1681 (detail). Paris, Bibliothèque nationale de France, département Cartes et plans, CPL SH 18E PF 122 DIV 2 P 0 Res.

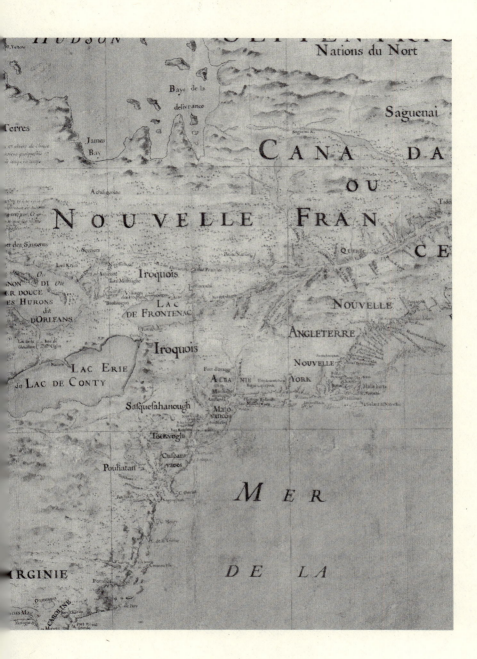

and violence. This describes one of the underlying discomforts vocalized in contemporary Canada when one considers changing names or sites of commemoration, because these names are viewed as historical and traditional, as rooting some identities to this nation and its colonial past, particularly because most Canadians have some sense of their family's pre-settler origins. Distributing hagiotoponyms or names inspired by biblical places across the Americas points to the namer's identification with various forms of Christianity; names celebrating royal or colonial authorities implicate the namer's white male background at the crossroads of imperial expansion; and some names construct the identity of the people who lived in a place, as the assignment of place names that commemorate European cities demonstrates. Settlements such as Windsor, Ontario (a French settlement, after the American Revolution it was renamed in commemoration of the British city by that name), and Selkirk, Manitoba (named for Thomas Douglas, 5th earl of Selkirk, located in Scotland), reflect the geographic origins of these cities' male colonizers. Canadians tend to cultivate some connection to these places, which reinforces the ties that bind settler-colonizers to Canada from the perspective of their identities primarily along patrilineal pathways.

Embodied Names

Women's presence in toponymy tends to be expressed through religious names, although exceptions are easily at hand, as the examples of Victoria and Regina demonstrate. Beyond well-known women, in this case both referencing monarchs, nearly no names commemorate everyday women, whereas a wealth of names points to ordinary men who owned land or staked a claim to it. A significant trend in gendered naming practices signals how women's bodies become transposed onto the landscape in ways that also allow them to be claimed, transacted upon, plundered of their natural resources, scarified with urbanization, and abandoned. As Mark Monmonnier observes, North American men in the trades during the nineteenth and twentieth centuries awarded names that today are deemed offensive or certainly referential to women.[20] The Teat Rocks (approved in 1946) in the Georgian Bay, Ontario, area "take their name from the shape of the southeastern rock, The Teat,"[21] which one infers was inspired by the shape of a woman's breast, whereas Breast-Work Hill, Alberta (1942), refers instead to the fortification, breastwork.

Nipples and breasts as geographic features require further consideration, particularly because geographers and cartographers have not agreed on the mammary as any form of topographical phenomenon. The Teton River's glacial headwaters rise in present-day Blackfeet Indian Reservation, from whence it flows into Alberta and Saskatchewan before veering south to meet with the Missouri River near Fort Peck Dam. Also called Milk River, it appears on maps in the nineteenth century after the Louis, Clark, and Fidler expeditions in the region.[22] The meaning of the river's name at first seems Indigenous, but it appears that its association with breast milk occurs only in the nineteenth century, and an examination of its origin contextualizes the use of human body parts in names.

The meaning of Teton River should also be understood through the name Tintonha that appears on Bernou's manuscript map of 1681 because the Tintonha people can be found west of this river system along an un-named river (presumably the Missouri). The toponym, like others on this map, signifies the name of a people, in this case the Blackfeet known also as the Teton today. Settlers have appropriated a Blackfoot name, Tintonha, and assigned it an etymology from romance languages associated with the breast, Teton, now also associated with the Blackfoot. The history of this river—according to Tom Bateman in his historical account of the river—begins with the Lewis and Clark expedition to the area in 1804–05. The eight flags displayed at a monument in the town of Milk River visualize the belief that history and presence begins with Europeans: there is a French flag, followed by that of Spain, then the United States, the Hudson's Bay Company, the British Empire, Canada's former Red Ensign flag, and finally the current Canadian flag.[23] No Indigenous presence is acknowledged nor any history that precedes the arrival of Europeans, which serves as a male-centred origin story.

Gender and Canada's Place Names   91

The visualization of breasts as topographic features of North America gives us pause to consider names that also connect place to person. Somatoponymy describes place nomenclature inspired by parts of the human body. In many European languages geographic features such as rivers are described as having mouths (Lac de la Bouche, Quebec, which is near Lac des Têtes and Lac de la Langue); seas have capes, which references the Latin word for head (Cape Fear, Newfoundland, and Cape d'Or, Nova Scotia); and mountains, depending on the position of the visitor, have feet. As Lee Irwin observes, once women's bodies become the land upon which men live their lives, and especially when likened to paradise and intimate areas of a woman's body, the possibility of a mythical journey or the necessity of a biblical pilgrimage arise. The symbolism reveals that "paradise is metaphorically likened to a woman's body, a fertile, beckoning promise as an earthly reward to the successful, reverent explorer—a visionary ground to be exploited and erotically possessed and used," and also abused.[24]

Hills categorized as breast-shaped do not themselves comprise an official form of geographical feature, but the phenomenon has nonetheless garnered sufficient recognition that it now boasts its own Wikipedia page.[25] The gendered character of these hills becomes clear upon associating elevation with the endowment of women's, as opposed to men's, breasts, and the vocabulary invoking breast imagery also varies. Twelve elevations named for nipples can be found on the Canadian map in British Columbia and the Yukon, all officially approved between 1924 and 1955. The British Columbia Geographical Names database categorizes The Nipples, northwest of Kitseguecla Lake, as "Peaks—Summit of a mountain or hill, or the mountain or hill itself. Plural of Peak (2)," which suggests that modern eyes have analyzed this toponymic data, as it now resides in a database online, but it was not flagged for future discussion.[26] The pairing of nipple-inspired names with twin peaks evidently reflects women's physical condition. In the same province, another "Plural of Peak (2)" elevation, called Nip and Tuck Peaks (1979), abstractly points to plastic surgery, presumably in the form of breast augmentation, through its name. And elsewhere in British Columbia's Monarch Mountain region is Concubine Peaks (1984), whose name describes two peaks, according to the person who filed the original name application in 1967, "in keeping with the royal theme."[27] This may be the only place name that refers to a courtly sexual companion in Canada.

An archaic English word for nipple, two sets of hills in Canada are called The Paps (Thunder Bay, Ontario, 1907) and Eskimo Paps (Newfoundland, 1953), the latter evidently also containing a dated term for Inuit people (there remain twenty-six places named for Eskimo across the country in English and French). While some names contain references to breasts and teats, it is often unclear whether there is any gendered element to them, as they may refer to a person's name, as with the example of Lac Bossum in Quebec (1988), whose place name commission categorizes it as a Cree name, reflecting the surname of a well-known chief. Most of these geographical features are remote locations accessed by mountaineers, miners, and related professionals in the field of natural resources, and for the most part predate the second wave of feminism. Without the opportunity to encounter these names, women and modern men beyond the staff of present-day naming commissions have yet to scrutinize their suitability for today's map of Canada.

In addition to women's physical features, some places were given names that personify people or animals in gendered ways.[28] These include *squaw*, used by white men, particularly in English but also in French, to denominate Indigenous women; the term is associated with sexual promiscuity and prostitution. The term remains so offensive that US Secretary of the Interior Deb Haaland (Laguna Pueblo), led a campaign in 2021 to have it removed from federal lands. There remain twenty-seven place names in Canada containing squaw, including Lac-de-la-Squaw in Bas-Saint-Laurent, Quebec (last approved in 1972), with others in Alberta, British Columbia, New Brunswick, Newfoundland and Labrador, Nunavut, and the Yukon. Other derogatory names that explicitly refer to women include Lac Bimbo (1972) in Quebec, and Bitch Lake (1939), Hag Lake (1933), Shrew Lake (1933), and Tease Lake (1936), all in Ontario.

Gender and Canada's Place Names

Indeed, there are many lakes located in northern Ontario whose names might attract extra scrutiny. Several places across the country refer to witches (whereas warlocks have yet to be honoured with a place name) and spinsters (yet there are even more places named for bachelors, as well as a qualitative difference in meaning between the two terms designating unmarried people).[29] Some places named for animals also possess secondary meanings associated with women's genitalia, in the case of beavers. While the double meaning may exist in some contexts, we acknowledge that it would be impossible to understand if the term was particularly gendered.

Nonetheless, two striking observations can be made about this sort of place name. First, the geographic features whose names might sound outdated or sexist tend to be located in remote spots and thus do not attract much attention within broader society. Hardly would we expect to find a large population who hails from Hag Lake, near Nipissing, Ontario, in Algonquin Park, without some disagreement about the name arising. There are no large population centres with problematic names in terms of depictions of gender—except for the overwhelming representation of male, often colonial or religious, commemorative names. Yet many of these marginalizing names were approved in more recent times, which suggests that committees with oversight over names did not find them problematic. In the case of Hag Lake, it was approved by the Ontario Geographic Names Board's predecessor in 1933. Lac Bimbo, whose name's meaning is the same in both English and French, in the Abitibi-Témiscamingue region of Quebec was approved by that province's place name office in 1972. Perhaps pointing to a discomfort with the name, the comparatively more visible street named Rue Bimbo in Montreal's suburbs had its name revised in 1990 to Rue Lauzanne.

It can also be proposed that some remote spots comprise ideal venues for gendered leisure and sport, for instance the hunting and fishing industries, which suggests that men would be more likely to hear the name of and interact in these spaces while engaging with leisure activities or natural resource extraction. Reinforcing this observation are the types of industry found on Rue Bimbo/Lauzanne, which include industrial facilities that produce moldings and signage, and services for paving as well as for vehicle repairs—all traditionally male vocations and workplaces. Second, the origins of these names remain obscure in that the provinces rarely acknowledge who proposed and approved them, which in some ways also obfuscates the responsibility of the namer to broader society and, in this case, frustrates a marginalized group when it comes to toponymy. Due to decades of underfunding, as well as our migration to online repositories of data, a history of the name often remains hidden away in bricks-and-mortar locations that are simply not accessible from a staffing and research perspective.

In this respect, gendered names also can be modified so that they resemble socially or culturally less-desirable forms. Taking the example of English-language place names that contain "woman," fifty-four names from nine provinces and territories exist. Of them, thirty-three describe geographical features and places using age: The Old Woman is a rock in Victoria, Nova Scotia (1975); South Old Woman River is found in Algoma, Ontario (1967), alongside Old Woman Bay and Lake, respectively (both approved in 1952); and the cape, Old Woman Head, is in Newfoundland (1953). None refer explicitly to youth or young and middle-aged women, and in contrast, only fourteen names use "woman" or "woman's" alone as a signifier of place—for instance, Woman Island in Algoma, Ontario (1970). Other curious adoptions include Medicine Woman Creek in British Columbia (1949), Fairy Woman Lake in Manitoba (1978), and the rock known as Naked Woman in Newfoundland (2013).

Perhaps not surprisingly, names that demonstrate possession are less common when the possessor is a woman (women's or woman's), exampled by Women's Buffalo Jump in Alberta (2015), which may point to the way women historically used a place or to the fact that women hunted. A total of nineteen names demonstrates possession of various geographic features and places using these two terms, sixteen of whose possessors were "old women." This observation exposes a known relationship between age

Gender and Canada's Place Names

and power, whether from an Indigenous perspective in terms of elders or knowledge holders, or from a settler-colonial one when viewed through the prism of economic power and wisdom.

In contrast, French-language names involving *femme*, which means both woman and wife, exhibit different trends in the eastern provinces. Of the seventeen names listed in Canada's national place-name database, four characterize their place as a "bonne femme," which highlights a valued characteristic of conjugal life. Five places are articulated as belonging to someone's wife, for instance Lac de la Femme de Givre (Lake of the Frosty Wife, or of the wife of Givre, being her husband's surname) in Sept-Rivières, Quebec (1989). While none seem to refer in any way to age, this is in part because *vieille* signifies old woman. Of the forty-four names in Quebec and New Brunswick, many of course describe old places such as churches (*églises*) and houses (*maisons*) that comprise female-gendered nouns in French that, when modified by an adjective, take the female form. At least sixteen of these names comprise spaces possessed by "la Vieille," being either an old woman or old wife, some of whom are named for their husband's surname, such as Lac de la Vieille-Ménard (Laurentides, Quebec). Previously called Lac Méduse, it was renamed in 1984 to remember "Flavie Ménard, nicknamed mother Ménard, who arrived in Val-David in about 1850. In addition to treating the infirm, she was a midwife. She regularly fished on this lake."[30]

These names for the most part do not refer to individuals but rather seem to adhere to a general sense of the female sex, whereas other names refer to specific individuals. Of the 100 places across Canada that refer to lady, many comprise commemorative names, such as Lady Franklin Bay in Nunavut (1910), named for explorer John Franklin's wife. When he was knighted, she received the title of lady, and after her husband disappeared in 1845, she launched several expeditions to locate him and the HMS *Erebus* and HMS *Terror*. When we study this name more closely, we detect two levels of commemoration. Not only is the woman as the wife and would-be rescuer of Franklin anchored to the map, but so is the husband himself, as she never travelled to this region of the world. Rather, her name here serves as a referent to her husband, with neither her first nor maiden name commemorated. This example reminds us that women's names have traditionally been erased through marriage renaming practices common in some regions of the Western world, here reproduced as a place name. The practice of referring to women using their spouse's name further erodes a sense of specificity, as a wife's married title would resemble that of her spouse's mother. Of these 100 names, thirty-seven comprise women's married names that commemorate men whose surnames will be familiar to most Canadians, including Banting, Douglas, Dufferin, Grey, Hamilton, Laurier, Macdonald, and Parry. Impressively, only two of this cohort refer to old ladies, which also points to the power of not just wisdom but also the class-based forms we associate traditionally with women who bear the title of lady. Other noble titles follow similar trends in Canadian toponymy.

Incidentally, there remain seven toponymic references to Medusa— the gorgon known for the snakes radiating out of her head who, if she gazed upon someone, would turn him to stone— in Newfoundland and Quebec. Certainly, mythological names broadly influence place nomenclature in Canada, despite the fact that these mythological figures have no relationship to this continent, and several of them are women. In fact, there are more Venuses than Zeuses, more Heras than Hermeses, and more Gaias than Eroses in Canada's place nomenclature, suggesting that women gods for some reason were preferred over male ones as place names, which contrasts with our findings for Judeo-Christian hagiotoponyms. One explanation for this difference may lie in the sexuality and eroticism invoked by these women deities, particularly in the myths associated with them, and thus their desirability. Viewed in this way, the use of female mythological figures coincides with the deployment of names that refer to women's body parts on the Canadian landscape. At the same time, few names refer to real women compared to female gorgons, gods, and biblical figures and saints (members of this last group, we recognize, may themselves have existed). The same cannot be said of names that commemorate real men, who as a typology occupy a significant percentage

Gender and Canada's Place Names   97

of this country's place nomenclature, in addition to names inspired by gendered mythological and religious beings and people.

Visualizing Gender

My study of bodies and gender thus far has omitted men, in part so that we may focus on the limited ways women are represented toponymically, but also because I struggle to find male analogues. There are no places named for distinctly masculine bodily features, nor places named for Dr. Beck's Husband. Indeed, only one place in Canada bears such a name, Husband Lake, Ontario (1957), and it does not refer in any way to his wife or her surname, and may in fact be a man's surname. Rather, we can point to some exceptional representations of masculinity that seem to be unparalleled in place nomenclature. The coats of arms adopted by settlements, provinces, and territories often feature explicit phallic references among the beasts that symbolize these places. For instance, Quebec's coat of arms was adopted in 1939 (Figure 3.3), and it features the fleur-de-lis and colours representing France, maple leaves signifying Canada, as well as a lion symbolizing the British crown. Both the lion's penis and testicles, which in armorial design terms are referred to as the pizzle, are included in the symbol. The coats of arms of Canada, Newfoundland and Labrador, and British Columbia all feature a similar lion. No analogous representation of female animals features their genitalia, and most provincial and municipal symbols have abstracted the pizzle so that it appears to be a lump or bulge extruding from the animal's genital region. Of all the provincial and territorial emblems, none include any representation of women among their symbolism.

Coupled with these anatomical observations is the fact that coats of arms comprise deliberately selected symbols organized into registers whose placement together characterizes their respective importance. Quebec's coat of arms references three polities—Canada, France, and Britain—whose symbols traditionally represent male-led monarchies and nation states, despite the coat of arms' creation between the reigns of

Figure 3.3 The province of Quebec's coat of arms, adopted in 1939.

Britain's two longest-serving women monarchs. Aside from symbolic beasts, many of the armorial shields that figure into the centre of a coat of arms are guarded or supported by lions, unicorns, deer, and other animals, some of whom exhibit the pizzle. And in recent centuries, some beasts have been replaced by male humans, and rarely women. When women do appear in armorial shields, they often represent symbols such as abundance, as seen on the coat of arms of the city of Guelph, Ontario, where a woman wearing a toga holds a cornucopia brimming with an array of fresh food (Figure 3.4). In this case, a neoclassical-styled woman represents a concept, opposite of whom is a white settler man. The shield upon which they lean unites two figures who could not exist together, given that personified concepts cannot be categorized as humans in the

Figure 3.4 The coat of arms for the city of Guelph, Ontario, adopted in 1978.

same way as the reality of a white settler man in the composition (which also features a pizzled lion and horse). The result is that most symbolic compositions that represent places offer an overtly masculinized program of visualization that almost entirely excludes women of any real variety.

This trend in the verbal and visual significations of places extends into the spatial realm to the sites that serve as the seats of local, provincial and territorial, and federal government power—at city and town halls, and at legislative sites. Lining the corridors of hallways leading to the offices of this country's public servants are portraits, typically of past lawmakers, who until recent decades were almost always men. These locations embody a place's symbolic representation and its history, as iterated in its place names and emblems, incorporating them into the interior and exterior architectural programming of the site, almost always designed and coordinated by men decades ago. An excellent example of this can be found at the provincial legislature of Saskatchewan, in Regina, built between

1906 and 1912, a location whose grounds later celebrated the monarch with the Queen Elizabeth II Gardens and Burmese, the latter being a commemoration of the species of horse she indicated was her favourite on the eve of her visit to the city in 2005. Elsewhere, the grounds offer a commemoration of unspecified generic religious women, in the Sisters Legacy Statue, who served as teachers and nurses to establish modern health and educational systems in the province. In the balance, the grounds offer monuments to male war veterans, former politicians, and at least one governor general. Inside the building, the Assiniboine Gallery features a series of fifteen portraits of Indigenous chiefs and leaders, none of whom are women.[31] Emanating from the ceiling of the rotunda, a central feature of the building, is a mural by John Leman in the 1930s titled *Before the White Man Came* that features Indigenous male hunters and their camp, also devoid of women.

Another example points to a location that includes women in more meaningful ways. The Famous Five Monument is located on the grounds of Parliament Hill in Ottawa, Ontario. A bronze installation dating from 2000, the monument is the only one at the facility to commemorate women whose contributions go beyond ceremonial and political activities. The five women (Henrietta Edwards, Nellie McClung, Louise McKinney, Emily Murphy, and Irene Parlby) advocated for the appointment of women to the Senate by overcoming the Supreme Court's ruling in 1928 that women were not persons and therefore could not serve in either the Senate or the House of Commons.[32] But this example is an outlier in most government houses across this country. Aside from recently elected women politicians and representations of women monarchs—particularly Queen Victoria and Queen Elizabeth II—women typically can be found in romanticized settler-pioneer scenes included in mosaics, murals, paintings, frescoes, and engravings as either Indigenous or white women, or as embodied concepts. In this way, unlike the Famous Five, they lack the specificity granted to male analogues as settler-colonizers and politicians whose historical presence anchors men, but not women, to these sites of place commemoration and collective identity.

Gender and Canada's Place Names

The state of this nomenclature and their visual analogues forces us to reflect upon the possibility of updating these racist and sexist terms, as Lac-de-la-Squaw did in 1985, to become Lac Sauvagesse (Savage Woman Lake), despite the outdatedness of the newer term in the year in which the Commission de toponymie rescinded squaw. Similarly, both squaw and *sauvagesse* obscure the fact that the Indigenous woman after whom the lake was named possessed an identity and likely came from a specific Indigenous community. In contrast, Lac de la Vieille-Ménard, updated from Lac Méduse, connects a specific woman (her first and maiden names absent, though) to a place where she lived and to which she contributed as a member of the community. Both name changes occurred within a year of each other and were approved by the same place-name board, yet they demonstrate the starkly uneven approaches to revising place names as well as some underlying bias. On the one hand, the nod to Ménard commemorates an everyday woman, but on the other, the treatment of a name referring to an Indigenous woman celebrates nobody specific and even reinforces a racist stereotype. In both cases, we can see how un-savoury terms referring to women were updated with new names that nonetheless maintained the characterization of the place as female. As will be explored in the penultimate chapter, the assumption that places named for racialized groups are masculine, such as Negro Creek, British Colum-bia, tends to inform any gendered aspect of the name when it is revised, whereas gender-specific names such as squaw may invite a revised name that maintains the same gender codes. A similar observation of the pizzle reinforces the normativity of this approach to representation: replacing more explicitly articulated depictions of genitals with less controversial ones only maintains gendered codes.

Asserting Women's Presence

To make commemorative material more inclusive from a gendered per-spective, structural, procedural, and philosophical changes must be made. First, place-name commissions must take a serious look at their membership from a gendered perspective. Without intending to criticize efforts made to date in the province and territories, as of 2021 the Geographical Names Board of Canada is chaired by a woman, but among the provincial and territorial members, there are nine men and four women who serve as provincial or territorial toponymist or director of a provincial or territorial geographical names commission. These women serve in roles that have traditionally been held by men, moreover, which may imply that the amount of work that remains to be done is possibly greater in some regions than in others. Certainly, if women have only come to these roles in the twenty-first century, this suggests that centuries of problematic and exclusionary names would comprise a significant archive that requires revising, in addition to the contemporary naming-related matters to which they attend. This recommendation also supposes that women might notice gendered issues more than men, which would be a faulty assumption. Many of these offices possess few to no staff members, which presents another structural barrier to revising our place names because the research and skillsets required to complete this work are expensive. That being said, by working with provincial and territorial universities, employing their students as research assistants, some headway may be made. Volunteer toponymists comprise another avenue that could be explored. Furthermore, the Geographical Names Board of Canada (GNBC) should consider appointing an expert equipped to assist in these gender-related matters who reviews all place-name proposals before they are approved and who flags concerns that must be addressed—for example, by creating an equality, diversity, and inclusion framework that the applicants for new names and name changes must complete.

At the procedural level, and as we will document in the last part of this book, revising and proposing place names follows a set of guidelines that vary from province to province. A limited-time moratorium on names that explicitly signify men while excluding women would compel all proposals for new names and revisions for existing names to consider inscribing women's presence in our place nomenclature. Similarly, the GNBC could work with its members to consider assessing duplicate names across the country, to encourage these towns and cities to embrace new or slightly adjusted names that better include women. For instance, there are twenty-five populated settlements that feature the name Windsor in some way, some of them in the same province. The name points not only to the European roots of this country's colonizers, but also to a patriarchal monarchy and noble line that do not originate from Canada, serving as the present queen's surname. These settlements should be encouraged to find ways of embracing new or altered names, perhaps through the creation of compound names that allow them to celebrate their distinctiveness.

One of the sticking points with changing names, however, is that most provinces and territories require some form of public support in order to enact any name change or assignment. Others typically expect that a proposed name has already become embraced by the community as an unofficial name. Usually, this support takes the form of a signed petition, plebiscite, or some other form of documenting public consultation and support that is included along with the application to adjust a name. Many of the most problematic names we have encountered are in sparsely populated and sometimes unpopulated areas of the country, where it would be challenging to amass the support required to change a name. Also, while many names invoking Windsor are populated settlements, others comprise geographic features whose name adjustments would not impact anybody's postal address nor their sense of identity in terms of their moorings to a place. Therefore, some streamlined procedures for adjusting names should be adopted by place-naming commissions across this country to make it easier to change the names of unpopulated places.

Finally, each place-name authority in this country must address what can be characterized as a philosophy of tolerance when it comes to our place names. In part, we tolerate outdated and colonial names because they connect with some of our identities, and the procedures outlined to change them presume that the status quo should be difficult to upset. Our naming procedures and their history, as we are exploring here, have white, patriarchal roots, and this demographic remains a significant one in Canada. How could our approach to naming be significantly different if it were influenced by more women? What sorts of names would we reach for when a new shoal required naming? Would we name it for our body parts? Or would we consider instead how names can honour and cherish people, values, moments, flora and fauna, and even objectives that we admire and remember? From another perspective, how can universities and other entities responsible for names address the overwhelmingly masculine nomenclature of buildings that is directly tied to male patronage and sexist economic conditions that maintain men as the predominantly wealthiest individuals in this country? If we want to cultivate a country where women feel equal and are equal to men, an adjustment to our naming philosophy is urgently needed.

In this chapter, I have outlined the ways that gender is asserted and sometimes operationalized through our place names while offering a history for gendered naming in Canada. I have taken a binary approach to gender, which leaves much room for further research and advocacy regarding non-binary gender and sexual identities as manifested in our toponymy. LGBTQ2S+ individuals will hardly see themselves in any name, such is the engrained and outdated conceptualization of gender in this sense. I have also offered some ways that gender, and particularly the inclusion of women, can be productively addressed by place name commissions, naming procedures, and by the Canadian public. In the next chapter, I build upon the analysis and observations made so far so to problematize Indigenous or Indigenous-seeming names when they become manipulated and appropriated by settler-colonial people.

CHAPTER 4

Indigenous Names in a Settler-Colonial Context

1492 Land Back Lane in Caledonia, Haldimand County, Ontario, epitomizes many of the recent critical issues in Indigenous–settler relations in Canada. After protestors felled a statue of Egerton Ryerson (1803–1882) in June 2021 at the Toronto university named after him, the statue's head appeared on a spike on Land Back Lane. In protesting the theft of their lands, the Haudenosaunee sequestered a settler-colonial monument associated with the country's Indian Residential School System through Egerton Ryerson's involvement with it. In tandem, the Haudenosaunee crafted a place name that encapsulates the ultimate objective of their protest, which began in July 2020. Despite being rendered in the colonial language of English, the name could belong to no group other than an Indigenous one, who for centuries witnessed their land illegally sold or stolen. The Haudenosaunee can point to the Haldimand Proclamation of 1784, an agreement between British authorities and the Six Nations that reserved the Haldimand Tract for their exclusive use; this agreement specified that the lands could not be sold or bought, which returns us to the grievance expressed by occupants of Land Back Lane.[1] This name, along with the recontextualization of a mutilated, settler-colonial symbol, weave together a place identity for a region of Caledonia that is distinctly unsettled.

Unlike the place knowledge explored in the first chapter of this book, much of Canada's Indigenous toponymy underlines the wounds inflicted by colonialism. To treat this topic, it is important to first acknowledge the defining foundations of the Indigenous–settler relationship in the form of treaties, agreements, laws such as the Indian Act, and declarations that have been embraced nationally or internationally, such as the United Nations Declaration on the Rights of Indigenous Peoples, which bear on place identity. Understanding these foundations will clarify the ways that Indigenous place knowledge and naming can be distinguished from names of Indigenous origins appearing on the map today. Many of these names, some of which may be embraced by the Indigenous communities from which they originate, exhibit a varying scale of authenticity in ways that should prompt us to question the suitability of certain Indigenous-seeming names, particularly given the richness of toponymic and place knowledge explored at the outset of this book. The remainder of this chapter will shed light on settler uses and conditioning of Indigenous names, while pointing to the ways in which Indigenous peoples have been reclaiming both names and spaces in examples such as the Six Nations and Land Back Lane.

Indigenous-Settler(-Colonial) Place Relations: Treaties, the Indian Act, and UNDRIP

Treaties between people define land use, access to resources, exchanges of people and goods, agreements about military support, and they use toponymy to define the areas included in a treaty. A significant treaty that impacted the colonial configuration of this country is the Treaty of Utrecht (1713), which saw much of North America surrendered, in the eyes of Europeans, to the British. The Treaty of Paris (1763) further reduced the French claim to lands in Canada. Both treaties are named for the European places in which they were signed. They were widely translated and disseminated documents that circulated in Europe, and they comprised agreements that excluded Indigenous groups as peer nations. Western governments and courts tend to view treaties as documents, whereas Indigenous groups in Canada have traditionally made these agreements in a variety of ways, for instance through wampum belts. The Hiawatha

108   *Canada's Place Names and How to Change Them*

Belt, discussed in the first chapter, represents the Haudenosaunee Confederacy. It documents the Peace and Friendship Treaty between its constituent nations and exists as an emblem of the Confederacy's territory.

In Canada, there are several varieties of treaties. The Peace and Friendship Treaties of the eighteenth century relate mainly to Indigenous peoples and their lands in Ontario, Quebec, and Atlantic Canada, whereas the numbered treaties of the nineteenth and twentieth centuries refer, for the most part, to regions and peoples to the west and north. Treaties can be understood as representations of international space in which boundaries between nations are defined and articulated. Their existence in Canada, in many cases, demonstrates a historical belief that these treaties involved nation-to-nation negotiations. The Two-Row Wampum Belt is an example of both the relationship of peer nations and their agreement to not interfere in each other's affairs and customs. The belt depicts two parallel lines of purple beads that represent separate Indigenous and colonial boats moving in the same direction. As Tehanetorens (Ray Fadden) describes the agreement, "One, a birch bark canoe, will be for the Indian People, their laws, their customs, and their ways. The other, a ship, will be for the white people and their laws, their customs, and their ways."[2]

As the Two-Row Wampum Belt demonstrates, many of these treaties become expressed in visual ways that are richly figurative and complex, while articulating relationships between the parties and the land. A similar treaty-making approach was taken by the French toward the Wendat and Algonquian peoples, as the British did with many other groups. The term "Covenant Chain" helps to characterize the range of broadly deployed colonial and Indigenous practices to formulate alliances and political relationships, particularly before the nineteenth century.[3] The Covenant Chain's North American origins can be found in the 1618 treaty initially created between the Mahicans and Dutch colonists in present-day New England. It became a model later embraced by many Indigenous peoples of the Great Lakes region following a period of unrest with the British, culminating in the Royal Proclamation of 1763 in which the Crown acknowledged Indigenous rights and title to their lands.[4] Signatories of the

Indigenous Names in a Settler-Colonial Context   109

ensuing Covenant Chain of 1764 and related Treaty of Niagara include the Anishinaabe to the west, the Haudenosaunee, and the Algonquian nations residing to the east, among them the Mi'kmaq. Councils convened for the purpose of forming the treaty, which included colonial officials, among them the Crown's representative for Indian Affairs, William Johnson (1715–1774). Johnson not only wrote down the treaty and presented it to the council of Indigenous leaders but he also gave the chiefs and elders of each nation a belt of wampum shells with the year 1764 on it, linking the treaty to the place and time where it was created.[5] The chiefs gave him a Two-Row Belt in exchange, sealing the parties' agreement on their nation-to-nation relationship.

The Covenant Chain relationship created what Bruce Morito calls a moral economy,[6] the health of which the treaty's parties had to keep balanced and where each would be held accountable. It is possible to see how these nation-to-nation relations existed by considering an example of the Haudenosaunee's treaty with the British. In 1684 the governor of New York learned that the Mohawk's allied nations had violated their treaty of 1643 by killing six colonists and their two hundred cows. The colonial administrator called a council meeting to discuss the violation and hold the Haudenosaunee accountable for violating their treaty. They were also accused of waving white flags (which the British erroneously interpreted as flags of peace rather than of war, because warriors wave them prior to launching an assault) and then of attacking colonists.[7] After apologizing and promising not to harm more colonists, both sides retreated for a number of days and renewed and polished the chain, this time with the enhancement of gifts for the governor, which included some hides and wampum.[8]

At first, visualizations of the Covenant Chain treaty were symbolized with a rope that moored a Dutch ship to a tree planted in Mahican territory.[9] The Mohawk reprised this representation in its treaty in 1643, but rather than rope, they used an iron chain, which no doubt was meant to emphasize the strength of the relationship or that of its parties compared to the weakened Mahicans. New York–based English settlers renewed

Canada's Place Names and How to Change Them

the chain in 1664 after replacing the Dutch in this region, and in 1677 two peace treaties negotiated at Albany, New York, rendered the chain in silver, making the chain stronger as well as more beautiful.[10]

As an Indian Agent and entrepreneur (he operated a wampum factory of some significance), Johnson participated in negotiating several treaties in the region of Six Nations in 1755. Part of his contribution was a speech that articulated the quality and strength of the alliance between the British Crown and the Haudenosaunee: "And tho' we were at first only tied together by a Rope, yet lest this Rope should grow Rotten and break, we tied ourselves together by an iron Chain—lest time and accident might rust and destroy this Chain of iron, we afterwards made one of Silver; the strength and brightness of which would be subject to no decay."[11] What changes in this version of the treaty is the mooring for the chain, because rather than a tree onshore in Indigenous land, it becomes fixed "to the immoveable mountains, and this in so firm a manner, that the hands of no mortal Enemy might be able to remove it."[12]

The replacement of the tree, which holds significant meaning to the Haudenosaunee and their Confederacy, with the mountains Europeans continued to expand into toward the west, cannot be overlooked, nor can the way in which Johnson inserts himself into the traditional symbolism of the Confederacy. For example, Johnson's professional stationary (Figure 4.1) features the tree associated with the Confederacy's core, Onondaga, with a chain slung from two branches like a garland, and a white heart featured prominently on the trunk, echoing some conventions used by Indigenous wampum makers, which reinforces my interpretation of the tree being Onondaga. To the right of the tree sit three Haudenosaunee men, and a fourth one approaches the fire (a third symbol of the Confederacy), who reaches out for a medal presented by Johnson, standing to the left of the fire, and behind him sit three of his men. Depictions such as this one also made their way into book engravings and onto treaty medals, the latter of which comprise gifts given to chiefs on the occasion of finalizing an agreement. They usually contained an engraved image of the British sovereign and were worn as a valued possession of honour.

Indigenous Names in a Settler-Colonial Context

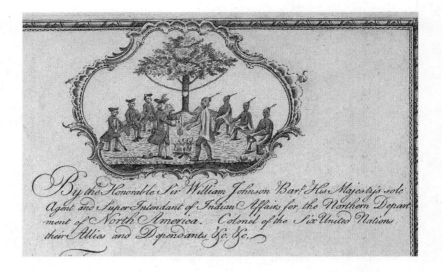

Figure 4.1 William Johnson's personal stationary depicting his relationship with the Haudenosaunee, from his Indian "Testimonial," engraved by Henry Dawkins, 1770 (reprinted at the New York Historical Society in 1946 using the original copperplate). Washington, DC, Printed Ephemera Collection, Library of Congress Portfolio 133, Folder 27f.

The legacies of these treaties anchor them to our present, making all Canadians and Indigenous groups treaty people. Their meanings are regularly shared within Indigenous communities and remain living treaties. For example, in 1851, Ottawa chief Jean-Baptiste Assiginack (1768–1866) related the meaning of the belt that Johnson gave his people in 1764. Johnson said their canoe floated on the other side of the Great Waters and that it was full of everything needed to nourish his children (the Anishinaabe in this context are characterized as Johnson's charges). All they needed was a place to anchor and the strength to pull this canoe across the Great Lakes to their territory.[13] In this way, Mark D. Walters contextualizes, "the Chain connected jurisdictions, but it was a connection defined by sacred duties of care and trust—and the British jurisdiction was moored at a distance until those living within Anishinaabe jurisdictions wanted to draw it nearer."[14] From another perspective, this arrangement entitled the Indigenous partners to the care and providing-power of the British, who could literally fill the Anishinaabe's canoes and satisfy their needs as allies would expect.

Concerning wampum belts as forms of treaties that express geographical relationships to people, not all of them relate stories and histories entirely focused on the land now known as Canada. In 1710, a Mohawk delegation that included Hendrick Tejonihokarawa (1660–c. 1735, who the British referred to as King Hendrick) went to England to request resources from Queen Anne to fight the French and Catholic missionaries who were encroaching on their territory. They were, in effect, exercising their nation-to-nation relationship according to the terms of their treaty. Once in London they were introduced to various members of elite society. A painting by John Verelst of Tejonihokarawa holding aloft the Peace Belt that he gifted to Anne reveals the level of public interest, in England at any rate, in the Indigenous delegation (Figure 4.2).[15]

In contrast, Thayendanegea, who also went by the name Joseph Brant (1743–1807), followed in the wake of Hendrick Tejonihokarawa and travelled to the country more than once with requests for the king. One request was for a tract of land in present-day southern Ontario, which was granted—and today Brant County remains a toponym in this region. One of the wampum belts created for Brant celebrates his transatlantic experience: a dark belt with two squares at either end, representing Britain and his home in North America, with a thick line connecting the two places.[16] In this way, Indigenous people actively used wampum as a means of depicting their own connection to the land they occupied, as well as to non-Indigenous spaces.

Many place names commemorate treaties, serving as a reminder about the boundaries and conditions they signify. Treaty Creek in the Cassiar Land District of British Columbia was adopted in 1930. According to the province's naming authority, it "refers to a treaty or convention between the Skeena and Stikine Indians—a sort of no man's land, and breeding

Figure 4.2 A mezzotint engraving based on John Verelst's portrait of Hendrick Tejonihokarawa holding the Peace Belt. Washington, DC, National Portrait Gallery, Smithsonian Institution (NPG.92.149). Photo by NMAI Photo Services.

ground for beaver between the two tribes; neither group are supposed to trap or occupy this area."[17] The Nisga'a and Tahltan Nations made this agreement in 1898 and drew a map defining their borders. Commemorating this peace is Treaty Rock, the place recently declared a Provincial Heritage Site, and one which nonetheless is not catalogued as a toponym by the province's naming authority. Similarly, many provinces have places named for wampum, another key means through which treaties were articulated.

After 1867, the year of Confederation, the federal government assumed an increasingly paternalistic relationship with the Indigenous peoples who had formed treaties with preceding settler-colonial representatives. The Indian Act (1876) is a document that uses blood quantum to define who is an Indian and what their entitlement to resources should be. It imposes governance structures in the form of band councils that have had significant impacts on Indigenous life and culture, particularly through requirements on children attending schools designed to interfere with the transmission of traditional knowledge ways. As a document, the Indian Act perpetuates centuries of inequality, both within Indigenous and settler societies, particularly for women, children, and people who experience intergenerational trauma. It banned cultural practices such as the potlatch and exerted controls not imposed upon other groups in Canada, for example in the form of temperance and prohibition under the belief that Indigenous people could not determine their own relationship with alcohol.[18] Importantly for this book, the Indian Act also describes the reservation system.

The reserve or reservation system describes a conservancy effort on the part of the federal government to remove Indigenous groups from their lands in the twentieth century and condense them into smaller areas. This strategy has its roots in the Spanish *reducción* (literally meaning "reduction"), which relocated Indigenous people, housed them in Spanish-style communities, educated them in Spanish language and Catholicism, and replaced their foodways with those of Europe. Like the Canadian reservation system, *reducciones* also had their own form of Indigenous governance and, in the balance, Europeans laid claim to and occupied land outside of the *reducciones*. French missions were also called *réductions*, and so we can see a similar strategy prior to the imposition of the modern reservation system in Canada.[19]

Canadians are often confused about reserves as designated spaces because they invariably are situated in the provinces and territories while remaining under federal jurisdiction, which has given rise to broad misunderstanding about resources and support given to Indigenous groups.

For instance, healthcare and education in Canada are administered by the provinces and territories, but the reservations are overseen by the federal Department of Crown–Indigenous Relations and Northern Affairs Canada (INAC). Harold Bherer, Sylvie Gagnon, and Jacinte Roberge mined the Indian Act for a definition of reserves and determine that they are "extra-territorial enclaves under the exclusive guardianship of the federal government, but still located in provincial territory."[20] Reserves were also named by the federal government, which has provoked much criticism over the decades on the part of Canadians, Indigenous groups, as well as international bodies, yet the provinces and territories are typically responsible for the awarding and updating of place names.

One of the 619 First Nations recognized by INAC, north of the Richibucto River in Kent County, New Brunswick, is Elsipogtog First Nation, whose name is not registered in the Geographical Names Board of Canada's (GNBC) federated toponym database. Instead, this reserve is catalogued as Richibucto 15; the number refers to the reserve being the fifteenth of twenty-eight in the province. This means that the federal database deliberately excludes the provincially registered name for this reserve, Elsipogtog (which means River of Fire in Mi'kmaq), whose former name was Big Cove—a name imposed upon it prior to the more recent name change in 2003.[21] After their ancestors signed a Peace and Friendship Treaty in 1761 with the British, the community became known as Richibucto Reserve in 1802. Today community members call it both Big Cove and Elsipogtog, which signals the reality that some communities have more than one name, and that historical names sometimes persist alongside updated ones. Importantly, nobody seems to refer to the community by its official name.

In this light, Indigenous place identity can be multilayered and involve several names that may or may not appear on the map. Métis scholar Chelsea Vowel points out that in the Indigenous world naming tends to be fluid in general, so Canadians should expect names to continue to change and not always as a response to colonialism. That being said, communities

116   *Canada's Place Names and How to Change Them*

across Canada, as Elsipogtog exemplifies, are eschewing names chosen by the settler-colonizer. As Vowel observes,

> One person can call herself Assiniboine, Stoney, Nakota Sioux, Stone Sioux, Asinipwât, Nakoda or Nakota, and Îyârhe Nakoda—all names that have been used for the same group of people. In addition to the group name, people will also identify themselves by which community they come from; in this case, it could be the Alexis Nakota-Sioux Nation in Alberta. Many of our communities have undergone name changes, too; so, depending on what generation you are in, you may use different names for the same community.[22]

She encourages Canadians to learn the historical names of local Indigenous groups and to devote effort to learning how their names are rendered within their own languages.

In addition to this effort, Canadians must learn the accepted and embraced orthography for Indigenous place names rather than rely upon settler-colonial expressions of those names, which may or may not be endorsed by the communities that they describe. An excellent example of this is the colonial spelling of Micmac or Mic Mac. While the Mi'kmaq have established how their people's name should be written, older forms nonetheless persist in street names and commercial venues such as Mic Mac Mall in Dartmouth, Nova Scotia. In colonial times, the name of a people rather than that people's name for their lands often labelled their territory in cartographic contexts, making Mic Mac the colonial analogue of Mi'kma'gi on Western maps well into the twentieth century. Today, there remain twenty places with the antiquated spelling, Micmac, in New Brunswick, Newfoundland and Labrador, Nova Scotia, and Quebec—some of which are communities where non-Indigenous people live.

In recent decades, pressure has been mounting on the Government of Canada to address its harmful and historical treatment of Indigenous

Indigenous Names in a Settler-Colonial Context

people, particularly the ways that it and its predecessors have attempted to sever Indigenous peoples' connections to their lands. By deciding who is "Indian,"[23] Canada effectively determines who possesses a pre-European connection with this land and thus a right to it. By obviating Indigenous names, the Government of Canada continues to silence Indigenous place identity, particularly with the notion that names need to be singular ·rather than plural or multivocal and official rather than community based. And, by appropriating Indigeneity in the form of names and symbols that then influence settler-Canadian identity and feelings of belonging, the Government of Canada supports a form of pseudo-Indigenization whereby the settler expresses their belonging using Indigenous referents, a topic to which I will return.

The United Nations has played a decisive role in recognizing calls for change developed by Indigenous groups around the world in recent decades, and in encouraging modern nations to cultivate fair and meaningful place relations with aboriginal peoples. The UN naming commission, for example, has developed recommendations about naming practices that relate to Indigenous groups. Peter E. Raper, on behalf of the UN's Group of Experts on Geographical Names, examined this issue states three recommendations regarding Indigenous names. First, Indigenous people should be invited to identify their geographical names and any related contextual information, so that they can be used or embraced as place nomenclature. Second, governments should consult Indigenous groups and adopt names in an agreed-upon textual form for use on maps and official publications. And third, it is recommended that more consideration by the UN and related bodies be given to discussing methodology for how these names are collected and recorded.[24]

These efforts have recently led to an important stance on the part of the UN, one that it asks the world to embrace: the United Nations Declaration on the Rights of Indigenous Peoples (UNDRIP), adopted by the UN's General Assembly in 2007.[25] Several articles problematize the Indian Act and the comportment of INAC. For example, article 10 declares that Indigenous people shall not be forcibly removed from their lands and article 13.1 insists that Indigenous people should designate and use their own names for their communities. This has propelled criticism on the one hand and action on the other about settler-colonial systems of names. In New Zealand, for example, Indigenous groups have been lobbying to change names. Most recently, the Māori Party petitioned the government to change the country's name to Aotearoa, a name that is increasingly appearing as a binomial way of describing the country: New Zealand–Aotearoa or Aotearoa–New Zealand. And the Indigenous name is also being recognized on its own. The use of Indigenous names fosters a climate in which reconciliation or a form of restitution can be made on the part of settler states. Could this country soon be known as some form of Canada–Turtle Island, and if so, who might be included or excluded by that name?

Settler (Mis)use of Indigenous Names

The collection of Indigenous place knowledge was recognized centuries ago as a useful practice when it came to wayfinding. Institutions such as the Hudson's Bay Company were tasked by the Crown, and later by themselves as a company, to catalogue Indigenous toponymy and knowledge about the land's resources. This practice grew beyond the ambition of expanding into areas hitherto not visited by Europeans. Christine Schreyer points to an HBC initiative to understand the names being given to the nine districts into which the company was divided in 1928. In this endeavour, the company requested each district's settler name, Indigenous name, as well as a translation of the latter toponym. From the survey, 188 places responded with this data, with 174 offering Indigenous names as well, which might suggest that some settler places had no Indigenous names or that Indigenous people had no knowledge of the place. But Schreyer concludes that it is more likely that these surveys simply were not completed accurately or fully. Her research also found that twenty-five Indigenous names were used by the HBC as names for their posts, and forty-nine of the 174 Indigenous names exist today as official names.[26]

Many of these Indigenous names comprise translations of the settler name or describe the settler relationship or activity that took place there. A good example of this is Vermilion Post, which translated to Yamen Woskican in Cree and T-see Dee Quan in Dene, respectively, both meaning "Red House."[27] For others, however, the English and Indigenous names share no relation: McKenzie, named for Nathanial Murdoch William John McKenzie (1857–1943), was translated as and became the toponym Washgageneesh, meaning "where one may trade."[28] This information was collected and provided by traders and postmasters who themselves may have been conversant in Indigenous languages, so it remains unclear whether they provided these translations or whether they consulted Indigenous informants. These names, once placed on the settler map, complicate Canadian identity and perpetuate colonial aims where the north remains a frontier, rather than a home or a people's territory. These names maintain associations of the north with resources and the physical difficulties aroused when attempting to harvest or access them, which also reinforces the settler-colonial gaze and the direction in which it looks, rather than an Indigenous one.

Scholarly attention on Indigenous place names appearing on the map also tends to be cursory and limited to attempts at providing either an etymology or a linguistic or phonetic representation of the word in its original language. These works of scholarship snowball over time because the next generation of scholars look to the work of the previous one. As a result, some Indigenous names end up with the same origin story narrativized through the pens of settler-colonial scholars decades or centuries ago. The study of Canadian toponymy, moreover, tends to focus on colonial names such as Vancouver, with little interest in the influence or contribution of Indigenous ones, and when they are treated, little knowledge is gained. One such work of scholarship examples this practice: "The Indian name for this province is easy to spell because it is

Canada's Place Names and How to Change Them

absolutely phonetic: Sas-katch-e-wan."[29] The author presumes his reader will be unfamiliar with the word's pronunciation; he exoticizes it while keeping it mysterious by not relating the word's Indigenous meaning, origins, or how it came to be embraced as a Canadian province's official name. Saskatchewan, from the Cree term *kisiskāciwani-sīpiy*, describing a fast-moving river, was used to name a district of the Northwest Territories in 1882, later becoming a province in 1905. Its Westernized name appears on an HBC map as early as 1795.[30]

Similarly, place-name history tends to rely upon the moment the name was made official or written down in some way. For example, many toponyms gleaned during the Lewis and Clark expedition of the early nineteenth century invariably reference the cartographic output of Peter Fidler (1769–1822).[31] Fidler worked closely with Indigenous informants along their routes, recording place names and topographical knowledge in much of the Canadian southwest and American west. Rather than view the informants as authoritative, scholars typically return to Fidler as the source, invoking him as an authority of the informants' place knowledge.

Many Indigenous names in Canada, like the Haudenosaunee's land, have been appropriated by settler-colonizers. We need not look farther than the name of this nation. Most popular history agrees that the name comes from the "Huron-Iroquois" term *kanata* (also a settlement in Ontario today) whose meaning is village—and specifically, when it was awarded as a name by Jacques Cartier in 1534, he was referring to the Indigenous village of Stadacona (Stadaconé/Quebec City).[32] The first issue with this designation is with the Wendat (Huron/Laurentian Iroquois) and the Haudenosaunee (Iroquois/Mohawk) origin of the name, because for centuries settler-colonizers have applied the term Iroquois to anybody who seemed to speak a language from the Iroquois language family—and not all groups identified with the Haudenosaunee, or for that matter the Wendat. The word *kanata*, as we can hardly call it a name, likely came from another people whom scholars now call the St. Lawrence Iroquoians, following their encounter with Cartier in the western St. Lawrence

Indigenous Names in a Settler-Colonial Context   121

River.[33] Cartier somehow transposed the word so that by the 1540s it occupied the entire area that is, was, or might be present-day Canada on European maps, being then *terra incognita* to people such as Cartier.

Cartier, thinking he was going to Asia, and thus quite disoriented, questioned Chief Donnacona and others about where he was. Despite having learned French, perhaps Donnacona's sense of humour was aroused at the moment he pointed toward the *chemin de kanata*, indicating the path toward the village, which Cartier converted into the Kingdom of Canada. This deliberate appropriation of a name that Cartier acknowledged in his travel relation signified village as a type of settlement was then used in his denomination of the St. Lawrence River, which he called the *rivière de Canada*. Even though the word existed before Europeans arrived in the Americas, the country's popular toponymic origin story dates from 1534 when Cartier, who did not speak Iroquoian languages, gleaned the meaning of a name that referred to no specific place, and certainly not a kingdom, but rather to a category of settlement. Viewed in this way, the modern nation's name reinforces the moment when *kanata* metamorphosed into Canada in Cartier's 1545 travel relation. With no little sense of irony, the Six Nations of the Grand River (Haudenosaunee) today have created a touristic experience whereby visitors can learn about First Nations culture and heritage at Kana:ta Village (Brantford, Ontario) through interactive opportunities to occupy and practise traditional ways of life as well as culture. The existence of this homonymously named place could be viewed as a reappropriation of not only a term, but also the space itself, which challenges the orthodoxy of settler-colonial time and presence. On a related note, there are five places in Quebec named for Chief Donnacona, including the town of just over 7,000 people located west of the City of Quebec; it was named in 1905. Citing Cartier, Quebec's name database defines Donnacona as "chef de paix" (chief of peace).[34]

Before the modern nation existed, the name also made its way into those of its British predecessors: Upper Canada (the Great Lakes watershed) and Lower Canada (Quebec and the Atlantic provinces) subsequently became the Province of Canada in 1841 until gaining its independence from

Britain, becoming the Dominion of Canada in 1867. Beyond the country's designated name, nearly 600 official toponyms spread across the provinces and territories also contain the term, for example, the neighbourhood of Le Petit-Canada, in Montmagny, Quebec. Made official in 2018, the latter name describes a neighbourhood of Montmagny found along Highway 132's Route des Navigateurs, that glides along the southern shore of the St. Lawrence River from Baie-du-Febvre to the Gaspésie, north of New Brunswick. This diminutive designation (*petit*) can be found in other places in Quebec (Sherbrooke, Thetford Mines, Abitibi, and the fishing hamlet of Cap-Chat in Gaspésie). The name in all cases denominates an area populated by impoverished or marginalized people; today it serves as Montmagny's industrial area, and nobody resides there any longer.[35] In this particular name, we see characteristics of the settler-colonial matrix when it attempts to define non-mainstream space as marginalized, ephemeral, in poor shape, undesirable, or as disappearing.

These elements are also present when we scratch beneath the surface of Qausuittuq National Park of Canada, in Nunavut. The park is located on Bathurst Island on the Northwest Passage, about eighty kilometers northwest of Cornwallis Island, where the hamlet of Resolute is situated. This hamlet was named for the HMS *Resolute*, one of the ships sent in 1850 to find the missing Franklin expedition. The community by this name was founded formally in 1953 after the region's inhabitants—including those on Bathurst Island—were forced to relocate in Resolute in what is now known as the High Arctic Relocation of 1953–55. The national park, whose name contains a formal claim as belonging to Canada— Qausuittuq National Park *of Canada*—was founded in 2015. Qausuittuq (Inuktitut for a place where the sun does not rise), according to the park's marketing material, is a "cluster of islands in a frozen sea, a home for the endangered Peary caribou, a traditional hunting and fishing area that has sustained the Inuit of Resolute Bay since the time of their relocation in the 1950s; Qausuittuq National Park is all of that and more."[36] The claim that species are endangered (and thus disappearing) reflects the reality that the traditional inhabitants of an area now claimed by Canada have

Indigenous Names in a Settler-Colonial Context   123

been disappeared by the same nation. By disappeared, I mean the verbal agency of the colonizer—in this case Canada—who employs deliberate and unintentional rhetorical and policy or legal strategies that reduce the appearance and actual presence of groups who resided in Canada prior to the European invasion.[37]

This simultaneous acknowledgement of endangered caribou and traditional Inuit presence on the part of Parks Canada unsettles and discomforts when seen from the perspective of a disappearance whose official objective is to preserve and conserve species and their environments. Since the nineteenth century, extinction and disappearance have been terms that settlers applied not only to fauna but also to Indigenous groups, in this case the Inuit. Coupling them together while describing a conservation and preservation project—a national park—emphasizes their entanglement with species that the government has classified as endangered. At the same time, the architecture of colonialism baldly informs us that a name, Qausuittuq, which was chosen in consultation with the local community and thus comprises one of its names—is of Canada, as are the people (nation) that were forcibly relocated from the area.

Another example demonstrates that this is a pattern on the part of Canada and sometimes the provinces and territories. Kouchibouguac National Park of Canada in eastern New Brunswick is situated on lands confiscated from the Mi'kmaq and Acadian people who lived there only decades ago. Its founding in 1969 required all residents to abandon their communities, homes, and traditional hunting grounds. One of these communities, Claire-Fontaine (1907), is still registered as an official place in the national and provincial registries, perhaps because one of its inhabitants waged a decades-long battle with the federal government to remain in his birthplace. Jackie Vautour (c. 1928–2021) continued to live in what became Kouchibouguac, even after authorities demolished his house in 1976, which he replaced not long afterward with a trailer, posting a sign in English and French for the park's visitors: "It is because of you that the government is making us suffer as you can see. Have a good look.

124   *Canada's Place Names and How to Change Them*

Warning: Parks Canada are ordered not to trespass."[38] Vautour grew up in an entangled community with two primary demographics—Acadians, who settled in the region in the seventeenth century and were expelled by the British in 1755, later returning in diminished numbers, and Mi'kmaq, who have lived there since time immemorial. Both groups have suffered the loss of their lands in this region, and they shared many cultural and social connections between each other.

When Vautour was arrested for fishing without a license in the park, he attempted to assert his Indigenous fishing rights as per the country's constitution, which landed him on the national stage. Ultimately, he and his son were convicted for illegal fishing because the court determined that the Vautours had failed to establish that an historical Métis (mixed-blood, Mi'kmaq-Acadian) community lived in Kouchibouguac, even though the demographics of the communities located there were well known to government and park authorities when they were forcibly removed.[39] In May 2021, the park evicted Vautour's widow, ending all permanent residency within the park. And while there are no Mi'kmaq or people of shared descent living there now, the park's Mi'kmaw name persists. The government's colonization of both the land and the name, as well as the forced removal of Indigenous and Acadian communities, point to wider issues impacting Indigenous place identity.

It bears noting that four of this country's ten provinces have names of Indigenous origin: Saskatchewan, Manitoba, Ontario, and Quebec. Like Canada, their origin stories also exhibit a disregard of their meanings and the places associated with them, and curiously, all of them refer to bodies of water or waterways—the same is true of three provincial capitals (Winnipeg, Toronto, and Quebec). Ontario, for instance, owes its name to a big lake. The Wendat word, *ontar*, meaning lake, and *-io* meaning large, certainly make the linguistic hybrid Lake Ontario somewhat redundant.[40] But after Jesuits began to use this name, a colonial one was imposed, and Lake Ontario was known as Lac de St. Louis or Lac Frontenac until the mid-eighteenth century. In 1792, Ontario County formed in Upper

Canada along the lake's eastern shores, and it officially became known by this name as a province in 1867 for the purposes of Confederation.[41]

Quebec's name comes from a term of Algonquian derivation, *kebec*, meaning "place where the river narrows," referencing the St. Lawrence River. Samuel de Champlain documents its meaning and location in one of his early seventeenth-century travelogues. However, according to the province's toponym authority, the origin story of Quebec begins not with an Algonquian term but rather with the Diocese of Quebec, which was established in 1674 and included Nouvelle France, which then also extended to Acadia and Louisiana. It points to the Royal Proclamation of 1763 that established the "gouvernement de Québec," and from there the name has colonized other places in Canada and abroad—a name used for streets and places located in England, France, Mexico, Spain, and the United States.[42] Unlike *kanata*, *kebec* describes a particular change in the river's girth that Champlain claims an Indigenous informant shared with him; in no way does it characterize the province of Quebec as a whole, nor do the Indigenous words used by the provinces of Manitoba, Ontario, and Saskatchewan.

This practice of projecting local names regionally and abroad, itself a form of colonization, bathes light on how settlers tend to abuse Indigenous names, and this can be seen throughout Canada at a more local level. One of the more common misuses of Indigenous names occurs when they find themselves far away from the people who speak and use them. For example, Hiawatha Beach (1976) in Hants County, Nova Scotia, on the Minas Basin is nowhere near Haudenosaunee territory but it joins places located in several provinces that nonetheless commemorate Hiawatha. In Oromocto, Sunbury County, New Brunswick—which borders the Oromocto First Nation and Canadian Forces Base Gagetown—one finds a street labelled with the Wolostoq word Waasis ("baby") bisecting Onondaga Street, another reference to the Haudenosaunee. In this town, there is also a Hiawatha Court, a MacDonald Avenue, a Huron Street, a Cayuga Street, a Mohawk Street, a Nootka Street, an Oneida Street, and a Haida Street.

Pseudo-Indigenous Names

As my exploration of *kanata* proves, not all Indigenous toponymies imply that the place was named by Indigenous peoples. In 1882, the Toronto Temperance Colonization Society founded a town on the South Saskatchewan River, and they struggled to find a name for the new settlement. One day, a young man associated with the effort came to the tent of the organizer, John Neilson Lake (1834–1925), with a pile of berries that the Dakota called Saskatoons, which then became the name given to the settlement.[43] In this way, settlers denominated places of their own creation using names extracted from Indigenous languages. In other words, it cannot be presumed that an Indigenous name comprises an authentic indication of Indigenous presence or agency in the bestowing of the name, or that it relates in any way to Indigenous place knowledge.

While some names become translated into English or French, offering a linguistically accessible name to the broader population, maintaining a name in its Indigenous language has other benefits. Cyril Meredith Jones observes that one of the benefits of using the Indigenous name rather than the English- or French-language translation of the name is that sometimes the original name is offensive or less beautiful once its meaning is made known to the English- or French-language speaker.[44] This poignant conclusion was recently made by Rebecca Sockbeson concerning the relationship between the S-word (squaw) and place naming, as explored in the previous chapter. Because the average Canadian may be unaware of the word's offensiveness—Sockbeson compares it to the N-word—they are less likely to care whether it persists or not.[45] As Jones observes, Winnipeg, whose meaning is dirty water, "is much more charming than some Anglicised form like Dirtywaterton!"[46] Other names are bestowed in geographical contexts divorced from the people to whom they refer. For instance, Wampum, Alberta, was randomly selected by the railway company during its expansion westward and when its stations required names. In this case, the cook in the construction crew's kitchen offered the name inspired by one of his favourite brands, Wampum Baking Powder.[47] Eight provinces and territories have places named for Eskimo,

Indigenous Names in a Settler-Colonial Context   127

Figure 4.3 Hayter Reed, deputy superintendent general of Indian Affairs, dressed as Chief Donnacona, and his stepson dressed in regalia for a ball on Parliament Hill, 1896. Ottawa, Ontario, Libraries and Archives Canada, Archives, Collections and Fonds, 3191522.

which is considered offensive or outdated, while 592 place names in English and fifty-two more in French contain a version of Indian, none of which appear to relate to people or things from Asia.

One of the more controversial uses of Indigenous names on the part of settlers is when they use them to "play Indian."[48] This occurs intentionally and unintentionally when settlers falsely claim Indigenous ancestry or espouse histories that conflate Indigenous and settler experiences, when they dress up in costumes that emulate regalia (Figure 4.3), or embrace other practices that replace Indigenous people with settlers. The demonym (the name for someone's place identity) for someone from Mississauga, for example, is Mississaugan, the same as the adjective that describes an Indigenous person from this nation in English. Maximilian

C. Forte, in his examination of Indigenous identity, explores contemporary issues arising from the perception of faking one's Indigenous ancestry and thus connection to the land: "New Indians. Born-again Indians. Hobby Indians. Wannabe Indians. Ersatz Indians. Indians of convenience. Generic Indians. There seem to be an awful lot of negative labels used in demarcating the zone of 'fake Indigeneity,' that is, of ways of answering the question of who is not an 'Indian.'"[49] "Indian" identity, as we saw with respect to the Indian Act, comprises a serious and fraught subject that is made more complex by the government's commitment to determine who is not "Indian," and the ease with which settlers play Indian.

The same process happens in reverse when Indigenous groups are given names that are not their own. Indigenous reservations are not surveyed nor included in the work undertaken by the Geographical Names Board of Canada. Rather, until recently they were exonymically assigned a name and have allonyms within the region and the Indigenous community itself that often exist in more than one language and thus exhibit orthographic variety—as the community of Richibucto 15/ Big Cove/Elsipogtog First Nation demonstrates.[50] While names of this variety originate from settler-colonial governments, sometimes non-Indigenous names are the preferred usage in their respective communities. This perspective should leave us questioning whether some place names containing settler-European signifiers were entirely awarded by non-Indigenous people because, as Greg Mitchell and Ihintza Marguirault theorize with respect to Canada's north, "To live and trade in a space that was increasingly multicultural and to adapt to that world, both linguistically and through personal expressions and attire, is a hallmark of Inuit persistence and resilience."[51]

This being said, we know that European place namers seeking to fill the map with toponymy conjured names from their Indigenous interlocutors. An Inuit trader known to the French as Captain Amargo was commemorated by Louis Fornel (1698–1745) with the place name Baye d'Amargo, which later appeared on a 1743 map of Labrador. It is now

Indigenous Names in a Settler-Colonial Context

called Hawke Bay, and none of Fornel's toponymy, nor this attempt to commemorate an Inuit trader, seems to survive on the map. Another example of this practice is in the surname Pompey in Labrador, which is used by or given to Inuit living there and remembered today among elders in the form of toponymy. Several places in Labrador bear this name, such as Pompey Island in Groswater Bay and Pompey Island in Sandwich Bay.[52] Both may be named for an Inuit man referred to as Old Pompey who was banished to an island after being found guilty of criminal activity. In this case, a European name was embraced by some Inuit and later became a familiar place name to the settler-colonizer. As this last example demonstrates, names can betray the encroachment of colonialism: how would the first century BCE Roman military figure, Pompey, react to knowing that his name would project across the western ocean to adorn faraway places and people? His era saw some of the earliest Western attempts to name places commemoratively. Today, there remain seven places named for Pompey in Newfoundland and Labrador.

Another variety of pseudo-Indigenous names relies upon referents associated with Indigenous lifestyle and culture. There are about a hundred places named for buffalo and bison in this country, mainly in British Columbia, Alberta, Saskatchewan, and Manitoba, where they once roamed, with nearly no place named for buffalo east of Ontario. Tasha Hubbard estimates that thirty to sixty million buffalo ranged on the Great Plains, stretching from Saskatchewan and Alberta to Mexico, and such were their numbers that the buffalo had a significant impact on the ecosystem and on human ways of life. The animal is a traditional food source of many Indigenous groups in Canada. Early evolution theorists such as Charles Lyell (1797–1875) argued that extinction due to human-related circumstances such as over-hunting is natural and should not be a source of preoccupation. Other scientists, such as Herbert Spencer (1820–1903), viewed "progress" as the imperial ideal before which no animal or people should stand. "By removing the means of survival," Hubbard contends, "the perpetrators of genocide succeed in removing Indigenous peoples."[53] Apologists for the near extinction of buffalo such as Lyell and Spencer were not troubled by how Indigenous bodies had become linked to those of buffalo as dehumanized obstacles to American and Canadian expansionism. Put another way, the presence of buffalo signalled the presence of Indigenous people; the disappearance of one would ensure that of the other in the minds of nineteenth-century settlers, all of which helped reinforce the narrative of disappearance and lasting that emerged in this century.

For some Indigenous peoples, the loss of traditional food sources became a second wave of trauma—the first being epidemic disease—that stabilized the European and settler-enabled genocidal course they were on and, in some ways, remain on. After so many died following exposure to European pathogens, many more perished of hunger after the herds disappeared. More than genocide of Indigenous peoples, the deliberate culling of buffalo also comprises an extermination of the animal itself, which many Indigenous groups consider the first people. Philip Sheridan (1831–1888), one of the architects of the buffalo extermination, particularly between 1865 and 1883, transformed the killing of buffalo into a patriotic practice whereby the removal of a buffalo was viewed as the removal of an Indigenous person. From another perspective, removing a people's traditional food source unsettles their nativism, superficially rendering them less Indigenous in some ways while making room for settler Canadians to cultivate the land so that it better served their interests.[54]

Hides also incentivized killing the buffalo because in the latter half of the nineteenth century demand grew along with supply in international markets. In this way, a commercial purpose for the buffalo served as a veil covering the impact their removal had on both the animal and Indigenous peoples. Furthermore, the number of buffalo killed in such a short time resulted in wasted meat and detritus. Colonel Richard Irving Dodge (1827–1895) boasts of the forty-five minutes it took him to slaughter 112 buffalo in a relatively small area with a gun: "Where there were myriads of buffalo the year before, there were now myriads of carcasses. The air was foul with a sickening stench, and the vast plain, which only a short twelvemonth before teemed with animal life, was a dead, solitary, putrid desert."[55] This sort of culling went on for a number of years, and by 1883,

Indigenous Names in a Settler-Colonial Context   131

buffalo had virtually disappeared from the Canadian landscape. This is the sort of story told at Head-Smashed-In Buffalo Jump in Alberta, now a World Heritage Site that explores Blackfoot history and what became of the buffalo in recent history.[56] The concentration of settler-assigned, buffalo-related names in the region where they once thrived anchors settler-colonial violence to the landscape.

Behind the buffalo came herds of cows now so rooted to Albertan identity, with hundreds of names in this part of the country referring to cows, calves, ranches, ranges, and to beef (such as Beef Trail Creek, British Columbia, named in 1954 for the cattle driven down the creek to market).[57] With the buffalo out of the way, cows that consumed the same source of food were free to flourish. Removing an Indigenous food source and replacing it with a European one is another way of nativizing the landscape so that settler food comes from this land as opposed to originating from Europe. This process works similarly for toponymy; the discarding of Indigenous names in favour of the bestowing of settler-colonial names fills the map and the landscape with names that define the origin of places and their contents. Names that refer to buffalo and beef should be read through this colonial lens and problematized as possible projections of colonial violence.

On a related note, names associated with Indigenous peoples in Canada pop up in unexpected places in the American Midwest. Initiated in the 1830s, a decades-long project unfurled across the United States alongside the buffalo extermination. Called the Trail of Tears or the Great Removal, hundreds of Indigenous communities were forced to move westward from eastern regions more populated with settlers to a designated space called Indian Territory. This region later became the states of Arkansas and Oklahoma. As a result, many place names in this region hail from other parts of the continent, for example names such as Oneida in Kingfisher County, Oklahoma. The post office for this settlement, which operated from 1892 to 1901, claimed that the "name is that of an Indian tribe of Iroquoian stock; the word means 'standing stone.'"[58] Many other names referencing Algonquian and Haudenosaunee groups can be found in this

132   *Canada's Place Names and How to Change Them*

region: Wyandotte in Ottawa County and Mohawk in Tulsa County, being just two examples.

Visual Place Identity and the Indigenous Body

Many more books could be written to add to existing work on settler-colonial appropriation of Indigenous cultural symbols such as regalia, objects such as bows and arrows, and physical characteristics.[59] In this final part of my examination of how the Indigenous intersects with settler-colonial place identity, I will turn to the design of flags and coats of arms that visualize Canada's towns, cities, provinces and territories, and the nation itself. A typical coat of arms consists of a shield, which forms a focal point with its defining symbols. Supporting or presenting the shield are two figures, often animals, but sometimes people, and usually a motto is included in either the upper or lower register.[60] These emblems attempt to capture the place's identity, geography, and history in ways that often inscribe Indigeneity, usually in problematic ways.

One category of representation relates to the display of Indigenous bodies, usually as the presenters of a place's shield. This can often lead to culturally insensitive ways of depicting often-fraught physical characteristics of individuals, such as hair or skin tone. Wetaskiwin, Alberta, exemplifies this practice (Figure 4.4). Founded in 1892 as the railway extended into the region and located about 100 kilometers south of Edmonton, the small Albertan city boasts both a pioneer museum and a museum that celebrates industrialization. The city's name comes from the Cree term, *wītaskiwinihk*, meaning "the hills where peace was made," commemorating a late nineteenth-century battle between Blackfoot and Cree warriors. Its coat of arms was granted in 2006 by Canada's chief herald, part of the Canadian Heraldic Authority, which is overseen by the governor general. This coat of arms features a Cree man supporting the city's shield; opposite the man is a grizzly bear, which creates an equivalency between the human and animal worlds not usually reflected in modern Western heraldry.[61] While this individual is meant to represent the aforementioned

Indigenous Names in a Settler-Colonial Context   133

Figure 4.4 The coat of arms of Wetaskiwin, Alberta, adopted in 2006.

battle from which the city draws its name, his skin colour has been whitened and thus he is re-racialized.

Nova Scotia's provincial coat of arms similarly depicts a whitened male Indigenous subject, and the province sometimes yellows his hair. The country's oldest coat of arms, it features the cross of St. Andrew, was first granted in 1625, and then re-adopted in 1929. Above the shield is a curious display of two hands, one armoured and one naked, representing agreement and cooperation between colonial and Indigenous peoples. Supporting the shield on the left side is a unicorn (which hails from Scotland's coat of arms) that is opposite a Mi'kmaw man, again creating a problematic equivalency between the pseudo-animal and human worlds. These depictions do not reflect Indigenous worldviews of partnership or coexistence between human and animal worlds but are more likely to reflect Eurocentric views of domain over animals and other races of people as resources. In the case of Nova Scotia's coat of arms, the original emblem described the man as a "savage." The province's motto, displayed above the emblem, is "one defends and the other conquers" in Latin.[62] A

134   *Canada's Place Names and How to Change Them*

Figure 4.5 A stained-glass version of Nova Scotia's coat of arms displayed in the province's legislature.

stained-glass panel acquired recently by the province's legislature, and displayed within the building, furthermore depicts the Indigenous man with Caucasian features, including lighter-coloured wavy tresses (Figure 4.5).

The representation of Métis also figures into the country's coats of arms. Edmonton's shield features a winged cog, representing industry, supported by Athena on the right side, representing education with the symbols of a book and torch. On the left side is a Métis trapper holding a rifle, indicative of the city's historical connection to the fur trade. Awarded in 1995, the Canadian Heraldic Authority describes the trapper as an "explorer [who] honours the origins of the city with the fur trade, as it was once known as Fort Edmonton, and the tradition of exploration established by the commercial concerns of fur trading companies. The explorer's brightly coloured sash is a reference to the Métis fur trade employers who played a major role in the success of this industry."[63] Depending on the representation, sometimes his features are darkened or lightened, while no changes to Athena's physical aspect have been documented. A similar pattern can be found in Thunder Bay's coat of arms. Its motto, "The Gateway to the West," features a voyageur as one of its shield's supports, as well as a canoe of fur traders heading westward, referencing the North West Company's symbolism and motto.[64]

Returning to the subject of Indigenous referents, many coats of arms feature bison or buffalo, as well as other animals associated with the fur trade, such as beaver, that were severely impacted by settler-colonialism. Manitoba's coat of arms, first granted by King Edward VII in 1905 and updated in 1993, features a bison on its shield, situated just below the cross of St. George, England's patron saint. A version of this shield also appears on the province's flag. Supporting the shield is a unicorn (on the left) and a horse (on the right), the latter wearing a beaded collar reminiscent of Indigenous beading creations. (New Brunswick's coat of arms employs a similar device by placing Wolostoq, meaning "friendship collars," made of wampum around the necks of two white-tailed deer. These were incorporated into this emblem in 1984.[65]) Above the shield on Manitoba's coat of arms is a beaver wearing a crown, which chafes against the motto, positioned below the emblem in Latin, "Glorious and Free," given how close both the beaver and the bison came to extinction in this region of the world.[66]

A refreshing approach to the coat of arms genre can be found in the most recently created emblem to represent a province or territory, that of Nunavut. Designed by Andrew Qappik and adopted in 1999, it may be one of the only emblems representing the provinces and territories that celebrates (rather than coopts) the presence and history of non-Western people (Figure 4.6). Its circular shield contains an inuksuk used for place finding and marking sacred places, a *qulliq* or stone lamp representing warmth of community, and stars arranged as a horizon topped with the *Niqirtsuituq*, or North Star, used for wayfinding. Above the shield is an

Figure 4.6 The coat of arms of Nunavut, adopted in 1999.

igloo, representing survival as well as the territory's legislature, and supporting the shield are two important species from the region—the caribou (on the left) and the narwhal (on the right). Using Inuktitut characters, the motto *Nunavut sannginivut* means "Nunavut, our strength."[67] It is the only coat of arms from a province or territory to include an Indigenous language. However, it is not the only coat of arms that employs an Indigenous rather than Western language at the municipal level. The emblem of Sault Ste. Marie, Ontario, adopted in 2014, includes the motto, "Ojibwe Gchi Gami Odena," which in Ojibway means "settlement near the Ojibwe's big lake."[68]

Making New Connections

The treatment of Indigenous presence in settler-colonial names and commemorative material has underlined the significant differences in

‧representation compared to the Indigenous place knowledge and naming practices explored in the first chapter of this book. Not only are Indigenous relationships to ancestral lands constrained by the contours of laws and documents to which they did not necessarily consent but so too are claims about the Indigeneity of place names, which are often exogenously defined by the federal government through tools such as the Indian Act. Yet, earlier treaties nonetheless provide the reader with context about the nation-to-nation relationship that still binds the Canadian government and all Canadians as treaty people with shared obligations. In light of settler-colonial naming practices, it is clear that non-Indigenous representation almost always ends in problematic constructions of Indigenous culture, history, and people. Exceptions such as the coat of arms of Nunavut have involved broad consultation and the involvement of non-settler groups in the creation of any identity-related symbol and label.

1492 Land Back Lane offers a sort of map to understanding this cleavage between settler and Indigenous place experiences, both in this descriptive name but also in the court challenges that backlight the Six Nations' assertion of their right to their territory. Thinking about Jackie Vautour's struggle to live where he was born and had property after the federal government expropriated land to create a national park, the proponents of Land Back Lane have mitigated and overcome similar difficulties. In 2015 Haldimand County, rather than creating a park, sold the Haldimand Tract, which is the land under dispute, to the housing developer Foxgate. The land belongs to the Six Nations as per the 1784 Haldimand Proclamation, which recognized their support of the British during the American Revolution. As Dania Igdoura shows, Six Nations land defenders' peaceful protest and re-occupation of their unceded territory are increasingly being criminalized, and the judicial process seems to prejudice the Haudenosaunee in the *Foxgate Developments v. Doe et al.* legal challenge to the occupation.[69] For example, the protestors' spokesperson, Skyler Williams, was found in contempt of court in October 2020 when he failed to comply with the judge's order to vacate the land. As a consequence, Williams was not allowed to participate in a hearing happening that same month on his people's right to the land, effectively silencing his defence. He was later ordered to pay the legal costs of both the county and the developer. As Igdoura observes, "there remains no legal avenue for Indigenous peoples to reclaim full jurisdiction over their lands. From this, one can tentatively conclude that the very notion of 'land back' is incompatible with Canadian domestic law ... By criminalizing land defenders for simply asserting their rights, this case demonstrates the ways in which Canadian courts continue to enable ongoing colonization in Canada."[70] As one journalist covering this saga notes, the Six Nations have lost 95% of the lands that were confirmed as belonging to them in eighteenth-century treaties. These lands have been flooded, converted into arable land or into housing, or transformed into the cities of Brantford, Cambridge, Dunnville, Kitchener, and Waterloo.[71] This example reminds us of UNDRIP's requirement that Indigenous peoples not be forcibly removed from their lands, and how Canadians continue to be at odds with this reality, despite the fact we are all treaty people and Canada claims it will adopt UNDRIP.

Land Back Lane also puts into relief many of the inequalities and forms of racism prevalent throughout the names and emblems examined in this chapter, which build upon the gendered issues with our means of articulating collective identity. Few emblems, for instance, represent Indigenous women; nearly all examples I have encountered relate to masculine Indigeneity, which echoes an observation that will be made in the next chapter with respect to race. In the next chapter, I turn to other marginalized groups—newcomers, settlers from areas of the world other than Britain and France, linguistic and religious minorities, and racialized groups, while examining some case studies that show us how offensive and dated names have been changed in recent decades.

Indigenous Names in a Settler-Colonial Context

CHAPTER 5

Marginalized Groups and Canada's Place Names

Canadian identity is often shaped by uncritical assumptions about what the average Canadian looks like, what their origin story might be, and how they fulfill or experience idealizations relating to national character. As explored in the last chapter, settlers attempt to Indigenize themselves, appropriating and often disrespecting pre-invasion names and place stories in order to strengthen their own invasive roots and fortify claims that they originate from here, as opposed to from Britain or France. Moored to some notion of tradition, history, and national pride, these assumptions reinforce white masculine place identity and, as we will see, have resulted in deeply offensive and violent names directed toward racialized groups. Put another way, Canada's place names can hide or render silent non-white presence. As Alberta poet Bertrand Bickersteth observes in "What We Used to Call It," the landscape as an element of Canadian identity presents a white space where non-whites are contained, surveilled, and defined:

> [...] have you seen this one this place this prairie's face look at its
> wide open spaces
> its Chinook arched above
> unclaimed coulees its snow covered skin [...]
> and that there is Nigger John's Creek but
> we don't call it that anymore [...]
> if I only knew

what that there is called.

I know what we used to call it.[1]

Unlike white settlers whose origin stories weave together some historical notion of Canada with that of the British and French empires and their precursors, more recent waves of immigration have created a second group of usually marginalized settlers who came from countries other than these so-called foundational ones. As linguistic and often ethnic and religious minorities, these groups also awarded and influenced place names. In the balance, sometimes harmful and racist names signalling their presence prevailed on the map of Canada. Furthermore, other minority groups—among them people living with disabilities, addictions, poverty, and so on— have remained much less likely to be reflected in the country's place nomenclature. In fact, none of the country's place emblems seem to acknowledge the presence of people of colour who are not Indigenous people, whether through cultural, racial, or cultural signifiers.

This chapter offers a panoramic study of how marginalized groups other than women and Indigenous people are represented by and exert influence over Canada's place names. In tandem, it offers some examples of how problematic names have been revised, which will serve us in the final part of this book as we study the implementation of name changes.

European Minorities

In nineteenth-century Europe, certain nationalities found themselves re-racialized by northern countries such as Britain, Canada, Germany, and the United States. Over the last two centuries, both Italy and Spain— whose histories include periods of Arab occupation and colonization— were increasingly othered and exoticized as orientalized corners of Europe. Their citizens were thought to have darker complexions and lower personal hygiene standards, and these countries were perceived as less modern. Their foods and cultural practices became projections of difference,

Canada's Place Names and How to Change Them

and in the case of Italy, to this day remain linguistically segregated in the way that some Anglophones pronounce "Italian" when referring to the country's cuisine (i.e., "eye-talian"). In contrast, "Spanish" remains a false denominator of Hispanic people and their cuisine, with many Canadians using the term to describe Caribbean, Mexican, South American, or even the cuisine of the US southwest rather than that of Spain. Slurs for othered white people are embedded in this country's place names, and include wop and dago, for an Italian person, as in Lac Wop, Quebec (1968), and Dago Gulch, Yukon (1983); and mick, for an Irish person, as in Mick Lake, Ontario (1968). Othering white people, often by grafting non-whiteness on them through essentialisms and stereotypes, becomes a means of re-racializing them. At the same time, there are slurs that happen to be surnames. Spick Lake, Manitoba (2020) commemorates Private Arthur Spick, who was killed in the First World War in 1917.[2]

Race-shifting describes a process whereby non-whiteness is either acquired or shed for reasons that may be complex.[3] In the last chapter, this process was explored in its use by white settlers to reinforce their connection to Canada and its landscape, while providing means for survival by relying upon Indigenous materials, practices for hunting, and sometimes their way of dress, protecting themselves from the climate. However, Europeans enrobing themselves in Indigeneity became important for more than their survival; it also allowed them, through the doctrine of discovery and court decisions, to argue their entitlement to the land and its resources. Race-shifting can become a powerful tool of subversion within settler society directed, in this case, toward groups with a connection to non-Anglophone and non-Francophone Europe.

In Canada and the United States, immigrants from several European countries lived in districts or barrios where their language and culture continued to flourish. While this ghettoization of immigrants presented barriers, it also resulted in some of the first toponyms associated with non-Anglophone and non-Francophone settlers. Little Italy and Greektown in Toronto—and there are many similar districts in medium and large Canadian cities—comprise two examples, whose presence may be as

Marginalized Groups and Canada's Place Names   143

familiar as that of Chinatown, discussed in due course. Toronto's Little Italy notably expanded after a second wave of immigration from Italy in the 1950s and 1960s. Italians settled in a working-class area of the city known as Little Britain. With more than 30,000 Italians moving there by 1961, the character of the community had remarkably shifted.[4] Its English-language name can be found on Google Maps and has been embraced as an official place name by the city but its street names remain distinctly un-Italian. The names of banks, restaurants, stores, and even the invitation to worship are expressed in Italian, which is one of the ways this neighbourhood's character is apprehended and reinforced. Another is in the architectural program of the area, which introduced features more common in Europe, such as stucco, columns, arches, and balconies, that differ from the typical look of Canadian infrastructure. Viewed in this way, assumptions about Little Italy's look emblematizes what one envisions they will find in a place with this name. In the context of the Second World War, moreover, the ghettoization of this group cannot be ignored in that Italians experienced internment in Canada, and more broadly Italophobia, as the enemies of Canada and its allies. Their neighbourhood became a locus for the expression of Italophobia and attracted dissenters and violence during and after wartime.[5] The use of the country's name follows the convention of naming places after the settler's place of origin, resulting in a form of colonial enclave. Italy also appears in the names of four place names, one of which includes Italy Cross in Lunenburg, Nova Scotia, adopted in 1937.

Greektown, whose other name is The Danforth (a commemorative name for the builder, Asa Danforth Jr., 1768–c. 1821), developed along similar lines after two waves of immigration from Greece in the first half of the twentieth century. Today, its street signs are not technically bilingual, but the names are expressed in the English and Greek alphabets. Like Little Italy, there are several analogous enclaves located in other parts of Canada—such as Greektown, Calgary. These neighbourhoods exhibit infrastructure particular to the Greek community too, such as an

144   *Canada's Place Names and How to Change Them*

Orthodox church, in addition to storefronts and services that use or refer to Greek terminology, all of which collectively characterize the neighbourhood in both a textual and visual way.[6] This community also experienced discrimination; they were considered foreigners and many of their shops were looted in the Toronto Troubles or anti-Greek riots of 1918.[7]

As these two names demonstrate, groups of immigrants craft or attract names that connect them with their place of origin. In doing so, they may be perceived either as less Canadian or this connection to the community's past may build a sense of unity and belonging. From a chronological perspective, we can see how naming practices in the hands of settlers have evolved in more recent times. While the French—the first wave of white immigration—municipalized saints such as Sainte-Anne-de-la-Pocatière in their settlement names, the British—the second wave of white immigration—used commemorative names such as Sackville and Moncton. The third wave of immigration by non-Anglophone and non-Francophone Europeans resulted in the imposition of toponymic facsimiles of the towns they left behind in Europe, which in turn impacted the place names they assigned to their new communities.[8] German Mennonites who settled in the Prairie provinces of Manitoba and Saskatchewan often chose commemorative names or awarded ones from their native language, as the examples of Gnadenthal ("Grace Valley"), founded in 1924, Reinland ("Clearland"), founded in 1875, and Schoenwiese ("Beautiful Meadow"), founded in 1880, demonstrate. And the same can be found among settlers from other countries, evidenced in Kiew, Alberta (1905), named for the capital of Ukraine.[9]

This tendency leads to tensions when external conflicts arise between the commemorated country of origin and Canada, and highly politicized times certainly influence the durability of this sort of place name. The First World War drew a line between several nations, thus dividing axis countries such as Austria-Hungary, Germany, and the Ottoman Empire from the allies, which included Canada, Britain, and France, among others. These tensions then became transposed upon Canadian soil in

Marginalized Groups and Canada's Place Names

ways that resulted in name changes, which reminds us that settlements have changed their problematic names in the past, in some cases offering possible models to follow for future name changes. Kitchener, Ontario, is located on the Haldimand Tract, part of Six Nations' territory, and in the nineteenth century German-speaking Mennonites migrated there from Pennsylvania, and later from Germany. Many street names and commemorative sites are named for the community's German American and German settlers, among them Joseph Schneider (1772–1843), after whom one of the country's largest and most well-known deli meat brands was named.

The settlement's name has an interesting history because it was previously known as the town of Berlin. In 1912, it grew large enough to be classified as a city, but with the political fallout from the First World War and in order to shed any affiliation with the allies' enemies, the city renamed itself Kitchener in 1916—after Herbert Kitchener (1850–1916), a British military figure with a noble title who had died in the war, in which he held several leadership roles for the allied forces. His unexpected death occurred at the moment in which a shortlist for names was being considered by the city, which is how it became a possibility. The city voted in a referendum to change the name, in which Kitchener beat out Brock (after Isaac Brock, another British military figure, but of the War of 1812) by a margin of ten votes. Unlike other democratic processes of the time—and keeping in mind male participation in the war—women voted in that election and thus influenced which name was eventually chosen.[10]

The choice of name also catches our attention for how quickly a recently deceased man was commemorated as a city's toponym, as is the fact that the town sent the British sovereign a telegram announcing the change. The region still exhibits several place names that commemorate Germany, including Heidelberg, Ontario, and stands out as an example of the isolation that newcomer communities experience, especially when politics settle close to home. And, while many communities today have war memorials for the First and Second World Wars, Kitchener also me-

146   *Canada's Place Names and How to Change Them*

morializes the 187 German prisoners-of-war whose remains were transferred to the city's Woodlands Cemetery in 1970. The rationale, reported in the city's newspaper, was that the place was "ethnically and geographically best suited" for the war graves, which previously were scattered across seven provinces, and thus they could be maintained more easily if located in one spot.[11] Monuments commemorating them, as well as an annual gathering of mourners, invoke Germany's loss and its connection to the community and collective identity in ways rarely seen in Canada.

Like Kitchener, towns across North America were de-Germanizing in response to the period's political climate, which gives us pause to wonder if names associated with colonial violence may one day be just as easily wiped off the map. Changes of this nature also emphasize how once-celebratory foreign toponyms such as Berlin and Little Italy found themselves less welcome on the Canadian landscape—might the same one day be true of London and Paris, Ontario, or Madrid, Saskatchewan?

Chinese, Japanese, and Other Asian Minorities

While the European ethnotype exhibits some variety in terms of physical appearance and assumptions that might be made about one's place of origin, as well as the social construct of whiteness ascribed to certain groups, many of the same xenophobic and political issues have impacted Asian communities as well, who in this country present as people of colour. As Stephanie Lewthwaite observes with respect to the growth of Los Angeles as a racially engineered (and thus structured) place not dissimilar to many of Canada's larger cities, "power relations, ideologies, and identities that dominated the region, and which supported ethnic and racial segregation, became embedded in the physical landscape."[12] In many North American cities that flourished during the late nineteenth and early twentieth centuries, similar demographic shifts occurred, although not all involving the same configurations of peoples. As waves of immigration from one part of the world to the Americas increased, communities and

Marginalized Groups and Canada's Place Names   147

neighbourhoods developed, and eventually became marked toponymically with some ethnic or racial stamp of identity, as often exampled by the proliferation of Chinatowns in North America.

The existence of racialized enclaves relative to Little Italys and other marginalized groups—especially Indigenous ones through the reservation system—prompts the question: how does toponymy acknowledge the presence of a group while segregating their presence in a particular area? For instance, a place named Indian River or Indian Road connects the location and its use to some Indigenous group, often within an historical rather than present-day context, through a generic name that refers to no specific group. "Indian" in Canadian toponymy never seems to refer to the presence of people who originate from or identify with India, which is notable given the 2016 census documented an Indo-Canadian population of 1.37 million people, compared to an Indigenous population of 1.67 million people. Like Chinese and Japanese settlers, Indians also settled in Canada in the nineteenth century; they worked on the expansion of the railway and in resource extraction for companies such as the HBC. However, references to India through its related adjective, Indian, seem to refer exclusively to Indigenous groups. In this way, toponymic identity expressed by the term "Indian" voids both the specific identity of an Indigenous group to which it refers and that of Indo-Canadian people to which it may well refer.

In contrast, any Chinatown may contain Chinese immigrants or their families, Chinese languages and culinary traditions, Chinese markets and imports, Chinese business associations and supports, and so on. At the same time, their presence in the city is toponymically contained. Outside of Chinatown, we do not usually find a China River or some analogue that might describe where a group of Chinese people live; or their neighbourhood's principal streets may have a completely unrelated name, such as Spadina Avenue, in the case of Toronto's Chinatown. Incidentally, Spadina comes from the Anishinaabe word for "rise in the land," *ishpadinaa*, and appears to date from the early nineteenth century. Recently, its Indigenous spelling has been implemented in the signage of one of

148   *Canada's Place Names and How to Change Them*

the city's most recognized street names.[13] In this respect, most Canadians do not read Cantonese and Mandarin, so signage in these languages may be less discernible than that which is found in the country's Little Italys, making the experience of being in Chinatown quite different for the Western gaze.

As this last example demonstrates, identity becomes layered upon a place. Language exercises significant control over place identity, as many naming boards and commissions specify that names must be expressed in one or more official languages. This requirement constrains the expression of a people and its culture by making them only spoken and heard, and written and read, in the official language, which ensures that linguistic colonization occurs at the level of racial and ethnographic diversification. This modus operandi and policy on the part of naming authorities effectively precludes official names from being in non-Romanized texts and syllabics, an issue that the Geographical Names Board of Canada is contending with and hopes to overcome. Doing so is urgently needed, as many Indigenous languages use syllabics or characters that are difficult to reproduce in software and databases because their orthographic symbols and characters are not included in most digital tools.

Some of these challenges also rest upon the way digital textual culture allows us to read, display, and write non-Romanized expression, such as when Cantonese names are spelled using the Roman alphabet (in the Pinyin system) rather than the language's characters, which makes Cantonese names pronounceable and possessable by people unable to read that language. This issue is manifested at the international level in terms of how place names transform into internet addresses. For example, Japan's ministry for the environment's Japanese-language website contains several English-language terms (https://www.env.go.jp/) where clearly the English-language name for the country, Japan (i.e., ".jp"), replaces the Japanese name, Nippon, and these are written not in Kanji but rather in Romanized text (Romaji). Overcoming the technological obstacles will no doubt allow for a better representation of names from minority language communities, both in Canada and abroad.

Marginalized Groups and Canada's Place Names

Ethnophaulisms (racial, religious, or ethnic slurs) as place names include dated terms referring to Asian and Pacific peoples and are readily available on the map of Canada. These can exist as official names, exampled by Chinaman Island, in Elbow Lake, Manitoba, adopted in 1979 as a means of acknowledging a mine developed by a Chinese businessman. They can also exist as historical or unofficial names, which is the case for Chinaman Lake, Peace River Land District, British Columbia. It was adopted in 1928 after being in use for many years, and then replaced in 2001 with Chunamun Lake after the Vancouver Association of Chinese Canadians complained.[14] The latter name commemorates John Chunamun, chief of the Dane-zaa, meaning "real people" (Euro-settlers called them the Beaver Indians), who lived on the lake in the late 1800s and early 1900s. Interestingly, its phonetics seem to resemble those of the original toponym, Chinaman, and even more ironic is the surveyor's comment in 1912 that "Chinaman's Lake [...] is a very picturesque spot, and the lake teems with trout and would have been a boon to settlers in the district."[15] Whether Chinese settlers were the intended target of the surveyor's remarks remains unknown, as there was much anti-Chinese sentiment during this period and a preference for white, Christian settlers over those from places such as China. Dozens of place names contain "China" across the country, but especially in western Canada.

In British Columbia, Chinese migrants worked in the canneries run by Euro-settlers, particularly in the late nineteenth century. As Lily Chow relates, seasonal work brought together people of different backgrounds to harvest salmon. Indigenous fishers harvested fish from the rivers and ocean, Indigenous women maintained nets and worked alongside Chinese cannery staff, while Japanese workers maintained the wharves and canning facilities.[16] Several place names in British Columbia commemorate the sites of these canneries, one of which was the Gulf of Georgia Cannery, which is now a national historic site and the location of a museum about the cannery and its industry. With knowledge about the intercultural labour environment of canneries in the western part of the country, we can re-code these places as having Chinese, Japanese, Indigenous, and women's presence through our knowledge of their contributions in that industry. This in particular may be a meaningful approach to revising place nomenclature because re-coding involves re-narrativizing, which then increases broader public awareness of a place's past through public history and education campaigns.

Some names also comprise transliterations of Chinese surnames when gold prospectors from all over the world flooded into the Fraser Valley in British Columbia in the late nineteenth century, creating claims to gold mines named "Ah Yott Claims" and "Hap Duck CO.," among others.[17] Sadly, these names never made it onto the map of Canada, so detecting Asian presence in that region of the country remains difficult if we were to rely upon toponymy alone. And when they did exist, names could be changed: China Creek in the Fraser Valley became Koster Creek in the mid-twentieth century, renamed after a white settler.[18] Chinese names and locations were also appropriated by Euro-settlers. The Chinese Wall, located in Kootenay Land District, British Columbia, was approved in 1963 by the province's naming authority. It describes an unbroken granite ridge that local guides say should not be crossed because of the treacherous terrain located beyond the ridge.[19] In this sense, the name's reference to the Great Wall of China was meant as a warning to trappers and climbers in the area to be cautious.

There are fewer instances of racial slurs referring to Asian people than to Black people, studied in due course, but when Asian slurs are uncovered, they seem more readily corrected. This mirrors trends documented by scholars in the United States for place names designating white people, Black and Indigenous people, Asian Americans, and Italian Americans.[20] For instance, all but one place name containing "chink," a slur of uncertain origin referring to a Chinese person, have been rescinded (Chink Lakes in Manitoba, last revised in 1977).[21] British Columbia in particular exhibits a dense array of slurs referencing certain Asian groups, such as Jap Lake, Range 1 Coast Land District (1952), which along with other references to Chinese in the province, likely reflect both the presence of those populations and that their places were named by white people. In

Marginalized Groups and Canada's Place Names   151

the case of the Japanese, the political landscape of the Second World War resulted in widespread anti-Japanese sentiment in Canada. Today there still remain three places named for "Jap," which is the same number of places that were renamed in the last twenty years after people complained about the anti-Japanese slur.

Even fewer names referencing Indian presence seem apparent today, with Lac Hindu in the Outaouais region of Quebec (1968) being one example, alongside a grouping of lakes named Lac Gandhi and Lac Delhi named the same year. Significant exceptions occur when it comes to commemorating influential and important Asian people at the local level, where parks, streets, and other features are named after them. The Parc Mahatma-Gandhi in Montreal (1989) commemorates Mohandas Karamchand Gandhi (1869–1948), who used non-violent protest to advocate for India's independence from the United Kingdom. This park was later joined by two others in the same vicinity that celebrate civil rights defenders, including Parc Nelson-Mandela (2016) and Parc Martin-Luther-King (2019). The latter one replaced Kent Park, which in itself reflects the choice to celebrate Gandhi while toponymically distancing the province from both English-language imperialism and British colonialism.

Some names also invoke religious minorities, and unlike hagiotoponyms, there are few places that overtly refer to these groups, with many of them—such as Muslim Lake in the Nipissing region of Ontario (1973) and Islam Creek in the Cassiar Land District of British Columbia (1986)—located in remote areas. This last toponym was proposed by the Columbia Cellulose Company, who argued it would complement the nearby Mosque Mountain (1940), named after its dome-like shape.[22] Other names create false connections with Asian communities. Nova Scotia has several places, including the community of Malay Falls in Halifax (1953), that seemingly describe Malay people. This name, however, is a white settler surname that dates to the late eighteenth century. And, finally, a dated term for the eastern part of the world from a Western perspective is Orient; places named for it can be found in Alberta and Ontario, which are certainly not eastern regions of the country, and several more in Quebec. Sometimes

152 *Canada's Place Names and How to Change Them*

the name implies the geographical orientation of a place as being east-ward, reflecting the Latin use of the word as a cardinal direction, but other times—such as Oriental Creek in the Coast Land District of British Columbia (1966), the name seems to refer to the "Far East."

Black and Afro-Descendent Minorities

European records acknowledge the presence of Black sailors on ships as early as Champlain's voyage to the country's eastern shores in the early seventeenth century, making this demographic among the earliest settlers and certainly so-called explorers of the region. In its 2016 census, Statistics Canada reveals that 3.5% of the population is Black, which comprises about 20% of the country's visible minorities, and it is a growing population.[23] Locating Black folks on the map, however, proves much more difficult, in part due to language. Unlike residents of Little Italy, which claims some relation with the country by that name, Black people are most often defined using varying terms disconnected from any ancestral or actual place of origin. There are no Little Ethiopias in Canada, although no doubt immigration in recent decades may make way for such a neighbourhood and related name. Categorical terms such as Black can ghettoize or designate spaces along racial lines while conflating especially non-white populations because, as discussed in the last chapter, Western geographical knowledge is limited, particularly of certain areas of the world.[24] As Michael D. Harris points out, the evolving vocabulary for describing Black people—the African/Negro/Black body—which have racist and racial implications not necessarily experienced by people from Greektown—contrasts with the visualization of Black people. A "veil of color" is what separates "whites and blacks, and each group was aware that blacks stood on the outside socially because American identity did not have dark skin anywhere in its definition."[25] This condition, which Harris associates with the United States, can also be detected in Canada where racialized references to white people do not denominate any settlement, but the same cannot be said of Black folks.

Chinatown and Indian Road as homogenizing generic labels are mirrored at the level of a Black community located in Nova Scotia. Called Africville, it was demolished by the province after its forcible depopulation. The toponym confines, acknowledges, and today commemorates a place where a racialized group lived. The container of Africa as a place whose geography remains relatively unknown to Westerners deserves some thought, as well as its bastardization in the name Africville, as there seems to be no other continent-inspired name of this nature in the country— no Europeville, Asiaville, or Mesoamericaville (although there are several places named for the god and moon known as Europa, and a handful of places that contain *Asian* from Indigenous linguistic influences, such as Asian Sakahikan in Quebec [1968], meaning "long lake" in Cree).

The terms for all continents in Western languages stem from Latin and its precursors, and should not be viewed as endogenous, making part of Africville—like the Americas named for Amerigo Vespucci (1451–1512)—as conceptually originating from Western antiquity. Former residents of Africville and their descendants, when asked about how the name came to be, agree that it was imposed upon them by fellow white Haligonians "since our forefathers came from Africa."[26] Another resident scorned the term and its disassociation of the community from their loyalist and American roots: "It wasn't Africville out there. None of the people came from Africa; you want to believe it. It was part of Richmond, just the part where the coloured people lived."[27] Richmond, previously an incorporated settlement, had become amalgamated into Halifax in the late nineteenth century, but many of Africville's residents continued to refer to their community as Richmond.

Richmond-Africville was founded and built by Black loyalists after they relocated from the United States, many themselves former slaves, in the outskirts of Halifax. By the twentieth century, the isolated community had been so underserviced by the city that its infrastructure was in poor shape, as modern developments in the form of roads, public works, schools, and new buildings had failed to materialize in the settlement compared to other parts of Halifax. A water treatment facility, a prison,

Canada's Place Names and How to Change Them

a hospital for infectious people, a garbage dump, a slaughterhouse, and railway systems nonetheless confined or crossed through Africville in the nineteenth and twentieth centuries, impacting the community's quality of life while allowing Halifax's other citizens to live away from these undesirable but necessary facilities.[28] These conditions, in addition to the community's poverty, constructed the justification for its demolition, which would also allow Halifax to build what it saw as important infrastructure projects for its port and highway system. The removal of the community occurred in the 1960s, precisely during the civil rights movement in Canada and the United States, with residents' property removed to other areas of Halifax using garbage trucks.[29] Today, a museum and park commemorate the site, and a formal apology was issued by the city in 2010. While the name now appears on the map in these two commemorative sites, the community itself no longer exists as it once did, making the name a reminder of a historic community—possibly the first Black one to thrive in Canada—and the injustices that it endured. In 1995, moreover, efforts to rename the area Seaview drew public outrage when a map proposed that Negro Point be replaced with Seaview Point, which would have further erased Black presence and white negligence in the region, and it remains Negro Point to this day.[30]

This last name also gestures toward a larger problem in racialized place naming and the temptation or need to revise names to eliminate offensive words. According to the BC Geographical Names Database, six remote features mostly located in the province's south were given what is the most offensive name in Western society for Black people—four creeks, one lake, and one mountain once inscribed Black presence with the N-word. While likely that some Black presence might have inspired this name, has the acknowledgement of Black presence been maintained in attempts to remedy racist nomenclature? From another perspective, when we reflect upon Seaview as a replacement for Negro Point, how is one name easier for the white gaze to rest upon than the other?

One such revision, Crayke Creek (Cassiar Land District, British Columbia), was introduced in 1967 when it replaced the original name

Marginalized Groups and Canada's Place Names   155

adopted in 1954. Crayke, the provincial toponymy database relates, is the name of a long-settled family of Telegraph Creek where they had a trapline. A last remaining son named John continued to trap there when this toponym was updated with his family's surname. Canadian census records in 1921 identify this region as inhabited by Dene (Stikine Indian Agency), with several individuals having this surname, which raises the complex issue of racial miscegenation.[31] Another creek originally sporting the N-word near Cranbrook (Kootenay Land District), approved in 1930, is located in the province's north; it flows into present-day Negro Lake (both the creek and lake were renamed with this now-outdated term in 1962).[32] Mid-province, yet another creek that flows into Cariboo Lake (Cariboo Land District) with this name was approved in 1939 and later revised to Pine Creek in 1967 after the Pine Creek Mining Company commenced operations in the area.[33] Nigger Mountain and Nigger Bar Creek (Kootenay Land District) were both adopted in 1950. The former had its name changed to Mount Jeldness in 1967. Norwegian Olaus Jeldness (1856–1935) was a skier and miner who settled not far from here in Rossland in 1896; he promoted the region as a ski destination.[34] The latter name became, in the same year, Goodeve Creek, after Arthur Samuel Goodeve (1860–1920), Rossland's mayor from 1889 to 1900 and the district's member of parliament.[35]

As these examples demonstrate, racist or problematic names referring to Black people often get replaced with names completely unrelated to this population, connecting the desire to remove hateful language with the commemoration of non-Black folks. At the same time, and returning to the hateful name mentioned in Bertrand Bickersteth's poem, the man named John was a former slave who had resettled in Alberta after gaining his freedom in the American South. John Ware (c. 1845–1905) became a famous cowboy, and several places were eventually named after him. On the occasion of updating these names in 1961, one journalist problematized the push on behalf of his descendants to revise these names while nonetheless acknowledging his "horsemanship, competence with cattle, feats of strength and endurance [that] won him friends and respect on a

156   *Canada's Place Names and How to Change Them*

long trail extending from Texas to the badlands of the Red Deer River."[36] The journalist disagreed with updating the racist name with the full name of the person being commemorated, pointing out the 4-H Club had also changed its name to the John Ware Club and his family home (John Ware's Cabin) had been moved to reside in Dinosaur Provincial Park in 1958, as examples of recent renamings. In Karina Vernon's assessment, the relocation of his home transformed it into another dusty relic that "is a testament to the difficulty of finding an adequate 'home' for prairie blackness."[37] It is in this context that the journalist in 1961 reasoned that "The name may be correct, but it is not the way his neighbors and contemporaries knew him. It may be official, but it denies an honest part of Western tradition."[38] This sort of nostalgia for and construction of the past is perhaps one of the greatest obstacles facing any attempt to revise toponymy, alongside refusals to use acceptable terminology such as Black or African-Canadian because it did not exist during Ware's lifetime.[39] Unfortunately, invoking anachronism as a reason for not changing a name that offends today has been reflected in other demographics' lack of place representation—what women or people of colour can be commemorated if white men have been credited with seemingly all significant accomplishments? For that matter, what is worthy of being commemorated and what is considered an accomplishment should also be examined closely.

While replacing racist names is not a bad idea, there are additional considerations when names are updated. In Grey County, Ontario, Negro Creek (1945) and Negro Lakes (1947), according to the province's place name database, in 1995 were "retained as official due to strong support from descendants of former black slaves who settled in the area."[40] This choice echoes that of the Halifax region to retain Negro Point. In the balance, changing a name does not necessarily correlate to any meaningful update of the map. In 2017, New Brunswick's toponymy officials changed five names that contained "negro" so that they positively represented Black presence by celebrating notable Black New Brunswickers. One of them, Nigger Lake, became Negro Lake (1965) and then Corankapone Lake (2017) in commemoration of a late eighteenth-century Black

Marginalized Groups and Canada's Place Names

loyalist and former slave from the United States, Richard Wheeler (born c. 1746), whose "African" name was Corankapoon (also spelled Coranka-pone).[41] He petitioned on behalf of several Black families to obtain land grants in the area, which were awarded by the Crown. This sequence of changes has maintained the place name's reference to Black presence in a positive fashion that also anchors this demographic to the landscape, and it was supported by more than one of the province's associations dedicated to supporting causes important to Black people. Despite these promising measures, however, New Brunswick's official map continues to use Corankapone Lake's previous name.[42] Google Maps similarly does not recognize the revised place name, in part because it relies upon state-sanctioned mapping tools such as GeoNB. Therefore, changing names—however well intentioned—does not necessarily equate to them being used for either wayfinding or informational purposes, leaving us to question what the real impact of name changes may be in certain contexts when old ones seem to remain in official use.

The other four places whose names were revised in New Brunswick in 2017 followed similar pathways, although noticeably absent from these celebrations of Black people is any attempt to commemorate women. Descendants of Frederick Hodges (1918–1999), a police officer and sup-porter of the labour movement in the mid-twentieth century, will see his name (Hodges Point) on signs near Saint John. Richards Lake is a second commemorative name for Richard Corankapoon. Lorneville Head seems to commemorate no Black person, but rather the pre-existing settlement of Lorneville, named for John George Edward Henry Douglas Sutherland Campbell (1845–1914), Marquess of Lorne, who served as governor gen-eral of Canada in the late nineteenth century. While the final name, Black Loyalist Brook, does not explicitly imply gender, normative assumptions nonetheless might be made about men as soldiers in the conflicts that preceded this community settling in Atlantic Canada.

Other pejorative references to Black people have flown under the radar of place-naming commissions, perhaps in part because their figura-tive meanings could refer to other subjects, but also because their words

158   *Canada's Place Names and How to Change Them*

are less clearly identified as racial slurs. Four provinces and territories reference Sambo and Samba in a variety of official names. Coon Creek, also in the Kootenay Land District of British Columbia, was adopted in 1965. In the same province, Ape Mountain, along with a series of related names in Tweedsmuir Provincial Park, was so-named because "When sighting the highest mountain in this area to obtain its position, it was noticed that the top resembled an ape's face."[43] This sort of discourse in place naming, according to my research, seems to only envisage the likeness of Black people when homonymous names are awarded, and ape is considered a racial slur. Take the example of Cape Negro Island in Shelburne County, Nova Scotia, which was officially adopted in 1975. The name, according to the province's place name database that cites a 1933 source for its origins, was inspired by sailors' perception that the rocks there "at low water look black and sailors passing compared them to negro heads."[44] Put another way, analogous features that resemble the heads of white people do not attract such names, which seem particularly prevalent in Atlantic Canada.

These name changes point to two historical movements that bear on Canada's racial makeup, and which we saw reflected in names referring to Asian folks. The first of these is the expansion of the mining and resource extraction industries, and thus the influx of settlers from North America and from Europe in pursuit of wealth and natural resources. The second movement comes about through the history of Black labour and life in the region, which dovetailed with increased migration from the United States to Canada to escape slavery and the ensuing violence against Black people in the Jim Crow era. Black loyalists settling in Atlantic Canada are just one example of a cohort of people who found new, if troubled, communities in Canada.

As the numerous streets celebrating Martin Luther King, Nelson Mandela, and Malcolm X attest, not all references to Black people deal with insults or outdated terminology. Mafeking, Manitoba, is a municipality of just under one thousand people whose name traces back to the Boer War. By the early twentieth century, as the railroad unfurled across

Marginalized Groups and Canada's Place Names   159

the province, the post office adopted this commemorative place name whose original location is Mafeking, South Africa, a predominately Black city in that country. The nearby town of Pretoria's post office similarly took inspiration from another South African locale.

In the end, no major settlement or feature is named for settler people of colour, which likely comprises the most significant inequality in terms of demographic representation identified in our exploration of Canada's toponymy.

People Living with Disabilities

It must be recognized that most Canadian toponyms existed in some official form by the mid-twentieth century, which predates the assertion of disability rights. As a result, when names were given before the civil rights movements of the 1960s, ableist namers did not consider commemorating individuals living with a disability. A shift in more recent decades to commemorating heroic acts, for instance during the First and Second World Wars, inscribes a disabled demographic within the country's place names in that some veterans develop disabilities during their service. In so doing, these names meant to honour, recognize, and give thanks reinforce the predominance of commemorating white males. Veteran, Alberta, is a village of just over two hundred people incorporated in 1914; the significance of this date in light of the toponym makes this town's name a monument to the survivors of and participants in the First World War. Hundreds of place names and monuments perform a similar office across this country, as we saw with Kitchener, Ontario, a name that commemorated a would-be veteran who found himself among the war's dead.

Diseases that cause disabilities and even death rarely find themselves the subject of place nomenclature, but there are important exceptions. The Baie du Choléra (2017) in the St. Lawrence River east of Quebec City in Montmagny, Quebec, was so named for the nineteenth-century quarantine island found in its midst, La Grosse-Île (previously known as Île de la Quarantaine), where many immigrants—particularly Irish—suffering

Canada's Place Names and How to Change Them

from sickness were forced to stay, and whose bodies—according to the province's toponymy database—were thrown into this bay after expiring from the sickness. Its name was also recently awarded and commemorates these tragic circumstances. Explicit references to the infirm can be found in Sick Lake in Kenora, Ontario (1968), and Lovesick Lake in Peterborough, Ontario (1953), but these are among the few such names in the country, with additional French-inspired or French-based versions found in Quebec and Newfoundland and Labrador.

Returning to disabilities caused by illness, there are ten places in British Columbia and Quebec named for Terry Fox (1958–1981), which echo an ableist narrative about disability as a condition that one overcomes or defies, and thus for which one becomes commemorated. Fox had had a leg amputated due to cancer, and several place names commemorating him were adopted the same year in which he died after lung cancer ended his attempt to cross Canada while raising awareness of the disease in 1980. Despite its reference to an astrological sign—many of which are used for place names—there are only three places named for cancer, perhaps due to negative views of that word itself, which makes it an unwelcome candidate for place nomenclature. Substances that cause disease are similarly undesirable as place names, as the town of Asbestos in southeastern Quebec has realized. Named for the carcinogenic material that was mined there, businesses in other sectors who hail from this location were experiencing difficulties attracting investors and partnerships due to outsiders' poor reception of the town's place name.[45] But the issue is even more complicated because Asbestos is an English word in a predominately French-speaking province with strict language protection laws and policies. In 2021, the town changed its name to Val-des-Sources, named for the town's location in a valley within the municipality of Les Sources. In doing so, it also makes itself a more attractive location for tourists, a subject explored in the final part of this book, who may have had concerns about stopping in Asbestos for any length of time.

Explicit references to disability also seem uncommon in the country's toponymy. Dated terms such as cripple nonetheless can be found in

Marginalized Groups and Canada's Place Names　161

thirty place names in British Columbia, Yukon, Alberta, Saskatchewan, Manitoba, Ontario, Nova Scotia, and in Newfoundland and Labrador. While the term itself has been around for centuries, after the civil rights movements of the 1960s, it acquired a pejorative meaning and now is considered outmoded (though the reclaimed "crip" is often being used by disability activists). Most of these names date from the 1930s to 1950s when the term described people living with physical disabilities, and the word was poorly received among this demographic. None of these places comprise towns or settlements, and most are geographic features such as lakes and creeks, where people may nonetheless live or vacation. Several names also gesture toward the nature of the disability invoked by the place name, all of which are physical in nature: Cripple Back Lake (2014), Cripple Leg Pond (2013), and Cripple Back Ridge (2019) are located in Newfoundland.

There are 102 places that explicitly refer to blindness in eleven provinces and territories. Blindness may refer not only to people with vision impairment but also to one's inability to see as a result of hidden obstacles or a vantage point that limits one's range of vision. Blind Bay (1981), in Harrison Lake, near British Columbia's northwestern Pacific coast, is characterized by the province's toponymy service as "named by local navigators" because the "bay is treacherous, with rocks, snags, etc. Not a good place to take a boat." This example highlights ways that names can describe conditions associated with disabilities in humans that are or might be caused by the geographical feature that bears the name. Disabilities associated with other sensorial impairments characterize other regions or features to be avoided, such as Deaf Man Shoal (1946) in Parry Sound, Ontario. The association of disability with dangerous obstacles such as shoals suggests that both the condition and the geographic feature are impediments that may invite naming dangerous features with words that iterate disability. Other names are perhaps more humorous in nature, such as the Rapides Three Blind Mice (2011) in Abitibi-Témiscamingue, Quebec. The name was inspired by three consecutive rapids found in the Kipawa River, each of which possess their own names (Rapide Huey,

162   *Canada's Place Names and How to Change Them*

Rapide Duey, and Rapide Louie). The relationship between the mice and Donald Duck's nephews remains unclear, except for the fact that both refer to children's cartoon and story characters. Other names refer explicitly to people, for example the shoals Blind Sister (1961) and Blind Tom (1976), both located in Halifax, although it remains unclear precisely who the individuals themselves may have been.

The assessment of who has a disability, and how disability has been defined, shifts over time: today we acknowledge the impacts of learning disorders and acquired conditions such as drug dependency as forms of disability. From an historical perspective, however, disability often remains unaddressed in scholarship, including place onomastics. As a result, certain people's biography and legacy, such as those that celebrate John A. Macdonald, who suffered from alcoholism, leave unacknowledged his disability. In the balance, scholars have been more likely to ponder the psychological state of Louis Riel (1844–1885), who Macdonald saw executed in 1885.[46] This framing suggests that disability, because it often goes undiscussed, might take up proportionately more space on the map of Canada than expected. Viewing Macdonald as disabled could resituate how we encounter and contextualize his name as an identifier of place, particularly if our goal is to envision a more inclusive Canadian toponymy. His disability allows us to destabilize the image of white masculinity as a symbol of power, humanizing and drawing imperfection into commemorative material to complicate and be more truthful about the man and his legacy, but also about Canadian society in general. While not desiring to defend the suitability of Macdonald as a source of commemorative names and material, his supporters—once apprised of his disability—can redevelop the picture of white masculine authority to include this usually silenced aspect that challenged the man and likely impacted his contribution to the country.

This positioning of disability as a challenge that could be overcome was precisely the approach that Franklin Delano Roosevelt (1882–1945) took during his political career prior to becoming the president of the United States in 1933. While he tried to hide his physical disability, a form

Marginalized Groups and Canada's Place Names   163

of paralysis caused by polio that required a wheelchair or other assistance in order to move, he also pushed the construction of his disability as a challenge he had mastered. Linking disability to a person's ability to dominate it, to live and work as a person who did not possess that disability, then became one of the reasons Roosevelt was commemorated in both the United States and Canada. Beyond street names and statues, the latter of which might hint at his disability through the inclusion of his wheelchair or the device of a cane, nine places situated in five provinces and territories bear his name. Unlike mental disabilities, Roosevelt's suitability for office was not questioned due to his physical disability, and the notion of beating or overcoming disability remains even today associated with normative masculinity in the Western world.[47] Ableist attitudes also may prevail when commemorating people with disabilities. For instance, the Larry Brander Bridge in Northport, Nova Scotia, was feted by the community when it was named in 2012 because it commemorated a local citizen who died prematurely in 2007 due to conditions associated with Down Syndrome. While no doubt some citizens celebrate Larry Brander as a person, from an ableist perspective, the bridge commemorates a person who contributed to his community despite his disability, not because of it.

Other examples of prominent Canadian officials who exhibited mental disabilities include William Lyon Mackenzie King (1874–1950) and John Diefenbaker (1885–1979), both of whom served as this country's prime minister in the mid-twentieth century. Their names adorn schools, streets, and certainly sculptural plaques across the country. Since their deaths, scholars have questioned the competencies and mental stabilities of these two politicians, with the former engaging in séances to communicate with the dead, and the latter attracting concerns about his sanity while serving in office.[48] The positioning of mental illness in scholarship has drastically changed in the last two decades, which we should see addressed in further considerations of renaming. Scholars subsequently have grown more aware of mental disabilities, which can allow their research to become coloured with a bias that associates a political figure's poor performance in office with their disability. In one way, these men remain commemorated likely as a result of their service leading Canada; in another way, however, their disabilities seem obviated from commemorative material and its explanations, tucked away and made invisible, just as Roosevelt had intended.[49] These "elephants in the room" today are increasingly drawn into public discourse as collective and individual challenges that society is asked to accommodate in order to support these individuals and ensure they participate fully in Canadian public, economic, cultural, and intellectual life. Historically, disability has been framed in a negative light, but in recent years awareness of disabled realities is becoming mainstream, perhaps led by the likes of Fox, who subsequently found himself commemorated precisely for his efforts to mainstream awareness of the disease that had disabled him.

On Canada's map, there are many off-colour references to mental and psychological disabilities. Presumably referencing some form of insanity, twenty-eight places invoke this condition through the word crazy, several of which modify humans, such as Crazy Kate Reef (1961) in Halifax, Nova Scotia, and Crazy Jane Lake (1971) in Kootenay Land District, British Columbia. According to the latter province's place name office, based on their research and interviews, the name comes from prospectors' legends told decades before. Named for a well-meaning sex worker who lived in the region and cared for miners who were ill or having a rough time, according to one interviewee, she "was fond of wandering off into the woods; one day [she] wandered off and didn't return."[50]

Names for Outsiders

A final group of rarely studied place names relates to tourists, who are often marginalized and segregated as a demographic who come from away, stay in purpose-built accommodations, and rely on the service industry and transportation networks in ways that most residents may not. Not all places have residents or citizens and their target constituents can be fluid and transient in the form of travellers who descend on a place from other parts of the country or from anywhere in the world. Locals recognize them because they may look different or speak another language; they arrive in campers or in cars donning far-away licence plates, all of which announce them as being from elsewhere—an experience that many Canadians know well when they visit a place.

Tourist attractions such as Canada's Wonderland, located outside of Toronto, Ontario, carefully don names that transform into signposts meant to characterize the place, the experiences it offers, and the place's brand identity—and there are three places that also celebrate wonderland elsewhere in Ontario and Manitoba, all invoking the well-known story, *Alice in Wonderland*. Touristic destinations, perhaps with the exception of parks or settlements named for famous locales, such as Niagara Falls, also comprise locations that are not catalogued by place-naming agencies. Yet, robust signage will direct tourists toward these places, assisting them in their wayfinding no differently than a toponymic sign informing the driver how far she is away from Toronto while travelling along an Ontarian highway.

As Asbestos/Val-des-Sources demonstrates, changing names offers a significant means of rebranding to attract tourists and their purse strings though a more appealing name.[51] The branding of wine country has been carefully cultivated to characterize a bounty of vineyards and presumably good-quality alcoholic beverages, as well as the visual culture one imagines along with this form of space: rolling green landscapes containing neatly arranged rows of vines, large villas offering luxurious tasting and eating experiences, as well as winery tours, the clean air of the countryside, and so on. In Canada, the Vintners Quality Alliance (VQA) has worked hard to create a quality standard associated with wine makers and, by extension, their locales through the notion of terroir. VQA terroir and its emblems can be found in British Columbia and Ontario, but not in any other province, making this brand exclusive while proffering to wine tourists a map pinned with award-winning wineries that they can visit. When wine tourists enter a VQA region, they see road signs authenticating that they are in VQA territory, and thus a region deemed by this authority to have high-quality wines. The visualization of a bunch of grapes indicates that there are wineries nearby; these signs, in conjunction with kilo-meter markers, lure tourists from the main road toward a nearby winery. Anywhere in the world, we expect this range of experiences and tools of wayfinding when we visit a wine-producing region that has linked its industry to tourism.

Naming and tourism also go together in the branding of cities and towns. The international relations maintained by a place name or emblem are embodied by the concept of the twin or sister city, whereby cities—normally from different parts of the world—link themselves for the purpose of cultivating tourism, commerce, a sense of shared heritage, or because they possess the same name, as the example of Stratford, Ontario (whose sister city is Stratford, UK) demonstrates. Both small cities with quaint downtown areas offer picturesque swans and international theatre scenes, and are in driving distance of their respective London, transplanting these geographical and cultural signifiers from the United Kingdom to Ontario. While there are examples of twinning going back thousands of years, the modern practice began toward the end of the Second World War in Britain.[52] By cultivating this connection between two places, citizens of either country acquire greater awareness of how the familiar—which encompasses the culture and industries, maybe even the climate and aesthetic character of their hometown—can be experienced abroad, which helps to make foreign lands seem more normalized and welcoming.[53]

By the late twentieth century, sister-city relationships began to form between Western and non-Western nations, which reflected the growing consequence of global trade and the rise of certain countries, for example Japan and China, in particular industries. Barrhead, Alberta (named for the Scottish settlement by that name), twinned with Tokoro, Japan, in 1991; it later became amalgamated into the larger Hokkaido city of Kitami. Both towns have populations of about 5,000 residents and share more than an interest in curling, with Hokkaido's strongest curlers having trained in Alberta. The province has cultivated other twin cities in the Hokkaido region, creating a constellation of places for Japanese tourists to visit while in Canada. These relationships are reinforced through

Marginalized Groups and Canada's Place Names   167

memorandums of understanding supporting university exchange programs, which bring students from Japan to study at Alberta's institutions of higher learning, as well as sports agreements, Japanese cultural investment into Alberta for the development of Japanese cultural institutions, joint industrial initiatives in key sectors, such as forestry and agriculture, among other connections. As a result, when Japanese tourists come to these regions of Alberta, they are also more likely to find welcoming signs from home during their stay, which incentivizes tourism.

The Next Frontier

As this broad array of names relating to racialized and re-racialized, disabled, and elsewhere groups demonstrates, a dearth of representation has been afforded in our names and emblems to significant numbers of Canada's people. While some problematic names, for instance of racialized people, have been corrected, the manner in which these changes have been implemented nonetheless provokes additional concerns. One of these is the implications of removing a name that describes marginalized presence, because people of colour and with disabilities remain invisible on much of the Canadian map. Renaming in this sense should somehow reaffirm marginalized presence rather than hide away the harmful behaviour of white namers. This was precisely one of the concerns voiced by residents of Negro Point, Nova Scotia, who chose to keep this name rather than change it to something else.

Perhaps not surprisingly, racist names join other offensive ones relating to disability and disease as drivers of economic misfortune. Recognizing the costs involved in not renaming a place that tourists and would-be residents or clients may find unsavoury, on the one hand, and the costs of rebranding a destination with more welcoming names and emblems, on the other, will be explored in the next and final chapter of this book. Certainly, settler groups from around the world have influenced place names in ways that not only inscribe their presence but also foment economic growth precisely through a named concentration of people possessing a certain background. Not only do people from China go to Chinatown to shop and do business but people from other backgrounds also benefit from these spaces in that they offer a form of local tourism that does not require travel to another part of the world.

In the next chapter, we take on the important task of changing, revising, or re-visioning our place nomenclature using some of the examples pursued throughout the book. While changing racist names may seem an unquestionable step to take in this endeavour, the steps toward realizing any change are not always straightforward and have other consequences beyond removing one name and installing another.

CHAPTER 6

How to Discuss and Change Names

The preceding chapters have hopefully stimulated interest in Canada's place names while complicating how we think about them relative to our identities and those of the people with whom we live, work, shop, worship, share meals, and interact within Canadian society more broadly. The last three chapters in particular highlight names that were problematized and later revised, giving us pause to wonder if and how these discussions might give rise to similar action in the future. The case studies contained in this final chapter model how names can be changed, what challenges were encountered along the way, what constituencies were involved in the process, and which laws and policies helped or hindered the endeavour. Media coverage of name changes provides rich context for this sometimes-fraught process as well as interviews with citizens who were impacted by the names. These lessons are organized by their methodological approaches toward possible solutions when it comes to contested, offensive, or inaccurate names. In addition to these case studies, I provide an overview of naming authorities in the country so that readers have starting points if they intend to propose either a new name or a revision for an existing one. I conclude by synthesizing recommendations made throughout this book for how place names can be assessed and discussed while encouraging community involvement at all levels.

What's Commemoration Got to Do with It?

Settler-Canadians and their European predecessors tend to prefer commemorative place names when places refer to people (especially non-Indigenous people). Perhaps that is, in part, because as humans we feel connected to each other and desire to celebrate the best and most accomplished among us, which then sheds a seemingly positive light on part of our own place identity.[1] As shown in the preceding chapters, commemoration is subjective and becomes re-evaluated over time—as the dismounted statues of Cornwallis, Macdonald, and Ryerson attest. Traditionally, Indigenous names do not commemorate individuals, but rather might project a people's name onto their land, which proclaims their connection to it and it to them. They tell of the history and contents of the land and inform us of the human experience in a place, among other facets of Indigenous place knowledge that could inspire settlements to embrace ways of naming that might be new to them.

In recent times, however, Indigenous people are becoming commemorated with place names, albeit in sometimes problematic ways, as Oneida Street in Oromocto, New Brunswick, Tom Longboat Elementary School in Scarborough, Ontario, and Queen's University's Patricia Monture Hall in Kingston, Ontario, demonstrate. This last name, which was proposed in 2020 but not yet approved, would celebrate Mohawk lawyer, professor, and activist, Patricia Monture-Angus (1958–2010), who graduated from the school decades before her name was considered as a suitable replacement for that of John A. Macdonald.[2] The university struck a committee to consider the name change at the request of the university's principal in response to a petition to take action against a name that students associated with racism. Essentially, the university was being asked to de-commemorate, and the institution's process in considering what action to take provides us with an instructive model regarding name changes.

The committee, composed of Indigenous and non-Indigenous faculty, staff, and students, undertook two months of deliberations and consultation with the broader university community, yielding a sixty-five-page report in which it weighed the benefits and detriments of the name

172 *Canada's Place Names and How to Change Them*

change, its sole mandate being to determine whether a name change was warranted.[3] The committee reflected on some key questions to understand the institution's relationship with the country's former prime minister: what connection did Macdonald have to the institution? Why did the university adopt his name for the law school and was there a rationale for embracing the name? And what impacts did his actions have, whether locally, nationally, or internationally?[4] At the same time, the committee considered the many objections to changing the name, which included concerns about so-called cancel culture, the performativity or triviality of removing the name, the importance of history, and the importance of recognizing Macdonald's contribution to the founding of Canada. The committee concluded that Macdonald had no connection to the university compared to the namesakes of other campus facilities, and this comparative approach may well assist others as they think about the suitability of names. The university has other instruments at its disposal as well to guide its decision making, including a naming policy approved in 1996 and the institution's strategic and academic missions, which express its values and objectives, including those relating to fomenting a campus that is inclusive. Committee members took the position that keeping the name was just as powerful of an action as changing it, a lesson that should give us all pause to think about the status quo of our names.[5]

Naming a building after an individual, albeit here after a Mohawk woman, still follows a Western paradigm for naming that has demonstrated a problematic tendency toward patriarchy and racism, and certainly does not reflect traditional forms of Indigenous place knowledge. At the same time, a deliberate shift toward commemorating marginalized groups allows the majority of the country's population living with marginalization (women, people of colour, Indigenous people, among other groups) to see people connected to their own identity celebrated. For this reason, and in the spirit of Canada's Truth and Reconciliation Commission's Calls to Action, the modus operandi of place naming in this country must be seriously rethought before awarding any name that might be commemorative in nature.

How to Discuss and Change Names

Commemorative place naming was typically undertaken by white men for and about other white men, and as the policies highlighted within this chapter demonstrate, rules about naming continue to support historical precedent. Indeed, the naming policy at Queen's University subscribes to commemorative naming as a form of honouring suitable individuals "who have rendered outstanding service to the University, the Province of Ontario, to Canada, or internationally. [The university] also welcomes the opportunity to honour individuals whose generous philanthropic benefactions make possible the construction or restoration of buildings, the establishment of endowed chairs, the development of programs."[6] Commemoration as a methodology tends to exclude others or reproduce the same harms when names are viewed over the course of time; it ensures that equalities gained closer to our present remain absent from our place identities, which tend to be moored to the past. In the case of Queen's naming policy, privileged people such as donors are favoured to be honoured, which narrowly confines the demographic representation of the campus's names to primarily white men. This issue can be seen on building names across the Canadian academic landscape and is not unique to Queen's University.

In recent years, Toronto's Ryerson University, which opened in 1948 as the Ryerson Institute of Technology, has attracted criticism for its name. Studying how it is dealing with concerns about naming demonstrates how de-commemoration takes place and, in some cases, how reconciliation, decolonization, and putting a stop to intergenerational trauma can be accomplished in a name. In 2017, the year of Canada's 150th anniversary of Confederation, a student-led campaign sought to see the university change its name due to Egerton Ryerson's involvement in the Indian Residential School System. They argued that the name was not only disrespectful and traumatic for Indigenous students, serving as a constant reminder of a violent past, but also that such a man did not deserve to be commemorated. A significant portion of the student body, however, objected to such a change, arguing that it was impractical and even disrespected Ryerson's memory. Such resistance underlines the importance of public will to rectify or address problematic names of this nature. With this division in the student body, the university administration was able to avoid taking a position on the matter, and it quietly faded from the media for a couple of years.[7] One of the obstacles to changing this name, some believed, were financial in nature, as plaques, school building and wayfinding signs, as well as its overall brand would have to be replaced, along with professors' email signatures and addresses, all of which donors may find alienating.

This last justification was used to defend McGill University's initial choice not to rename its sports team, the Redmen, due to the nostalgia that alumni expressed about the name and the sense of tradition that they sought to uphold with possible donations on their part.[8] The concern about this name, which originally was not intended to refer to Indigenous people, is that in subsequent decades the term nonetheless became a racial slur. Its new name, the Redbirds, only came into effect in 2020, yet it has retained the component that some viewed as a racial signifier by combining it with an avian species. The lesson gleaned from this university's choice should serve as a warning when names are corrected in that problematic language cannot simply be repackaged so to have the offensive bits erased. Red remains a signifier of Indigenous race, which is how some people interpreted the team's first name; by remaining part of the name, the racism stays in plain sight, even if the human signifier, men, has been removed.

Returning to Ryerson University, three years later the discussion was resurrected with petitions to change the institution's name and remove their namesake's statue; the latter was vandalized and moved to 1492 Land Back Lane. In fall 2021, the university agreed to change its name, which introduced issues other than finding a new name. The matter of financing the rebranding is a significant issue, one that perhaps a generous donor could resolve. Western University, for instance (my alma mater), rebranded itself from the University of Western Ontario in 2012, and dropping On-

How to Discuss and Change Names

tario from its name, according to *Maclean's* magazine, cost $200,000.[9] Today, both the old and present names are synonymous, with graduates such as myself using the old name with which we are more familiar. This suggests that renaming places may be an intergenerational project in that a new name will eventually gain traction with younger generations. A telling detail about this name change is that the university maintained the same address structure—www.uwo.ca—and this is reinforced on its diplomas and in email addresses and signatures used by staff, students, and faculty. A complete rebranding would not only have been much more costly it also may well have been on a scale not supported by the university when they adopted its new name. Ryerson University, which announced its new name in May 2022—Toronto Metropolitan University—therefore finds itself in a difficult and expensive position because as it rebrands itself the costs will be wide-ranging and likely damaging for donor relations, many of whom offer money and their own names to build new infrastructure on campus. How will they feel seeing a commemorated Ryerson discarded, and might that happen to their own names down the line? No doubt donors to Queen's University have expressed these same concerns.

Other institutions that have changed their name include Malaspina University-College, now known as Vancouver Island University. It began as Malaspina College in 1969, becoming a university-college in 1988, and in 2008 it rebranded itself. Named for Alessandro Malaspina (1754–1810), who attempted to claim land on British Columbia's western coast in the name of Spain, the university's motto is "Discoveries in education," and it appears in the institution's coat of arms underneath a floating Spanish corvette, last updated in 2019. Despite rebranding itself, several referents to navigation and the so-called age of discoveries remain—its athletics team is called the Mariners, the school's colours are blue and white, the university's magazine is titled the *Portal*, and its student paper *The Navigator*. These elements demonstrate how difficult rebranding is for organizations and settlements, on the one hand, and how associated names buttress the name that was initially found to be problematic or in need of revision. In this case, while the institution came under some scrutiny for the colonial origins of its name, it was rather their depiction of quality education that gave rise to this name change. The justification for changing the name rested on the sole use of "university" in the institution's brand, which resulted in increased enrolments due to its disassociation from its status as a college, which Canadian and international audiences usually view as being a trade-focused form of higher education.[10] These elements nonetheless suit the university's choice to embrace the island's name, bestowed in commemoration of British naval officer, George Vancouver (1757–1798). The university effectively traded one colonial invader for another when it completed its most recent rebranding.

Beyond Ryerson and Malaspina, several other Canadian institutions share similar connections to the colonial past, from Laval and Dalhousie Universities to hospitals named for royals, such as Queen Elizabeth II Health Sciences Centre in Halifax, Nova Scotia. This reality should be recognized in the balance of any institutional commitment to "decolonization," which describes the attempt to remove colonialism at the institutional level. Decolonizing will impact both the structure and functioning of educational, medical, and justice systems, among others—including their colonial names. Cape Breton University, like Vancouver Island University, takes its name from one of the country's first European-derived toponyms, which appeared on maps in the early 1500s, for the western French fisher people (Bretons) who frequented the region. Both the settlement and the university feature a European vessel on their coats of arms, which reinforces the intersecting identities that institutions and settlements exhibit with the places with which they share names.

Yet, as Western University and Land Back Lane demonstrate, changing names seems more possible at the local level. The recent changes to team names in sports leagues emphasize the power of focusing on local changes. The Edmonton Eskimos, a Canadian Football League franchise founded in 1949, renamed itself the Edmonton Elks in 2021 after years of pressure from fans, the general public, and sponsors. The process involved

How to Discuss and Change Names   177

consulting with thousands of interested parties, who also proposed new names for the team, and yielded a new team logo. In this case, the team chose to maintain the same initials while entirely omitting the offensive term referring to Inuit people and instead replacing it with a traditional Indigenous food source.

Values and Collective Identity

Rather than using commemorative names, one innovative approach to naming might acknowledge, instead, our values or goals and hopes for the future. Reconciliation Bridge in Calgary, Alberta, is an example of this practice. This name replaced the Langevin Bridge, named for Hector-Louis Langevin (1826–1906), who was a proponent of the Indian Residential School System and a so-called father of Confederation. The name change comprised one of the final recommendations of the city's *White Goose Flying* report, published in 2016 as a means of advising the city on how to respond to the TRC's Calls to Action.[11] The city voted in favour of changing the name in January 2017, with all but one councillor supporting the initiative. Calgary's then mayor, Naheed Nenshi, believed that the change would help heal past harms while offering a symbol of this objective in the form of both the name and the bridge as a connection between two peoples.[12] Interestingly, the notice of motion for the name change acknowledges the traditional name of the city, Moh'kin sstis, being "the traditional land of the Treaty 7 people, and of the Métis Nation of Alberta Region 3 and the home to Urban Indigenous peoples"[13]—a name that the city might consider embracing as a replacement for, or modification of, Calgary. Council furthermore voted in favour of creating a plaque that explains the bridge's naming history, the Indian Residential School System, and the impact it had on Indigenous peoples as a means of facilitating dialogue between the city's citizenry and its Indigenous neighbours. A year later, a renaming ceremony celebrated the adoption of the new name, with elders congregating at the bridge's north entrance. They offered prayers to the Creator asking for spiritual healing and harmony

Canada's Place Names and How to Change Them

before walking across the bridge to the south side where drumming, speeches, songs, and dancing ensued.[14]

The city of Calgary offers a tool for naming that many settlements lack: a policy. While its overall purpose is to provide oversight and guidance on commemorative naming for events and people with outstanding achievements, service, or contributions to the community, it nonetheless outlines the process of implementing a new or different name. The policy also offers the opportunity to purchase or sponsor naming rights as a revenue stream to support municipal services. Sponsored names must celebrate notable people from the city, country, or from abroad, politicians who have retired or died, or people who have donated to the city.[15] As we know, these categories predominately favour white men, so it will be no surprise that the city's new names will likely continue the existing patriarchal toponymic practices that Reconciliation Bridge disrupts. That being said, sponsorship also offers an opportunity because cultural associations representing marginalized groups could approach the city and offer to sponsor a name they deem suitable for commemoration.

The process for awarding names is clearly laid out in the city of Calgary's naming policy. Interested parties propose a name to the relevant department, a planning technician evaluates the name and provides feedback, then the naming policy steward makes a determination, after which their recommendation goes to the Calgary Planning Commission with the final decision being made by council.[16] Public consultation, even for naming rights that are sold to third parties, is an essential element of the city's naming process, as is transparency with respect to the names under consideration. The policy also provides advice about avoiding divisive names: "When an individual or group is identified by a name, best efforts should be taken to ensure that the name is not seen as linked with discrimination, oppression and systemic racism nor in violation of community standards as they exist today."[17] This last criterion—community standards of today—suggests that names must respond to the community's contemporary values, which provides the community with an important justification in support of changing or adopting a new name. Applicants

How to Discuss and Change Names   179

are advised to propose names that celebrate people or the region's flora and fauna or, in the case of roads, that relate to the community's name or its history. Excepting numbers and hyphens, non-Roman characters are not allowed, much like rules from provincial toponymy offices. Calgary's policy states that existing names will not normally be renamed except under exceptional circumstances, as Langevin Bridge proves. As this last guideline demonstrates, many naming policies offer means of maintaining the status quo.

The city's guidelines also suggest other ways that names can be revised. First, while renaming roads is not normally allowed, the policy does permit awarding secondary names. This possibility could not only allow more communities to view naming more flexibly through the co-existence of more than one name but it might also become the means through which changes happen over time, as communities become accustomed to new names, hold future votes to embrace them, and discard old ones. Second, the name Reconciliation Bridge was proposed as a result of the *White Goose Flying* report's recommendation that a name symbolizing historical harm should be revised. Inviting focused assessments of local names, as will be detailed in due course, is a powerful tool that puts weight behind the revising of names.

Many name-change deliberations are sparked by a petition demanding change. Across this country, committees of city staff have been created in response to public requests to de-commemorate or to use names to express values and hopes for the future. Their research inevitably points to other municipalities undertaking similar self-studies in advance of council meeting votes to remove a name and then to adopt a new one. This is precisely the process used by the city of Toronto as it votes on a new procedure for recognizing and commemorating individuals, all of which came from the impetus to change the name of Dundas Street, one of the country's most recognized urban arteries, named for Henry Dundas (1742–1811).[18] The call to rename the street rested on the man's reticence to abolish the transatlantic slave trade, and research into Dundas and his

180   *Canada's Place Names and How to Change Them*

history took place alongside public meetings and the city's affirmation of its commitment to fighting anti-Black racism and supporting equality and inclusion. The city approved the removal of Dundas from its nomenclature in June 2021; this action will certainly impact other civic assets across the city, which will also need new names.[19]

These issues confronting our towns and cities have given them cause to think about their values relative to naming. Toronto has drafted a statement on its commemorative principles that acknowledges the inequality of its names and the way values change over time. It promises to take a "three-Rs approach: rename (e.g. a street), remove (e.g. a monument), or reinterpret (e.g. a street name, monument, or artwork)."[20] For those whose values include historical memory, the city promises that any changes or removals will be preserved and documented in the city's archival and historical collections for future scholars and educators to learn about. This recourse is an important one for enabling name changes and helps to assuage concerns about so-called cancel culture. The city is careful to distinguish between history and commemoration as an expression of today's shared values rather than an anchor to a past that may not be universally moored to everybody's identity.

Bilingualism and Language Nationalism

Canada has two official languages, which can complicate place onomastics in this country because generics—the category of feature being named in the toponym, such as a river, bay, or lake—may need to be translated and because the name's orthography may vary considerably between English and French versions. Guidelines for treating geographical names in English and French were most recently revised by the Geographical Names Board of Canada (GNBC) in 2011.[21] This resource is joined by other guidelines set by the provinces' and territories' place-name offices, which are easily available on their respective websites and are synchronized with those of the GNBC. All provinces and territories are bound by the guidelines laid out by the GNBC, but they approve names within their own jurisdictions. As such, regulations on creating and changing toponyms share many similarities across the country.

Returning to the example of Asbestos in southeastern Quebec, a town of just over 7,000 people, the renaming process it followed provides an excellent model for settlements who wish to change their names in the context of undesirable names as well as language nationalism. The toponym dates from Anglophone occupation of that region of the province, whose name—were it spelled in French—would be Amiante or possibly Asbeste, but not the English word Asbestos. The province's naming commission recommends against translating names, giving the example of "the city of Québec" as an official spelling in English of the province's capital, Québec, which many Anglophones refer to as Quebec City.[22] And this works the other way around too—English names must not be translated into their French variants, with the exception of border features where an official name in English may be used in other parts of the country, called pan-Canadian names—Baie d'Hudson and Hudson Bay being excellent examples of this practice. The province furthermore recommends against using bilingual names because the generic would make the name confusing, as Baie James Bay demonstrates. The requirement to translate or not translate, depending on the province or territory, nonetheless reinforces the systemic racism embedded in toponym policies because Indigenous generics are forced—with some exceptions explored in due course—into English or French, as with Lake Ontario (meaning "Lake Large Lake").[23]

The name Asbestos came about when a post office opened in 1884, giving rise to a descriptive name for the substance that was being mined there.[24] While the town could have embraced a bilingual or French version of its name, its connection to a British colonial past as well as a harmful substance gave the community reasons to consider changing its name. Doing so, it was believed, might bolster the town's prosperity by distancing itself from an undesirable, cancer-causing substance, thereby making the town more inviting for new residents and businesses.[25] The name was also associated with a declining industry, whose main source of asbestos as well as good paying jobs—the Jeffrey Mine (named for its founder William Henry Jeffrey)—closed in 2011.

The town took about a year to look at this issue after town residents, politicians, and businesses vocalized their concern about the name, all leading up to the fall of 2020 when the name change would eventually be implemented. In September 2020, a soft launch of four names appeared on the town's Facebook account, attracting criticism. Greenpeace Canada had proposed Apalone as a replacement (referring to a species of turtle), but residents found the name inadequate, with one remarking, "I wouldn't be proud to say that I live in a soft turtle city."[26] Jeffrey was another possibility that was thoroughly criticized for maintaining the town's connection to the mine, not to mention colonialism, and on social media residents complained about a lack of transparency with respect to the first list of names, prompting the city to enter into a period of consultation with its residents. This process resulted in an expanded final shortlist of candidates: L'Azur-des-Cantons, Jeffrey-sur-le-Lac, Larochelle, Phénix, Trois-Lacs, and Val-des-Sources, with the status quo of Asbestos not making the ballot.[27] The town council determined that residents fourteen years of age and older could vote on the town's new name in October of that year, and 51.5% of the vote went to Val-des-Sources (Valley of the Springs), which described the town's location at the source of three nearby lakes, and overall the new name has been positively received among residents. The voter turnout was fairly high, with about 50% of eligible voters participating, although a demographic disparity between supporters and dissenters revealed itself throughout the revision process, with older generations being less supportive of the change. The demographic divide reflects the difficulty in using new names, one that I experience with respect to my alma mater, as I struggle to remember its new name and favour its old one.

This observation points to another issue that arises in the GNBC's naming guidelines. Its second principle on naming states that "First priority shall be given to names with long-standing local usage by the general public. Unless there are good reasons to the contrary, this principle should prevail."[28] The consequence of this principle is the reinforcement of the names that are sought to be changed. If by "general public" we are to understand the normativity of white settler society, then Indigenous names, and certainly new names meant to correct problematic ones, have less standing. The fact is that communities such as Val-des-Sources created an entirely new name for itself without the new name being commonly or broadly used before the process to revise its name was initiated. This may well be a necessary step to take while changing names, which implies that the GNBC, along with the provinces and territories, may need to reconsider how some of its principles reinforce the settler-colonial status quo. Its fifth principle regarding the use of personal names, for instance, states that "The person commemorated should have contributed significantly to the area where the feature is located," and such names should be in the "public interest."[29] And while it discourages naming places after their owners, the board nonetheless excludes past examples of this practice, which again reinforces the masculine identity of the country's existing nomenclature. On this last subject, the board's sixth principle makes explicit the masculine approach to naming unnamed features in recommending that "pioneers," the war dead, and people associated with "historical events" in the area be considered.[30]

Returning to Val-des-Sources, it was approved in December of that year by the Ministère des Affaires municipals et de l'Habitation, with the name officially updated in the GNBC and provincial registries in March 2021. Technically, names become official once they are published in the *Gazette officielle du Québec*, and the GNBC will accept any new or revised names once approved by the provinces and territories. Name revisions of this nature also incur other costs unrelated to government and staff wages for their efforts to re-name: all street and highway signage, letterhead, envelopes, and related objects and places where the name may appear will need to be replaced. For Val-des-Sources, it was estimated that these costs would amount to about $133,000, which is no small sum considering the town's population. It should also be noted that, despite its namesake as a post office and later town, Asbestos remains an official post office in keeping with the GNBC's third naming principle: "Names for facilities established by postal authorities, railway companies, and major public utilities shall be accepted."[31] Like its second principle, this third one effectively cements the presence of antiquated names selected during the industrialization of the country within our toponymy. This fact is particularly evident when one studies a post-office map of Quebec where many of the post offices were denominated before the establishment of a Francophone government and naming office. Many provinces and territories acknowledge, in their jurisdictional place-name guidelines, that they have no authority over legislated names, names given by postal services, railways, or utility companies, motor vehicle transportation routes, and regional or municipal streets, communities, parks, and buildings.[32] So one critical area that must be urgently addressed by the GNBC and its provincial and territorial affiliates is to undertake an assessment of institutional names, such as post offices and railway stations.

The province's Francophone mandate, moreover, raises another issue when it comes to place names in Quebec that are not necessarily as contested in other regions. While the province certainly exhibits a range of Anglophone names, the fact is that the Commission de toponymie upholds the province's linguistic charter, which is one reason why generics must be expressed only in French. This is the same charter that states that a toponymy office will be established to ensure linguistic oversight and the protection of the French language. In fact, all toponymy signage must be in French, which complicates the inclusion of any non-French words used for specifics while a generic French term must be used.[33] A great example is the recently revised Lac-de-la-Squaw studied in this book's third chapter, which became Lac Sauvagesse. In this term, the gender of the specific (Squaw or Savage) is expressed, so if one did not know the meaning of this hateful term, they would nonetheless interpret its gender as a noun. In June 2021, Quebec's naming authority revised it with an Innu term, *innushkuess*, meaning "young Innu woman."[34] The average Canadian would not recognize the word's meaning, so its update may have less impact than the negative reaction against its preceding name. In contrast, at

How to Discuss and Change Names   185

the local level, the name change should have much greater impact while occasioning broader awareness of the reasons for revising the toponym.

From another perspective, Lac-de-la-Innushkuess still has some issues in that the reference to no specific Innu woman demonstrates how genericity obscures marginalized identity by leaving it undifferentiated rather than individualized as a commemorative name would. The choice to make this designation youthful, moreover, rather than wizened or motherly, also merits some consideration, as commemorative names favour older and experienced individuals rather than younger ones. What would that woman for whom the lake was named have been doing there—hunting to feed her family, teaching children how to harvest birch bark, or was that location her favourite place to swim? The province still has a way to go when it comes to eliminating names offensive to Indigenous women, as its eleven places containing Sauvagesse attest. While the province's toponymy office is in the process of dealing with this group of names, it nonetheless acknowledges that the term is poorly received, should no longer be used, and promises that "Savage will be replaced little by little with Indian, Aboriginal, and by Amerindian, which are more neutral terms. Today, the name Savage is no longer in current use except in a historical context for Quebec."[35]

The only officially bilingual province or territory in Canada is New Brunswick, whose logo embraces the generic in both languages (New/ Nouveau Brunswick). As a result, some settlements and geographic features also possess bilingual names, as Grand-Sault–Grand Falls in the province's northwest demonstrates. The name betrays the region's colonial history, as French settlers gave it its French toponym in the late seventeenth century, for the remarkable waterfalls and river that run through the town. After the British invaded and spread throughout the region, an English-language version of the name emerged. The coexistence of a name in both languages powerfully allows both Anglophones and Francophones to see themselves represented in a place's name and thus identity, which has no doubt served a role in reconciling these populations after two centuries of difficult relations. But Wolastoqiyik people will likely not identify with the name in either language; the waterfalls in question are called chik'un'lk'a'bik (place of destruction). The expansion of the province's bilingualism mandate to include Indigenous languages will be an essential contribution to reconciliation, particularly given the province's existing willingness to use more than one name for a settlement in order to be linguistically inclusive. This may well comprise a significant direction for Canadian toponymy and, as bilingual English and French names in New Brunswick demonstrate, a means of reconciliation after difficult periods of intercultural relations. Certainly, bi- or multilingual names can play a critical role in creating more inclusive place names.

Certain provinces have legislation that deals with their toponymy.[36] New Brunswick requires that municipalities propose a council-approved name along with a plebiscite through which more than 50% of the settlement votes in favour of the change. Several other provinces and territories, such as the Northwest Territories, also require a plebiscite, whereas Nunavut allows the minster to make the final decision about a name.[37] In New Brunswick, the minster of local government and local governance reform then approves the change and asks the lieutenant-governor in council to change the name. According to the province's toponymist, any decision regarding names closely follows the GNBC's guidelines of 2011, which has prepared guidance on how to propose a name.[38] The form for name proposals requires several categories of information, including the names and addresses of five long-time residents who can discuss the proposed name's history and confirm its well-established use. This requirement returns us to the intergenerational project implied by a name change in that older populations are less likely to support revising a toponym and they may have less difficulty with the problematic names with which they grew up. Several provinces at the moment are in the process of updating their guidelines, laws, and the procedures for proposing or changing a name, whereas others, such as Manitoba, have decided to list its naming principles and procedures on its website but not to circulate a guide like other provinces and territories have long done. All of them, with the exception of the territories, struggle to include Indigenous languages and nations in any equitable way, favouring instead the languages of English and/or French for both generics and descriptive names.

A Place with Two or More Names

Most provinces and territories conform to the GNBC's twelfth principle on generic terminology that states that the generic term—lake, mountain, falls, point, cove, and so on—will not be provided in more than one language. As shown in the fourth chapter's discussion about the settler-colonial appropriation of Ontario (Wendat for "large lake") for the lake that bears this name, limiting our use of generics to English and French creates redundancies in the feature's name in ways that are ignorant of Indigenous languages.

There is some hope on this front when we read closely the GNBC's advice concerning generic terms, which are to "be recorded in English, in French or in an Aboriginal language by the names authority concerned."[39] Yet, it also advises that fusion names exampled by Lake Ontario are acceptable: "Occasionally a name of Aboriginal origin has fused with the specific, a generic term that is similar in meaning to the French or English generic of the toponym," meaning it sees no issue with an evident redundancy.[40] Some provinces nonetheless have been approving the use of Indigenous generics while following the guidelines to not translate them, as Suzanne Bung'hun (Cariboo Land District) in British Columbia demonstrates.[41] A lake named in 1997, its Carrier linguistic origin was supplied by Nak'azdii Band chief Robert Antoine. *Bung'hun*, meaning "lake" in Nak'azdli Dakelh, seems to suggest that it commemorates somebody named Suzanne.[42] When the name is viewed on a map, moreover, it becomes evident that the generic, lake, is rendered in an Indigenous language yet the designation itself is clearly expressed in visual form, comprising a means of translating Indigenous generics. In this sense, Lake Suzanne does not exist, but Suzanne Bung'hun does. This practice underlines a discrepancy in how English and French generics are treated, as they would typically be translated. By not translating Indigenous generics, the names may be less available in textual form to broader audiences (which may not necessarily be a negative outcome). At present, there seems to be different rules or guidelines in place that impact the representation of Indigenous names when it comes to generics, so some work on promoting linguistic equality should be invested into this area of place nomenclature.

Willingness to accept Indigenous names lacking any English- or French-language component has unfolded across the country, and Indigenous groups have been leading this charge.[43] In 2017, the Stoney Nakoda Nation wrote to the province of Alberta to request that several of its signature place names be replaced with ones from their language, rather than the Cree and English ones that occupy much of the map of that province's southern region: Calgary should be Wichispa Oyade (elbow town); Canmore should be Chuwapchipchiyan Kude Bi (named for a hunter who imagined he saw a wolf in the woods where there were only willows); Bow River should be Ijathibe Wapta (a literal translation) or Mini Thni Wapta (cold river); as well as several others that have been proposed.[44] A possible way forward is to promote bi- or multilingual place names, exampled by the 1984 adoption of Mount Laurie (Îyâmnathka), whose name means "the flat faced mountain." Its Stoney name, Yamnuska, appears in Google Maps and other material used by hiking enthusiasts, including on signage pointing travellers toward the trail and mountain that bear this name. The co-existence of the official Indigenous name, Îyâmnathka, with a popular orthographic but not official variant, Yamnuska, defies the GNBC's call for uniformly spelled names and reminds us that places have different names due to the distinct languages and dialects spoken by the people holding this place knowledge.

This movement to change names also addressed offensive ones in southern Alberta. In 2020, a group petitioned to revise Squaw's Tit, at the top of Mount Charles Stewart in Canmore. The name itself is unofficial, which is why it is not in the GNBC's database, so it will be considered a new unnamed feature that was until recently findable in Google Maps by its unofficial name. Two previous proposals to change the name to "Tit" and "Mother's Mountain," both of which infer the location's original namesake, were not approved by Alberta's place-name office, which desired an Indigenous name for the location. After several years advocating for a change, the matter went to the town of Canmore, whose council minutes provide insight into its deliberations on this name.

Canmore's city council discussed the name change in August 2020 at the request of its mayor, John Borrowman. The town had previously expressed support for the TRC's Calls to Action for planning purposes and serves as another model for Canadian municipalities to follow. According to the town, this commitment was meant to "Guide the municipality in advancing the progress of Canadian reconciliation, strengthen right relations with the Stoney Nation and Indigenous Peoples with respecting their right to heal, and create a more culturally comfortable space to increase the level of inclusion of Indigenous Peoples in our community."[45] Impetus to change this name came from the community's settler and Indigenous residents, in consultation with the Stoney Nakoda Nation, whose support to change the name was obtained. After the nation consulted with elders to understand traditional names for the peak in question, Anû kathâ Îpa (Bald Eagle Peak) was selected and eventually endorsed by the region's government, and in September 2021 the province officially adopted the name.[46] Once a municipality proposes a change, the province is responsible for formalizing its adoption as per the Alberta Municipal Government Act: "The Lieutenant Governor in Council, on the request of a municipality's council and on the recommendation of the Minister, may change the name of the municipality."[47] A similar process was followed by Quebec when Asbestos requested its name change, and in Ontario, a municipality seeking to change its name must first have its council approve a bylaw that it then sends to the director of titles and the minister concerned.[48]

One possible explanation for the delay is that names involving Indigenous groups must be approved at the federal level as well. In the meantime, Google Maps has updated the place's name without any government approval at the provincial and federal levels, which speaks to contemporary naming authorities' irrelevance when the majority of Canadians consult non-governmental and, in this case, commercial sources of place knowledge. Rather than the proposed one expressed in Stoney, however, Google Maps marks the location of Bald Eagle Peak in English. As a result of this process to revise a name, a collection of official and unofficial names for the same place have emerged, some of which are adopted by authorities beyond those of the province's naming office, such as businesses, municipalities, and hiking enthusiasts. These varying naming practices seem to defy the province's policy on the awarding of toponymy, which follows other jurisdictions in providing rules about spelling, language, the local or popular use of a name, and regarding commemoration, which again speaks to the irrelevance of traditional settler place-name authority.[49]

Allowing places to grow beyond having only one name affords us many opportunities when it comes to embracing name changes. The cost to Canadians is low. While we could maintain the status quo of our toponymic knowledge, what is more likely with time and broader exposure to additional names is that our toponymic vocabularies will expand, making places recognizable by more than one name and allowing us to choose which name we wish to associate with ourselves. This practice has already come into effect for individuals who choose to state that they come from Turtle Island, rather than Canada, whereas some choose to link these names (Canada-Île de la Tortue-Turtle Island, or vice versa, Île de la Tortue-Turtle Island-Canada). That being said, not all Indigenous people agree that Turtle Island in any language would be a suitable replacement for Canada. In this light, Calgarians could choose to hail from Wichispa Oyade or from its Anglicized form, Elbow Town, or by the name given to the land Calgary occupies by the Blackfoot, Moh'kin sstis (meaning elbow), or create a hybrid name that includes Calgary. The impetus to embrace a name therefore empowers the individual to choose which name they wish to use. Educating citizens about their choices in this respect will give rise to greater awareness of the range of name possibilities

How to Discuss and Change Names   191

while broadening toponymic knowledge through this solution of layering names. Over time, this awareness will graft one or more names onto our collective identity.

While joining settler and Indigenous names in this fashion might help to correct historical issues with our toponymy, Mount Laurie (Îyâmnathka) flags our attention for another reason. The practice of positioning an Indigenous name in brackets after one that celebrates settler John Laurie (1899–1959) should be rethought, as the brackets suggest that the name is parenthetical or secondary to the settler name. A more equitable approach would see the names joined by a hyphen and, whenever possible, ordered in such a way that reflects either the name's age or alphabetical (albeit Roman) order, with a preference for a chronological ordering whenever possible. In this case, the traditional name used since time immemorial, Îyâmnathka, would come before Mount Laurie, a twentieth-century name, in both ordering systems.

Regarding the subject of values, many settlements deliberating on their place names reach for policy and statements about equality, diversity, and inclusion. These policies do more than promote social and cultural relations. When policy is implemented and impacts the settlement's decision making—for instance, which infrastructure projects it supports—it may become a more attractive place for new residents. Names comprise just one aspect of a settlement's place branding, which it uses to attract both future citizens and tourists.[50] This form of strategic planning dovetails with broader knowledge of the demographic representation among residents, which ultimately spurned places such as Toronto to remove names that might alienate certain groups. If they were to commission an assessment of their streets, buildings, neighbourhoods, parks, rivers, lakes, and other named features, a clearer picture of the inequality and exclusion perpetuated by nomenclature would emerge. Once settlements understand the percentage of names that commemorate white men compared to women, people of colour, and Indigenous peoples—in addition to other groups, such as people living with disabilities—they can determine whether a plan to use nomenclature to promote inclusion is warranted.

Canada's Place Names and How to Change Them

Initiating a naming policy that strives to reflect the demographic mixture of the settlement—for example, if 52% of residents are women then 52% of names referring to people should be named for women—is one action that could be implemented. This possibility does not imply that more than half of all names would be named for women, as in the balance many names are descriptive or named for flora, fauna, or geographic features. Reducing the number of names that commemorate white men may also help to achieve a better balance in terms of demographic representation, either by removing them and replacing them with a name relating to a marginalized group, or by doing away with commemorative names and adopting, with permission, Indigenous or descriptive ones. Consulting marginalized groups and ensuring that they lead any naming process would be an essential element of any action taken by settlements to address their names. This approach was modeled by the city of Vancouver when it adopted its 150+ Place Naming Project in 2017. The motion brought before council noted the disparate number of names for women, the problematic use of Indigenous names, and other concerns that were at odds with the demographic representation and the history of the city and the land that it occupies.[51] Since that time, demographic considerations have impacted the city's naming choices.

Authority, Respect, and Consultation

Thus far, the idea of a naming authority has been situated primarily in government offices at all levels, although it is becoming apparent that non-governmental bodies have become instrumental in changing or updating names. In New Brunswick, Oromocto's name was created when the town was laid out in 1956 by engineers; called a model town, its name derives from the Wolostooq word *welamukotuk* (meaning "deep water"). In its present form, the name is a Western, Francocized appropriation or reinvention of an Indigenous term. Like Elsipogtog First Nation in the same province, Oromocto First Nation has a colonized place identity with respect to its name, which is officially registered by the GNBC as Oromocto 26, being the 26th Indian Reserve in the province. Both names—like Big Cove and its official geographic signifier, Richibucto 15—have been imposed upon this Indigenous group, who instead calls themselves Welamukotuk. Evidently, UNDRIP's recommendation that Indigenous people determine their own names has yet to impact the GNBC or provincial authority's naming practices in some ways, although nothing has stopped Welamukotuk from using this last name.

Rather, we should consider what procedures could be in place to ensure that settlers have permission to use Indigenous names and to determine what form they should have. The example of Oromocto puts into relief how Indigenous names have been appropriated and reshaped in the hands of settlers while Welamukotuk, located in the same area, has effectively invalidated its neighbouring town's name, perhaps raising the possibility of Oromocto adopting Welamukotuk. It should not do so, however, on its own accord; consultation and permission must be requested, as Indigenous groups have authority over their knowledge, language, and names. Embracing Indigenous names may be controversial, particularly in a country where many lands are unceded and occupied by settlers despite acknowledgement that they belong to Indigenous groups. But with their use may come greater awareness of Indigenous rights and presence.[52]

By consulting Indigenous groups and asking for their permission and advice about place names used by settlers, Canadians will not only show respect for Indigenous knowledge and culture but this step may also lead to a meaningful form of reconciliation. In particular, settlements and the provinces bearing Indigenous names should reach out to local Indigenous groups to inquire about the name's meaning, history, and the spelling used by that group. They should ask whether it remains acceptable to use the name, whether permission to use it was ever granted, and if not, would consent to use this name be granted today, and under what conditions. Names may need to be slightly revised so to exhibit the orthography embraced by the nation or nations consulted. A similar measure might be taken by settlements that, like Asbestos, desire to change their name and consider the possibility of applying Indigenous place knowledge, should

Canada's Place Names and How to Change Them

permission be granted for this purpose. Conditions for using Indigenous names might include an agreement that settles disputed land title and claims, funding for Indigenous-created spaces within the settlement, Indigenous authority over resource extraction and use, and autonomy and support for Indigenous-led climate-crisis mitigation, among other possibilities.

Consulting and gaining permission to use names will avoid what Red Indian Lake in Newfoundland experienced as a result of not consulting people impacted or implicated by a name change that explicitly refers to skin colour associated with Indigenous people. In 2021, Red Indian Lake's name was about to be revised to Wantaqo'ti Qospem, which in Mi'kmaw means "peaceful lake," a change that garnered widespread criticism when it was brought before the province's house of assembly for approval. The socio-political circumstances in which this name change was attempted have proven themselves to be fraught. Centuries ago, Europeans took Beothuk and other Indigenous remains to the United Kingdom where they have remained treated as museum artifacts. In recent years, efforts to see these ancestors return home are making inroads and it is expected that repatriation will only increase as time goes on. But controversy continues about where their remains will rest—in a St. John's museum, The Rooms, or in a place cared for by Indigenous people.

When the name was revised without consulting the province's Indigenous population, they felt disrespected and naturally distrustful of the government's intentions.[53] While not against renaming the lake's racist toponym, Mi'kmaq and non-Indigenous locals nonetheless wanted to be involved in determining the new name. Consultation in this case should have reached beyond a mayor, chief, or elder who were consulted. Instead, the entire community should have been apprised of the movement to change the name, been invited to contribute possibilities for its new name, and asked to either vote for or somehow represent their preferred choice before a final decision was made. As a result of media reports on the matter, the government halted the proposed name change. Broader consultation ensued, led by the province's office of Indigenous affairs and reconciliation, which conducted public hearings or engagement sessions, and the name was revised to Beothuk Lake in November 2021.

Like Oromocto First Nation's use of another name, the impacts of adopting a new name could impact local businesses, hiking and camping groups and trail maps, and have a knock-on effect that results in several other companies and bodies accepting the new name. At the same time, there was resistance to changing Red Indian Lake. Many Mi'kmaq and settler supporters of the status quo who signed a petition against revising the name have stated that they were born in Red Indian Lake and feel not only a connection to it but also are proud to come from there. One resident reasons, "I would like the name to remain Red Indian Lake. If the name must change I would support Beothuk Lake to recognize and remember those who lived on these waters before us. To change it to a Mi'kmaq name, Wantaqo'ti Qoospem, does not sit well with me as the last recollections [that] the Beothuk peoples had on that lake were anything but peaceful."[54] This resident's reflection on the Beothuk acknowledges their presence prior to that of the Mi'kmaw, a fact that seems to have escaped local authorities while initially attempting to change the name.

Like Dundas Street in Toronto, efforts to change names where people reside must involve consultation. This could take multiple forms: an open session of town council, a series of social media posts inviting feedback and name suggestions from the public, a presentation in schools to discuss name changes with groups who may not have any voting rights, and focused consultation of certain groups when the name change directly impacts them. In the case of Toronto, the city reached out in particular to Black communities, and Red Indian Lake should have reached out to its Indigenous population using numerous forms of consultation. Once broad consultation is undertaken—which means going beyond the leaders of a group, for instance the chief, to consult with everyday citizens—the feedback should be synthesized and shared broadly. This is the step that Queen's University took after it struck a committee to look at the name of its law school. Transparency with respect to naming helps raise confidence that everyone's opinion was heard and considered, even if the

Canada's Place Names and How to Change Them

outcome does not please everyone; it exposes what the majority believes while underlining the harms and benefits behind a name, thus educating individuals who may be poorly informed about others' perspectives and experiences.

Beyond transparency, reporting allows the process to be documented, and for other sources of guidance in the form of policies or values statements to be referenced. At present, this documentation remains siloed on municipal websites and poorly integrated into provincial and federal toponym databases, which is one of a number of areas that requires additional resources. Some place-name authorities, such as Quebec's toponym agency, invite the public to submit information regarding the origins of place names. This is an excellent opportunity for settlements to submit their existing name's history, along with any debate about it, so that it becomes part of a larger toponymic history in digital form. Digitization offers the broadest access to place-name data yet, while analogue sources such as gazettes remain difficult to access, even today—and most provinces and territories have invested into databases for managing information about place names. Reporting in this sense need not always be linked to a name change; it can also be an excellent opportunity to archive place knowledge while making it available to others. Such an approach decentres the authority of place-name agencies while allowing local groups to have greater impact. This approach would allow more than one name to co-exist and point to the same location, which is a more democratic and certainly more inclusive means of managing place nomenclature.

Place Emblems in the Twenty-First Century

At several points throughout this book, place emblems have provided additional insight into our place identities. As a medieval genre of visualizing identity, coats of arms and flags are codified in complex, transhistorical, and transcultural ways. Not only do they represent often-romanticized versions of a history that do not necessarily include everybody's experiences but they also reinforce colonial elements of place identity, often through explicit references to European colonizers and their vestiges on Canada as a modern nation. Traditionally the purview of professional heralds who regulated and approved the visual signatures obtained by cities and nations, as well as corporations, place emblems have also grown throughout the twentieth century to become logos and brands.

A significant observation about our place emblems is the normativity of problematic representation of marginalized groups alongside representations of abundance and bounty. I argue that there is a strong connection between the two when viewed through the prism of colonialism. Nearly every Canadian place emblem features flora, fauna, industry, natural resources, and the labour to extract them, each of which comprises a justification or outcome that compelled exploration, colonization, and settlerism. Those that feature non-white people usually construct their physical and cultural features in such a way that anchors them, almost entirely, to the past. And this historical skein overall characterizes most place emblems, with some exceptions, as the coat of arms for Nunavut demonstrates. This symbol, approved at the dawn of the twenty-first century, foreshadows what could become a transformation of our visualized place identities as we ask our towns, cities, and provinces or territories to think about each component of their emblems and to assess whether they must be updated.

In the digital age, moreover, coats of arms have been re-deployed online using graphic design. This has allowed some minor changes to creep into the average coat of arms, which the average person might not notice. Not only have the colours become vibrant but also unsavoury features such as the pizzle have been de-emphasized. These changes are as a direct result of the technological innovation in design and computing that has compelled designers to create higher-quality and -resolution versions of place emblems and logos. But there is much more work that needs to be done on this topic, which in itself will likely comprise a book-length study. Changing place emblems so that they avoid colonial, racist, or sexist imagery seems natural and easy enough, but unlike place names, there is no policy and little precedent for doing so.

A final consideration is whether we should be using a European medieval genre of visualization today—might it be time to do away with the structure of the coat of arms and flag? If so, what sort of codified place symbol would we embrace? Who would determine whether it reflects all of us, and how would it be generated, assessed, and adopted? Can we look to Indigenous forms of self-visualization as a possible source of inspiration and wisdom? The subject certainly warrants asking our communities about place emblems and whether they should be modernized to better reflect Canadians' values and objectives today.

Taking the Next Step

As this final chapter has demonstrated, individuals interested in lobbying for name changes at any level have resources at their disposal. First, they can seek out policy and process-related guidelines provisioned by their institution, settlement, and province or territory. These resources will outline how name proposals can be brought forward and the authorities involved along the way. While many cities have naming policies or recent precedents for awarding names, smaller settlements may not. Where this material has yet to be developed, citizens can approach their council and municipal staff and request that this documentation be created. Many of the name-change proposals discussed in this chapter required research on the part of municipal staff, who looked at how other settlements handled name changes or what sorts of initiatives were launched to help address diversity issues with commemorative names and emblems. Places that have not had name changes of their own can also look to other settlements' naming policies as sources for inspiration.

While staffing resources may well present a problem for some settlements, it bears noting that town staff may not be the only resource for performing this research. For example, the students in one of my courses have partnered with the town of Sackville, New Brunswick, where our university is located, to perform an assessment of its place names and monuments. While the report and recommendations we generated will be submitted to the town to do with them as it sees fit, my students had the opportunity to assess who and what are represented by our names. By working with the town and university archives, in addition to historical societies and local museums, students researched the history behind these names and monuments before synthesizing this information in a statistical format that shows concretely which demographics are represented and which ones are not, relative to the town's demographic makeup.

Performing this analysis helps to build the justification for changes in the future while pointing to possible themes and values that the town might want to consider endorsing or fortifying, particularly given existing policy relating to inclusion, Indigenous populations, the town's strategic plan, and other elements it uses to construct its identity or brand. Recommendations generated by this exercise could extend to the modification of names. For example, where names celebrate men through their surnames, which is often the case for street names, the town could consider modifying the name by pointing to a woman who had the same surname. If Stanley Drive was named for George Stanley (1907–2002)—the man who founded the Canadian studies program at Mount Allison University, served as the province's lieutenant governor, and has been credited with designing the Canadian flag—the name could be modified to commemorate his successful wife. Ruth Stanley (1922–2017) was an award-winning and nationally recognized lawyer who was one of the first women in Canada to hold a law degree; she was awarded the Order of New Brunswick along with several other honours. Ruth Stanley Drive offers residents the status quo by retaining the surname while allowing all women in the settlement to see a celebrated example from their demographic represented by a street name. Hybrid naming may well comprise a significant tool that place-naming authorities at all levels can use to make their names more inclusive, and it is one that has been implemented in other post-colonial regions, such as New Zealand. Adopting a second street sign will also allow people to get used to a street's new name, to begin to use it in their wayfinding, and to understand its meaning or origin, so that

Canada's Place Names and How to Change Them

in time the new name prevails over the old one, whose sign may or may not be removed. Moreover, research completed by the students resulted in a profile for the celebrated woman that can then be fleshed out in the town's marketing and educational materials, possibly even in the local school system, to raise awareness about the contributions of people other than white men.

Some names were created in an ad-hoc fashion when a town was incorporated and may have no connection to a place, while others celebrate people that have become controversial in recent decades. For both of these categories of names, which might be completely removed, Indigenous names might be considered, or possibly names that better articulate the town's relationships with other communities, particularly those that could foster recognition between the student body and their own place identities, as most university students do not come from the town in which the university is located. For example, if a significant stream of students comes from Bermuda, perhaps awarding a name that makes the town more familiar to them would make them feel more at home, which could result in community growth. This also might be accomplished through a sister-cities relationship whereby more explicit and formal links to such communities are cultivated. Names, as we have seen with respect to tourism and changes made to enhance a place's prosperity, powerfully impact a place's brand. Similarly, religious names in many Canadian settlements favour Christianity. If a town decides to keep religious names, it may want to broaden the representation to include other faiths, particularly in a community where people of other faiths live. The strategic use of names can thus help cultivate a more welcoming, friendly place for people to settle.

A municipality undertaking such an assessment may also need sources of inspiration for names that are less likely to be controversial as the decades pass. It may also want to implement a policy that limits any further commemoration of white men until such a time as greater representation of other groups has been achieved. It may also need to assess any name that might refer to Indigenous people. As we have seen, this is particularly

How to Discuss and Change Names 201

true of Indigenous names that have been appropriated and mangled by settlers. Researchers could approach local Indigenous communities to develop partnerships that would result, ideally, in sharing place knowledge and a commitment to using Indigenous names whenever possible using the orthography that they determine is correct and not necessarily that which is proscribed by the provincial or territorial naming authority. An attempt to develop this sort of relationship was initiated by the city of Mississauga when it decided on its name in 1968. At the ceremony marking the name that citizens had voted in favour of adopting, Chief Fred King of the Mississaugas of the Credit First Nation presented the city's mayor, Robert Speck, with a medicine stick as a symbol of good luck. The mayor reciprocated with a key to the city and a scroll representing their ancestors' treaty allowing settlers to live there.[55]

In exchange for this knowledge, municipalities should offer Indigenous partners something in return. It is not enough to ask for and use their names; reciprocity is an essential component of this partnership. Municipalities could concede to Indigenous groups the authority to develop and execute environmental policy and planning or invite them to take ownership of the historical narrative used by the municipality with respect to its settler-colonial history. Similarly, when approaching a local Black cultural association, inquiring after possibilities for commemorative names would likely result in a one-way relationship in that research and discussion would be undertaken by the association and not necessarily by the municipality. In the spirit of reciprocity, the municipality should consider what it can give to that association—using a name that represents a certain demographic after consulting them is not necessarily enough in this respect. They could be invited to contribute to the town's next equality, diversity, and inclusion policy discussion and to make recommendations that the municipality is bound to follow. Marginalized groups should also be remunerated for their time. The settlement could promise to focus their next infrastructure project in an area predominately inhabited by the group with which they wish to partner. Another possibility involves

Canada's Place Names and How to Change Them

inviting an artist from a marginalized community to create a statue or installation that relates to the type of remediation the settlement wishes to facilitate, therefore anchoring them more explicitly to the place.

Finally, research into names and emblems can be undertaken by all age groups and would comprise an excellent, grassroots project for schools and community groups. While costs for new signage may present a short-term obstacle for some communities, the reality is that signs are replaced frequently, and they may be updated on a rolling basis. Funds to invest in equality, diversity, and inclusion initiatives could easily be directed toward signs and emblems that contribute to these objectives, as could community fundraising initiatives and community improvement money and grants from all levels of government.

Throughout this book, I have exposed the settler-colonial architecture of Canada's place names while articulating a naming history that goes back centuries. By connecting our present to our toponymic past, the status quo of this country's names becomes destabilized and prompts everyone to assess whether the names we use today are suitable, desirable, and representative of ourselves, our neighbours, our colleagues, and our fellow Canadians. One of this book's objectives has been to frame out our place ecumene as a multivalent and transhistorical body of knowledge that responds to and reflects our diverse, intersectional, and sometimes conflicting identities as Canadians. Each of the identity-related chapters has pointed to the ways that women, Indigenous people, and people of colour are, or are not, represented by Canada's place names and emblems, while pointing to the need to develop policies and practices that cultivate greater inclusion moving forward.

Names, as it turns out, are complex anchors of identity. The thought of changing them can be deeply upsetting for some, and uplifting for others, making certain names divisive. Nowhere is this more apparent than in racialized names, such as Negro Point, Nova Scotia, or in commemorative names, such as Ryerson University. Commemorative naming practices appear to be a relatively new naming practice in the Western world, one articulated by Columbus in his initial voyage to the Caribbean when he bestowed names that reflected the identities of his patrons. While not likely the first person to deploy commemorative naming as a means of securing titles and benefits for himself, the practice nonetheless grows exponentially in the decades that follow, with Amerigo Vespucci seeing his name projected onto these continents, and later the founding of colonies, settlements, and named features followed suit. It is difficult in this light not to see commemorative naming as a tool that furthers the aim of colonization, not just by occupying space using toponymy, but also by asserting a place identity that reflects white patriarchy.

Resisting the reaches and harms of colonization can be accomplished by removing names and emblems, as the example of Ryerson's statue (and head) prove. In this case, progress was borne upon the shoulders of Indigenous and allied protesters who struggled against institutional and legal processes and authorities to see this symbol of colonial violence removed. Its desecration with paint and the severing of the statue's head, which appears to have been accomplished without any legal ramifications on the part of the protestors, may well be an indication that Canadians more broadly are ready to think about the symbols with which we enrobe ourselves as a people.

While removing statues and names will not directly redress historical harms that are perpetuated today by our place names and emblems, addressing problematic symbols nonetheless offers everyone a future where they may see less violence and experience less harm at institutional and public-facing levels. Put another way, white men in this country for the most part do not encounter names or symbols that celebrate their oppressors because, with some exceptions, this demographic has not experienced oppression. Whereas, in the balance, women, people of colour, and Indigenous groups continue to shoulder that burden, to see their bodies, culture, and history created in textual and visual form by and for primarily male audiences and not by and for themselves. Before us lies an opportunity as a people to broach this topic in public discourse and to think about alternatives to the status quo that weave together a more complex and realistic place identity that better reflects who we are.

NOTES

INTRODUCTION

1 Settler-colonialism describes the occupation of space by people or their ancestors who at some point settled in Canada, fossilizing in this location their culture, languages, values, and knowledge in ways that undermine the propagation of these same elements in Indigenous societies. While scholars often focus on white settler-colonialism and its European roots, increasingly the term applies just as easily to people with roots elsewhere in the world who live in places such as Canada.

2 Rich bodies of scholarship relating to the politics and racial implications of naming in Apartheid and post-Apartheid South Africa have resulted in frank discussions as well as action on the part of the public and government. For instance, refer to P.E. Raper, *Toponymical Practice*, trans. R.F. Purchase (Pretoria: South African Centre of Onomastic Sciences, 1977); P.E. Raper, G.S. Nienaber, and J.S.B. Marais, *Manual for the Giving of Place Names* (Pretoria: National Place Names Committee of the Department of National Education, 1979); and E.R. Jenkins, P.E. Raper, and L.A. Möller, *Changing Place Names* (Durban: Indicator Press, 1996).

3 Studies offering a synthesis of scholarship on toponymy, for instance in the form of a bibliography, are a related subset of this variety. Refer to, for example, Richard B. Sealock and Pauline A. Seely, *Bibliography of Place-Name Literature: United States and Canada* (Chicago: American Library Association, 1967).

4 An example of this form of scholarship can be found in James Kari, *Ahtna Place Names Lists*, 2nd ed. (Fairbanks: University of Alaska and Alaska Native Language Center, 2008).

5 One excellent example of this sort of study, which decentres the meaning of place names and instead considers place knowledge in the hands of women, is Judith Tyner, *Women in American Cartography: An Invisible Social History* (New York: Lexington Books, 2020). Although it deals more with the United States, its methodology will serve scholars of Canada in due course.

6 As explored in the first chapter, language plays a critical role in determining the knowledge conveyed by place stories. Refer to Nancy Turner, *Ancient Pathways, Ancestral Knowledge: Ethnobotany and Ecological Wisdom of Indigenous Peoples of Northwestern North America*, vol. 1 (Montreal: McGill-Queen's University Press, 2014), 220.

7 Place storytelling is found in many disciplines and for our purposes can be exampled by the following works: Edward Sapir and Morris Swadesh, *Nootka Texts: Tales and Ethnological Narratives with Grammatical Notes and Lexical Materials* (Philadelphia, PA: Linguistic Society of America, 1939); Florence C. Shipek and Rosalie Pinto Robertson, eds., *The Autobiography of Deflina Guero, A Diegueño Indian, As Told to Florence C. Shipek, Interpreter Rosalie Pinto Robertson* (Los Angeles, CA: Dawson's Book Shop, 1968); Jean E. Speare, ed., *The Days of Augusta* (Vancouver: J.J. Douglas, 1973); Alan Rayburn, *Naming Canada: Stories about Canadian Place Names* (Toronto: University of Toronto Press, 2001); and Peggy Brock, *The Many Voyages of Arthur Wellington Clah: A Tsimshian Man on the Pacific Northwest Coast* (Vancouver: UBC Press, 2011).

8 Refer to the essays in Lawrence D. Berg and Jani Vuolteenaho, eds., *Critical Toponymies: The Contested Politics of Place Naming* (Burlington, VT: Ashgate, 2009), as well as in Reuben Rose-Redwood, Derek Alderman, and Maoz Azaryahu, eds., *The Political Life of Urban Streetscapes: Naming, Politics, and Places* (New York: Routledge, 2017). Also refer to Derek H. Alderman, "Street Names as Memorial Arenas: The Reputational Politics of Commemorating Martin Luther King, Jr. in a Georgia County," *Historical Geography* 30 (2002): 99–120; and Derek H. Alderman and Joshua Inwood, "Street Naming and the Politics of Belonging: Spatial Injustices in the Toponymic Commemoration of Martin Luther King Jr.," *Social and Cultural Geography* 14, no. 2 (2013): 211–33.

9 Robert Fuson, *Fundamental Place-Name Geography*, 2nd ed. (Dubuque, IA: Wm. C. Brown Company Publishers, 1970).

10 Theodore Binnema, *Common and Contested Ground: A Human and Environmental History of the Northwestern Plains* (Norman: University of Oklahoma Press, 2001).

11 Mark Monmonier, *From Squaw Tit to Whorehouse Meadow: How Maps Name, Claim, and Inflame* (Chicago: University of Chicago Press, 2006).

12 Gwilym Lucas Eades, *The Geography of Names: Indigenous to Post-Foundational* (New York: Routledge, 2017), 20–22. The term has historically referred to the toponym awarded to a city, from the Greek term, *oikonym*. Here I deploy the more contemporary definition and use of the term relating to how the environment informs our place names and identities.

13 Eades, *The Geography of Names*, 24.

14 At the time of the publication of this book, the CNBC database can be found online at http://www4.nrcan.gc.ca/search-place-names/search.

15 BC Geographic Names Information System, https://apps.gov.bc.ca/pub/bcgnws/. Accessed February 2022.

16 Banque de noms de lieux du Quebéc, https://toponymie.gouv.qc.ca/ct/accueil.aspx. Accessed February 2022.

17 While certain provinces do offer databases of place names, no contextual information is offered through them that would be particularly useful for place-name studies of this nature.

18 A recent study demonstrates increasing interest in the genre, however. Refer to Jonathan S. Lofft, "'Some Heraldic Propriety of Composition': Solving the Mystery of the Origin and History of the Armorial Achievement of the County of Wellington, Ontario," *Ontario History* III, no. 2 (2019): 55–68.

19 See Dominic Medway, Duncan Light, Gary Warnaby, John Byrom, and Craig Young, "Flags, Society and Space: Towards a Research Agenda for Vexillgeography," *Area* 51, no. 4 (2019): 689–96.

20 Michael D. Harris, *Colored Pictures: Race and Visual Representation* (Chapel Hill: University of North Carolina Press, 2003).

21 See, for example, Martin Waldseemüller, *Universalis cosmographia secundum Ptholomaei traditionem et Americi Vespucii alioru[m]que lustrationes*

(Strasbourg (?): n/p, 1507), and Johannes Ruysch, *Universalior cogniti orbis tabula ex recentibus confecta observationibus* (Rome: Bernardinus Venetus de Vitalibus, 1508).

22 I use the term "imagined community" as explored in Benedict Anderson, *Imagined Communities* (New York: Verso, 1983).

23 The province's coat of arms, however, does acknowledge its British colonial connection. Refer to Geneviève Zubrzycki, *Beheading the Saint: Nationalism, Religion, and Secularism in Quebec* (Chicago: University of Chicago Press, 2016), 188–89.

24 The Loi sur la laïcité de l'État (also known as Bill 21) was adopted by Quebec in 2019.

25 Eva Mackey, *The House of Difference: Cultural Politics and National Identity in Canada* (New York: Routledge, 1999), 63–103.

26 Of course, some European nations still possess overseas territories in the Americas, as France's continued possession of the archipelago located just south of Newfoundland, St. Pierre and Miquelon, demonstrates.

CHAPTER ONE

1 William A. Lovis and Robert Whallon, "The Creation of Landscape Meaning by Mobile Hunter-Gatherers," in *Marking the Land: Hunter-Gatherer Creation of Meaning in Their Environment,* eds. William A. Lovis and Robert Whallon (New York: Routledge, 2016), 3.

2 Keith H. Basso, *Wisdom Sits in Places: Landscape and Language among the Western Apache* (Albuquerque: University of New Mexico Press, 1996), 108.

3 Robin Wall Kimmerer, *Braiding Sweetgrass: Indigenous Wisdom, Scientific Knowledge and the Teachings of Plants* (Minneapolis, MN: Milkweed Editions, 2013), 206.

4 An excellent exploration of this ecological philosophy and form of science, sometimes referred to as Traditional Ecological Knowledge, at the intersection with language in western regions of Canada, can be found in Nancy Turner, *Ancient Pathways, Ancestral Knowledge: Ethnobotany and Ecological Wisdom of Indigenous Peoples of Northwestern North America* (Montreal: McGill-Queen's University Press, 2014).

5 Kimmerer, *Braiding Sweetgrass*, 206.

6 Frank Pokiak, "From Tuktoyaktuk—Place of Caribou," in *When the Caribou Do Not Come: Indigenous Knowledge and Adaptive Management in the Western Arctic*, eds. Brenda L. Parlee and Ken J. Caine (Vancouver: UBC Press, 2017), 34.

7 Leona R. Shaw and Jane P. Young, "Ethnobotany of the Tl'azt'en Nation: Plant Use and Gathering Site Characteristics," *Ethnobiology Letters* 3 (2012): 2.

8 Karen Heikkilä, "Teaching through Toponymy: Using Indigenous Place-Names in Outdoor Science Camps" (master's thesis, University of Northern British Columbia, 2007), 43–44.

9 Heikkilä, "Teaching through Toponymy," 84–85.

10 Turner, *Ancient Pathways, Ancestral Knowledge*, vol. 1, 220.

11 BC Geographic Names Information System, https://apps.gov.bc.ca/pub/bcgnws/names/16809.html. Accessed February 2022.

12 Shaw and Young, "Ethnobotany of the Tl'azt'en Nation," 4.

13 Heikkilä, "Teaching through Toponymy," 100–20.

14 Robert Jarvenpa and Hetty Jo Brumbach, "Initializing the Landscape: Chipewyan Construction of Meaning in a Recently Occupied Environment," in *Marking the Land: Hunter-Gatherer Creation of Meaning in their Environment*, eds. William A. Lovis and Robert Whallon (New York: Routledge, 2016), 13–44; and by the same authors, "Ethnoarcheological Collaborations: Hunting Societies, Interethnic Relations, and Gender in the Northern Latitudes, Part 1," *Ethnoarcheology* 6, no. 2 (2014): 149.

15 Jarvenpa and Brumbach, "Ethnoarcheological Collaborations," 141.

16 Jarvenpa and Brumbach, "Ethnoarcheological Collaborations," 141.

17 Brenda Parlee and Micheline Manseau, "Using Traditional Knowledge to Adapt to Ecological Change: Denésǫłiné Monitoring of Caribou Movements," *Arctic* 58, no. 1 (2005): 32; Jarvenpa and Brumbach, "Initializing the Landscape," 22.

18 Parlee and Manseau, "Using Traditional Knowledge to Adapt to Ecological Change," 31.

19 James G. Smith, "Chipewyan," in *Handbook of North American Indians*, vol. 6: *Subarctic*, ed. June Helm (Washington, DC: Smithsonian Institution, 1981), 273.

20 For Chipewyan–Cree conflict lore, refer to Robert Jarvenpa, "Symbolism and Inter-Ethnic Relations among Hunter-Gatherers: Chipewyan Conflict Lore," *Anthropologica* 24, no. 1 (1982): 43–76.

21 Jarvenpa and Brumbach, "Initializing the Landscape," 20–21.

22 Gerald A. Oetelaar, "Places on the Blackfoot Homeland: Markers of Cosmology, Social Relationships and History," in *Marking the Land: Hunter-Gatherer Creation of Meaning in Their Environment*, eds. William A. Lovis and Robert Whallon (New York: Routledge, 2016), 45–46.

23 Joan Kennerly, Carmen Marceau, Doris Old Person, and June Tatsey, *Old Man Napi: The Indian Reading Series* (Portland, OR: Pacific Northwest Indian Reading and Language Development Program, 1978), 7, 34.

24 Oetelaar, "Places on the Blackfoot Homeland," 46–47.

25 Sweet pine is occasionally consumed or used as medicine by the Blackfoot, and mostly has ceremonial uses relating to Medicine Pipe bundles gifted to them by Thunder, the master of summer, who told them to open it after the spring's first thunder to pray for rain and healthy crops of Saskatoon berries. The pine is used in smudging and related rituals while seeking protection from thunderstorms. Oetelaar, "Places on the Blackfoot Homeland," 48–50.

26 Oetelaar, "Places on the Blackfoot Homeland," 52.

27 Oetelaar, "Places on the Blackfoot Homeland," 53.

28 Patricia Steepee Barry, *Mystical Themes in Milk Rover Rock Art* (Edmonton: University of Alberta Press, 1991), 25.

29 Oetelaar, "Places on the Blackfoot Homeland," 55.

30 Oetelaar, "Places on the Blackfoot Homeland," 56.

31 A similar practice can be found on Blackfoot painted tipi. Refer to María Nieves Zedeño, "Art as the Road to Perfection: The Blackfoot Painted Tipi," *Cambridge Archaeological Journal* 27, no. 4 (2017): 631–42; Oetelaar, "Places on the Blackfoot Homeland," 57.

32 Oetelaar, "Places on the Blackfoot Homeland," 59–60.

33 Oetelaar, "Places on the Blackfoot Homeland," 60.

34 Gerald A. Oetelaar and D. Joy Oetelaar, "People, Places and Paths: The Cypress Hills and the Niitsitapi Landscape of Southern Alberta," *Plains Anthropologist* 51, no. 199 (2006): 376.

35 Claudio Aporta, "Markers in Space and Time: Reflections on the Nature of Place Names as Events in the Inuit Approach to the Territory," in *Marking the Land: Hunter-Gatherer Creation of Meaning in Their Environment*, eds. William A. Lovis and Robert Whallon (New York: Routledge, 2016), 67–68. Also refer to Valerie Alia, *Names and Nunavut: Culture and Identity in the Inuit Homeland* (New York: Berghahn Books, 2009).

36 There is some debate about the date of their arrival, which may have occurred earlier. Certainly, like Indigenous peoples of the southern regions of what is now known as Canada, Inuit presence on the land was well before the arrival and invasion of Europeans, which is why they, along with First Nations and Métis, are considered to be amongst the Indigenous peoples of Canada.

37 Peter Whitridge, "Inuksuk, Sled Shoe, Place Name: Past Inuit Ethnogeographies," in *Marking the Land: Hunter-Gatherer Creation of Meaning in Their Environment*, eds. William A. Lovis and Robert Whallon (New York: Routledge, 2016), 90.

38 Aporta, "Markers in Space and Time," 71–72.

39 Whitridge, "Inuksuk, Sled Shoe, Place Name," 104.

40 Aporta, "Markers in Space and Time," 72–74.

41 Aporta, "Markers in Space and Time," 76.

42 Guy Bordin, "What Do Place-Names Tell about Non-Human Beings among Canadian Inuit?" *Journal of Northern Studies* 11, no. 1 (2017), 15–16.

43 Sophie McCall, Deanna Reder, David Gaertner, and Gabrielle L'Hirondelle Hill, eds., *Read, Listen, Tell: Indigenous Stories from Turtle Island* (Waterloo: Wilfrid Laurier University Press, 2017), 198–208.

44 Aporta, "Markers in Space and Time," 82.

45 Greg Mitchell and Ihintza Marguirault, "The Onomastics of Inuit/Iberian Names in Southern Labrador in the Historic Past," *Newfoundland and Labrador Studies* 33, no. 1 (2018): 84.

46 Mitchell and Marguirault, "The Onomastics of Inuit/Iberian Names," 88.

47 The founding narratives and relating meanings of the Haudenosaunee have been recently published by Mohawk scholar Brian Rice in *The Rotinonshonni: A Traditional Iroquoian History through the Eyes of Teharonhia:wako and Sawiskera* (Syracuse, NY: Syracuse University Press, 2013).

48 Joe Sheridan and Roronhiakewen "He Clears the Sky" Dan Longboat, "The Haudenosaunee Imagination and the Ecology of the Sacred," *Space and Culture* 9, no. 4 (2006), 366–68.

49 Rice, *The Rotinonshonni*, 187.

50 Anne Molloy, *Wampum* (New York: Hastings House, 1977), 39.

51 In Rice's account, however, it is Mohawk Ayenwatha (Hiawatha) who discovers how to make beads from lake clam shells. Refer to Rice, *The Rotinonshonni*, 233.

52 William N. Fenton, *The Great Law and the Longhouse: A Political History of the Iroquois Confederacy* (Norman: University of Oklahoma Press, 1998), 224.

53 Molloy, *Wampum*, 12–13.

54 Tehanetorens (Ray Fadden), *Wampum Belts of the Iroquois* (Summertown, TN: Book Publishing Company, 1999), 12–13.

55 Tehanetorens, *Wampum Belts of the Iroquois*, 21–22.

56 Fenton, *The Great Law and the Longhouse*, 236.

57 Tehanetorens, *Wampum Belts of the Iroquois*, 69.

58 Turner, *Ancient Pathways, Ancestral Knowledge*, vol. 1, 339–40.

CHAPTER TWO

1 Margaret Atwood, *Selected Poems, 1966–1984* (Oxford: Oxford University Press, 1990), 60.

2 Angel Delgado-Gómez, *Baptizing the New World: What's in a Name?* (Providence, RI: John Carter Brown Library, 2010).

3 Bartolomé de las Casas, *Viajes de Cristóbal Colón*, ms. c. 1552. Madrid, Biblioteca Nacional de España, Vitr/6/7, fols. 1v–2r.

4 In various places in Columbus's writing, both the diary shaped by Bartolomé de las Casas (1474–1566) and in his own writing to colleagues, Columbus reinforces our observation that he could not communicate with and did not understand Indigenous peoples he met in the Caribbean; refer to Christopher Columbus, *Carta a Luis Santangel* (Barcelona: Pedro Posa, 1493).

5 William Least Heat-Moon and James K. Wallace, *An Osage Journey to Europe, 1827–1830: Three French Accounts* (Norman: University of Oklahoma Press, 2013).

6 Evelina Gužauskytė, *Christopher Columbus's Naming of the 'Diarios' of the Four Voyages (1492–1504): A Discourse of Negotiation* (Toronto: University of Toronto Press, 2014), 12–16.

7 An excellent example of this rare practice can be found on a tripartite, east-oriented medieval map contained in a psalter created in the late thirteenth century; rather than visualize the locations relative to one another, the cartographer instead lists all the major cities for each continent. Refer to *The Map Psalter*, London, UK, British Library, Add. MS 28681, fol. 9v.

8 Martin Waldseemüller, *Universalis cosmographia secundum Ptholomaei traditionem et Americi Vespucii alioru[m]que lustrationes* (Strasbourg (?): n/p, 1507), and Johannes Ruysch, *Universalior cogniti orbis tabula ex recentibus confecta observationibus* (Rome: Bernardinus Venetus de Vitalibus, 1508).

9 These anxieties were also experienced by Spaniards relative to British and French expansion, as evidenced by a Spanish-language manuscript map of the St. Lawrence River and how it connected with the Great Lakes and Mississippi River. Refer to *Croquis de la costa del Seno Mexicano desde la bahía de San Bernardo hasta Nueva Francia, y los cursos de los ríos San Lorenzo y Colberto* (late seventeenth century), Seville, Archivo General de Indias, Mapas y Planos, México 62.

10 Raymonde Litalien, *Champlain: The Birth of French America* (Montreal: McGill-Queen's University Press, 2004), 26.

11 For a recent study on this subject, refer to Robert J. Miller, Jacinta Ruru, Larissas Behrendt, and Tracey Lindberg, *Discovering Indigenous Lands: The Doctrine of Discovery in the English Colonies* (Oxford: Oxford University Press, 2010), especially part 4, "The Doctrine of Discovery in Canada," 89–125. Also refer to Jamie S. Scott, "Cultivating Christians in Colonial Canadian Missions," in *Canadian Missionaries, Indigenous Peoples: Representing Religion at Home and Abroad*, eds. Alvyn Austin and Jamie S. Scott (Toronto: University of Toronto Press, 2005), 21–54.

12 A nineteenth-century concept, *terra nullius* has been well explored by scholars. Refer to Andrew Fitzmaurice, *Sovereignty, Property, and Empire: 1500–2000* (Cambridge: Cambridge University Press, 2014).

13 David Matless, "The Uses of Cartographic Literacy: Mapping, Survey and Citizenship in Twentieth-Century Britain," in *Mappings*, ed. Denis Cosgrove (London: Reaktion Books, 1999), 193–212. For the use of cartography

as a means of conquest and capitalist development, refer to Elizabeth Sutton, *Capitalism and Cartography in the Dutch Golden Age* (Chicago: University of Chicago Press, 2015).

14 Thirty years ago, J.B. Harley and David Woodward acknowledged that scholarship has and continues to favour Western perspectives on the nature of our world, which in turn leaves a dearth of scholarship (consulted, that is, by Western scholars) with broader objectives. J.B. Harley and David Woodward, "Preface," in *The History of Cartography*, Volume One: *Cartography in Prehistoric, Ancient, and Medieval Europe and the Mediterranean*, ed. J.B. Harley and David Woodward (Chicago: University of Chicago Press, 1987), xix.

15 Jean M. O'Brien, *Firsting and Lasting: Writing Indians out of Existence in New England* (Minneapolis: University of Minnesota Press, 2010), 145.

16 Modernity as an ongoing project typically implies the scientific, legal, cultural, and technological innovations associated with the notion of progress, particularly after 1492.

17 Ashley Glassburn Falzetti, "Archival Absence: The Burden of History," *Settler Colonial Studies* 5, no. 2 (2015): 138.

18 Christopher Columbus, *Epistola de insulis nuper inventis* (Rome: Stephan Plannck, 1493), n/p.

19 Refer to, for instance, Leandro de Cosco's edition titled *Epistola de insulis repertis de nouo* (Paris: Guyot Marchant, 1493) and Giuliano Dati's versified version titled *Lettera delle isole nuovamente trovate* (Florence: Lorenzo Morgiani and Johannes Petri, 1493).

20 A more complete study of these dictionaries cannot be undertaken here, however a representative list relating the Spanish language to other European ones includes Nebrija's Spanish–Latin dictionary (1495; 1516), a Spanish–Tuscan dictionary (1570), Percival's English–Latin–Spanish dictionary (1591), and Pallet's French–Spanish dictionary.

21 Little research has been done on this topic. One work that comments on past research but otherwise contributes little to understanding how the meaning of discovery transformed in the early modern period is Wilcomb E. Washburn's "The Meaning of 'Discovery' in the Fifteenth and Sixteenth Centuries," *The American Historical Review* 68, no. 1 (1962): 1–21.

22 Jacques Cartier, *Brief receipt, & succincte narration, de la navigation faicte es ysles de Canada, Hochelage & Saguenay & autres, avec particulieres meurs, langaige, & cerimonies des habitans d'icelles* (Paris: P. Roffet & A. Le Clerc, 1545).

23 Jacques Cartier, *Relation originale du voyage de Jacques Cartier au Canada en 1534*, eds. H. Michelant and A. Ramé (Paris: Librairie Tross, 1867), 34.

24 Refer to, for instance, Michael Lok's well-known map of present-day North America that extracted toponymy for Canada from a range of sixteenth-century accounts, *Illvstri Viro, Domino Philippo Sidnæo Michael Lok Civis Londinensis hanc Chartam Dedicabat: 1582* (London: Thomas Woodcocke, 1582).

25 Roland Barthes, *S/Z* (Paris: Éditions du Seuil, 1970), 11–12.

26 Samuel de Champlain, *Les Voyages du sieur de Champlain Xaintongeois, capitaine ordinaire pour le roy, en la marine, divisez en deux livres : ou Journal tres-fidele des observations faites és descouvertures de la Nouvelle France : tant en la descriptio[n] des terres, costes, rivieres, ports, havres, leurs hauteurs, & plusieurs declinaisons de la guide-aymant ; qu'en la crea[n]ce des peuples leur superstition façon de vivre & de guerroyer: enrichi de quantité de figures* (Paris: Chez Jean Berjon, 1613).

27 This project also extended to documenting Africa and Asia, known as the *Petits Voyages* (1597–1633).

28 Samuel de Champlain, *Les Voyages de la Nouvelle France occidentale dicte Canada faits par le Sr de Champlain* (Paris: Chez Pierre Le-Mur, 1632). Lescarbot, in his relation, is explicit that "n'ayant peu bonnement arranger en peu d'espace tant des ports, iles, caps, golfes ou bayes, détroits, & rivières, desquels [...] te les indiquer par chiffres, ayant seulement chargé la Charte que je te donne des n/oms les plus celebres qui soient en la Terre-neuve & grande riviere de Canada" (with so little space within which to arrange so many ports, islands, capes, gulfs, bays, straits, and rivers [...] they are indicated for you using numbers, so I could fill the map with the most famous names located in Newfoundland and the St. Lawrence River). Refer to Marc Lescarbot, *Histoire de la Nouvelle France* (Paris: Jean Milot, 1609), 236.

29 Titled *Carte de la Nouvelle-France, augmentée depuis la derniere, servant à la navigation faicte de son vray meridien par le Sr. de Champlain Capitaine pour*

le Roy en la Marine, it was published in *Les Voyages de la Nouvelle France occidentale* (1632).

30 Diego González Holguín, *Vocabulario de la lengua general de todo el Peru llamada lengua Qquichua, o del Inca* (Lima: Francisco del Canto, 1608), 25.

31 Gabriel Sagard, *Dictionaire de la Langue Huronne* (Paris: Chez Denys Moreau, 1632), n/p.

32 This concept of the long eighteenth century reflects important moments in the expansion and protection of the British Empire as well as the influences of particular monarchs, which have been accepted as having had a significant impact on this country and its Enlightenment.

33 Rachel Alpha Johnston Hurst, "Pro Pelle Cutem: Photographing Furs for the Hudson's Bay Company's 250th Anniversary Celebrations in Canada," *History of Photography* 42, no. 2 (2018): 110.

34 Robert K. Barney and Michael H. Heine, "'The Emblem of One United Body ... One Great Sporting Maple Leaf': The Olympic Games and Canada's Quest for Self-Identity," *Sport in Society* 18, no. 7 (2015): 819.

35 BC Geographical Names Database, https://apps.gov.bc.ca/pub/bcgnws/names/3599.html. Accessed February 2022.

36 The Tłıchǫ Yatıì Enı̀htł'è/ Dogrib Dictionary was published by the Dogrib Divisional Board of Education in 1996 and can be accessed through the following link: http://tlicho.ling.uvic.ca/users/mainview.aspx. Accessed February 2022.

37 Advice for place naming while in the field was the subject of a government-supported work published in the late nineteenth century. Refer to Hélène Hudon, *A Manual for the Field Collection of Geographical Names*, trans. L.M. Sebert (North York: Queen's Printer for Ontario and the Ministry of Natural Resources, 1987).

CHAPTER THREE

1 Walter D. Mignolo and Catherine E. Walsh, *On Decoloniality: Concepts, Analytics, Praxis* (Durham, NC: Duke University Press, 2018), 158, 198. Literature on African place naming practices has focused more intently on gender. Refer to, for example, Szinashe Mamvura, Itai Muwati, and Davie E. Mutasa, "Toponymic Commemoration Is Not for One Sex: The Gender Politics of Place Renaming in Harare," *African Identities* 16, no. 2 (2018):

429–43, and Dorcas Zuvalinyenga and Liora Bigon, "Gender-Biased Street Naming in Urban Sub-Saharan Africa: Influential Factors, Features and Future Recommendations," *Journal of Asian and African Studies* 56, no. 3 (2021): 589–609.

2 E.R. Jenkins, P.E. Raper, and L.A. Möller, *Changing Place Names* (Durban: Indicator Press, 1996), 7.

3 Lauren Beck, "Early-Modern European and Indigenous Linguistic Influences on New Brunswick Place Names," *Journal of New Brunswick Studies* 7, no. 1 (2016): 17.

4 Two excellent studies on this topic include Edmundo O'Gorman, *The Invention of America: An Inquiry into the Historical Nature of the New World and the Meaning of Its History* (Westport, CT: Greenwood, 1972) and José Rabasa, *Inventing America: Spanish Historiography and the Formation of Eurocentrism* (Norman: University of Oklahoma Press, 2015).

5 Norman Pounds, *The Medieval City* (Westport, CT: Greenwood Press, 2005), 15; Tesse Stek, *Cult Places and Cultural Change in Republican Italy: A Contextual Approach to Religious Aspects of Rural Society after the Roman Conquest* (Amsterdam: Amsterdam University Press, 2009), 134–38.

6 For an overview of this topic, refer to Andro Linklater, *Owning the Earth: The Transforming History of Land Ownership* (New York: Bloomsbury Press, 2015); Anthony Pagden, "The Struggle for Legitimacy and the Image of Empire in the Atlantic to c. 1700," in *The Oxford History of the British Empire*, vol. 1, ed. William Roger Louis (Oxford: Oxford University Press, 1998), 34–54; and Patricia Seed, *Ceremonies of Possession in Europe's Conquest of the New World, 1492–1640* (New York: Cambridge University Press, 1995).

7 G.P.V. Akrigg and Helen B. Akrigg, *British Columbia Place Names* (Vancouver: UBC Press, 1997), 29–30.

8 Guy Puzey and Jani Vuolteenaho, "Developing a Gramscian Approach to Toponymy," in *Names and Their Environment: Proceedings of the 25th International Congress of Onomastic Sciences*, vol. 2: *Toponomastics II*, eds. Carole Hough and Daria Izdebska (Glasgow: University of Glasgow, 2016), 66–77.

9 Lawrence D. Berg and Robin A. Kearns, "Naming as Norming: 'Race,' Gender and the Identity Politics of Naming Places in Aotearoa/New Zealand," in *Critical Toponymies: The Contested Politics of Place Naming*, eds.

Lawrence D. Berg and Jani Vuolteenaho (Burlington, VT: Ashgate, 2009), 19–51.

10 Iris Shagrir, *Naming Patterns in the Latin Kingdom of Jerusalem* (Oxford: Prosopographica et Genealogica, 2003), 47–48.

11 For Canada, these include the Geographical Names Board of Canada's Canadian Geographical Names Database (https://www.nrcan.gc.ca/earth-sciences/geography/place-names/search/9170); provincial ones such as the Commission de toponymie Québec's Banque de noms de lieux du Québec (http://www.toponymie.gouv.qc.ca/ct/ToposWeb/recherche.aspx?avancer=oui); and while not Canadian, another useful tool for our place nomenclature is the United States Board on Geographic Names' Geographic Names Information System (https://geonames.usgs.gov/apex/f?p=138:1:811237943199). Accessed February 2022.

12 Jean-Yves Dugas, "Évolution de l'hagiotoponymie municipale québécoise (1980–1987)," *Onomastica Canadiana* 70, no. 2 (1988): 51–58.

13 Kathleen Sprows Cummings, "American Saints: Gender and the Re-Imaging of U.S. Catholicism in the Early Twentieth Century," *Religion and American Culture* 22, no. 2 (2012): 205.

14 Erik R. Seeman, *The Huron-Wendat Feast of the Dead: Indian-European Encounters in Early North America* (Baltimore, MD: Johns Hopkins University Press, 2011), 6–7.

15 Philip J. Deloria, *Indians in Unexpected Places* (Lawrence: University Press of Kansas, 2004), 6.

16 Robert M. Leavitt and David A. Francis, eds., *Wapapi Akonutomakonol. The Wampum Records: Wabanaki Traditional Laws* (Fredericton: Micmac-Maliseet Institute, 1990); Barbara E. Mundy, *The Mapping of New Spain: Indigenous Cartography and the Maps of the* relaciones geográficas (Chicago: University of Chicago Press, 2000); and Laura L. Peers and Carolyn Podruchny, eds., *Gathering Places: Aboriginal and Fur Trade Histories* (Vancouver: UBC Press, 2010), 23.

17 Jodi A. Byrd, *The Transit of Empire: Indigenous Critiques of Colonialism* (Minneapolis: University of Minnesota Press, 2011), xv–xxxix.

18 Geoffrey Plank, *An Unsettled Conquest: The British Campaign against the Peoples of Acadia* (Philadelphia: University of Pennsylvania Press, 2001), 140–56.

19 On this particular commemorative act and the need to revisit who is publicly commemorated and how, refer to Daniel N. Paul, *We Were Not the Savages: A Micmac Perspective on the Collision of European and Aboriginal Civilizations* (Halifax: Nimbus, 1994), 112.

20 Mark Monmonier, *From Squaw Tit to Whorehouse Meadow: How Maps Name, Claim, and Inflame* (Chicago: University of Chicago Press, 2006).

21 Service hydrographique du Canada, *Guide Nautique Baie Georgienne*, 12th ed. (Ottawa: Ministère des Pêches et des Océans, 1986), 72.

22 See in particular Three Feathers (Ac-ko-mok-ki) and Peter Fidler, *An Indian Map of the Different Tribes that Inhabit on the land & West Side of the Rocky Mountains*, 1801, Winnipeg, Hudson's Bay Company Archives G.1/25; and Patrick Gass, *A Journal of the Voyages and Travels of a Corps of Discovery under the Command of Captain Lewis and Captain Clarke of the Army of the United States from the Mouth of the River Missouri through the Interior Parts of North America, to the Pacific Ocean during the Years 1804, 1805, & 1806* (Pittsburgh: for David McGebian; and London: for J. Budd, 1808), 120–21 and 137–38.

23 J. Tom Bateman, *The Milk River Man: The Life of Alva Bair* (Calgary: The Conservation Education Wise Foundation, 2002), 5.

24 Lee Irwin, *Coming Down from Above: Prophecy, Resistance, and Renewal in Native American Religions* (Norman: University of Oklahoma Press, 2008), 63.

25 Wikipedia article "Breast-Shaped Hill," https://en.wikipedia.org/wiki/Breast-shaped_hill. Accessed February 2022.

26 "The Nipples," BC Geographical Names Database, http://apps.gov.bc.ca/pub/bcgnws/names/14378.html. Accessed February 2022.

27 "Concubine Peaks," BC Geographical Names Database, http://apps.gov.bc.ca/pub/bcgnws/names/29506.html. Accessed February 2022.

28 The literature on this subject has been deepening in recent decades and representative studies include Anne Baker, *Heartless Immensity: Literature, Culture, and Geography in Antebellum America* (Ann Arbor: University of Michigan Press, 2006); Magali Marie Carrera, *Imagining Identity in New Spain: Race, Lineage, and the Colonial Body in Portraiture and Casta Paintings* (Austin: University of Texas Press, 2003); Claire Dwyer and Caroline Bressey, eds., *New Geographies of Race and Racism* (Burlington,

Notes to pages 87–93 221

VT: Ashgate, 2008); Peter Jackson, ed., *Race and Racism: Essays in Social Geography* (London: Allen & Unwin, 1987); and Ilona Katzew, *Casta Painting: Images of Race in Eighteenth-Century Mexico* (New Haven, CT: Yale University Press, 2004).

29 That being said, in the last century, "bachelor" has also been used as a euphemism referring to gay men. The degree to which place names might refer to single men of non-heterosexual orientations requires further study.

30 "Flavie Ménard, surnommée mère Ménard, qui est arrivé vers 1850 à Val-David. En plus de soigner les maladies, elle était sage-femme. Elle avait coutume d'aller pecher à ce lac." Refer to "Lac de la Vieille-Ménard" in Quebec's Banque de noms de lieux du Québec, http://www.toponymie.gouv.qc.ca/ct/ToposWeb/Fiche.aspx?no_seq=135638. Accessed February 2022.

31 For more on this facility, refer to Rhona Goodspeed, "Saskatchewan Legislative Building and Grounds," *Journal of the Society for the Study of Architecture in Canada* 32, no. 1 (2007): 61–88.

32 This fight for equal rights was also called the Persons Case (*Edwards v. A.G. of Canada*).

CHAPTER FOUR

1 These agreements were usually drawn up between chiefs and British colonial authorities. Several of these, dating from the late eighteenth century in the Great Lakes region, articulate the scope of these deals whereby hundreds and sometimes thousands of square kilometers might be sold for a few thousand pounds in cash or in kind (i.e., merchandise). Refer to "Treaty Texts—Upper Canada Land Surrenders," Department of Crown–Indigenous Relations and Northern Affairs Canada, https://www.rcaanc-cirnac.gc.ca/eng/1370372152585/1581293792285. Accessed March 2022.

2 Tehanetorens (Ray Fadden), *Wampum Belts of the Iroquois* (Summertown, TN: Book Publishing Company, 1999), 74.

3 Bruce Morito, *An Ethic of Mutual Respect: The Covenant Chain and Aboriginal–Crown Relations* (Vancouver: UBC Press, 2012), 19.

4 There is some debate about the lands indicated in the proclamation for Indigenous use and possession, likely caused by a lack of awareness about the

geographical coverage defined at the outset of the proclamation as British territory, which stretched beyond the Mississippi river at that time. For more about which lands were most impacted by the Royal Proclamation of 1763 and which provinces attempted to abdicate responsibility from ceding title to Indigenous groups later on, refer to the essays in *Aboriginal and Treaty Rights in Canada: Essays on Law, Equality, and Respect for Difference*, ed. Michael Asch (Vancouver: University of British Columbia Press, 1997).

5 Mark D. Walters, "Rights and Remedies within Common Law and Indigenous Legal Traditions: Can the Covenant Chain be Judicially Enforced Today?" in *The Right Relationship: Reimagining the Implementation of Historical Treaties*, eds. John Borrows and Michael Coyle (Toronto: University of Toronto Press, 2017), 190–91.

6 Morito, *An Ethic of Mutual Respect*, 22–23.

7 Colours conveyed universal messages. Purple conveyed sorrow and death; red on white is a declaration of war. When that wampum also had a hatchet and was accompanied by some tobacco, it became an invitation to the receiving nation to join the Iroquois in war against a common enemy. Refer to Tehanetorens, *Wampum Belts*, 98.

8 Morito, *An Ethic of Mutual Respect*, 22–23.

9 Gilles Havard, *Montreal, 1701: Planting the Tree of Peace*, trans. Phyllis Aronoff and Howard Scott (Montreal: Recherches amérindiennes au Québec and McCord Museum of Canadian History, 2001), 21.

10 Jaye Frederickson and Sandra Gibb, *The Covenant Chain: Indian Ceremonial and Trade Silver. A Travelling Exhibition of the National Museum of Man* (Ottawa: National Museum of Man, National Museums of Canada, 1980), 11.

11 Frederickson and Gibb, *The Covenant Chain*, 15.

12 Frederickson and Gibb, *The Covenant Chain*, 15.

13 The Anishinaabe traditionally are comprised of Ojibwa, Chippewa, Ottawa, Mississauga, and Potawatomi, and reside in present-day Ontario and Manitoba.

14 Walters, "Rights and Remedies," 197.

15 Anne Molloy, *Wampum* (New York: Hastings House, 1977), 94.

16 It can be found in the National Museum of the American Indian in Washington, DC. Refer to Molloy, *Wampum*, 100.

17 BC Geographical Names Database, https://apps.gov.bc.ca/pub/bcgnws/names/22015.html. Accessed February 2022.

18 For an overview of this documentation, refer to Keith D. Smith, *Strange Visitors: Documents in the History of Indigenous and Settler Relations in Canada from 1876* (Toronto: University of Toronto Press, 2014).

19 Havard, *Montreal, 1701*, 11.

20 Harold Bherer, Sylvie Gagnon, and Jacinte Roberge, *Wampum and Letters Patent: Exploratory Study of Native Entrepreneurship* (Halifax: Institute for Research on Public Policy, 1990), 11.

21 Refer to Lauren Beck, "Early-Modern European and Indigenous Linguistic Influences on New Brunswick Place Names," *Journal of New Brunswick Studies* 7, no. 1 (2016): 15–36. Also refer to the white paper prepared by Michael W. McDonald and Angel Julian, "Elsipogtog First Nation," https://www.apcfnc.ca/wp-content/uploads/2020/06/Elsipogtog_First_Nation_article.pdf. Accessed February 2022. My thanks to Patrick Augustine for bringing this last resource to my attention.

22 Chelsea Vowel, *Indigenous Writes: A Guide to First Nations, Métis, and Inuit Issues in Canada* (Winnipeg: Portage & Main Press, 2017), 12.

23 This term is used in this fashion here to reflect the status of Indian described in the Indian Act.

24 Peter E. Raper, *United Nations Documents on Geographical Names* (Pretoria: Names Research Institute, 1996), 67.

25 United Nations Declaration on the Rights of Indigenous Peoples, http://www.un.org/development/desa/indigenouspeoples/wp-content/uploads/sites/19/2018/11/UNDRIP_E_web.pdf. Accessed February 2022.

26 Christine Schreyer, "Canadian Geography as National Identity: Hudson's Bay Company Place Names and their Aboriginal Counterparts," *International Journal of Canadian Studies* 49 (2014): 318–19.

27 In this sense, Indigenous toponyms were created by translating the English toponym.

28 Schreyer, "Canadian Geography as National Identity," 322–23.

29 Robert Fuson, *Fundamental Place-Name Geography*, 2nd ed. (Dubuque, IA: Wm. C. Brown Company Publishers, 1970), 10.

30 Refer to Bill Barry, *People, Places: Saskatchewan and Its Names* (Regina: Canadian Plains Research Centre, 1997).

31 For an excellent study on Fidler and his cartographical works, refer to Barbara Belyea, *Peter Fidler: From York Factory to the Rocky Mountains* (Denver: University Press of Colorado, 2020).

32 Natural Resources Canada, https://www.nrcan.gc.ca/earth-sciences/geography/origins-canadas-geographical-names/origin-names-canada-and-its-provinces-and-territories/9224. Accessed February 2022.

33 James F. Pendergast, "The Confusing Identities Attributed to Stadacona and Hochelaga," *Journal of Canadian Studies* 32, no. 4 (1998): 149–67.

34 Banque de noms de lieux du Québec, https://toponymie.gouv.qc.ca/ct/ToposWeb/Fiche.aspx?no_seq=18836. Accessed February 2022.

35 Banque de noms de lieux du Québec, https://toponymie.gouv.qc.ca/ct/ToposWeb/Fiche.aspx?no_seq=434681. Accessed February 2022.

36 Parks Canada, https://www.pc.gc.ca/en/pn-np/nu/qausuittuq. Accessed February 2022.

37 For more on disappearance, refer to Jean O'Brien, *Firsting and Lasting: Writing Indians out of Existence in New England* (Minneapolis: University of Minnesota Press, 2010).

38 Ronald Rudin, *Kouchibouguac: Removal, Resistance, and Remembrance at a Canadian National Park* (Toronto: University of Toronto Press, 2018), 5.

39 The full decision can be found in *Vautour et autre c. R.*, 2017 NBCA 21. https://www.courtsnb-coursnb.ca/content/dam/courts/pdf/appeal-appel/decisions/2017/05/20170504VautouretalvR.pdf. Accessed February 2022.

40 For more on names such as this one, refer to Lauren Beck and Chet Van Duzer, *Canada before Confederation: Maps from the Exhibition* (Wilmington, DE: Vernon Press, 2017). Also, it can be observed that redundant names such as this one are common in colonial and post-colonial milieus.

41 Alan Rayburn, *Place Names of Canada* (New York: Oxford University Press, 2009), 206–207.

42 Banque de noms de lieux du Québec, https://toponymie.gouv.qc.ca/ct/ToposWeb/Fiche.aspx?no_seq=151227. Accessed February 2022.

43 Cyril Meredith Jones, "Indian, Pseudo-Indian Place Names in the Canadian West," *Onomastica* 12 (1956): 11.

44 Jones, "Indian, Pseudo-Indian Place Names," 11.

45 Rebecca Sockbeson, "Honored and Thriving: The Squaw Law and Eradication of Offensive State Place-Names," *American Indian Culture and Research Journal* 40, no. 2 (2016): 123.

46 Winnipeg comes from the Cree term for dirty or mucky water. Jones, "Indian, Pseudo-Indian Place Names," 14.

47 Jones, "Indian, Pseudo-Indian Place Names," 14.

48 This expression echoes Philip J. Deloria's treatment of the subject in *Playing Indian* (Hartford, CT: Yale University Press, 1998).

49 Maximilian C. Forte, "Introduction: 'Who Is an Indian?': The Cultural Politics of a Bad Question," in *Who Is an Indian? Race, Place, and the Politics of Indigeneity in the Americas*, ed. Maximilian C. Forte (Toronto: University of Toronto Press, 2013), 41.

50 E.R. Jenkins, P.E. Raper, and L.A. Möller, *Changing Place Names* (Durban: Indicator Press, 1996), 19–20.

51 Greg Mitchell and Ihintza Marguirault, "The Onomastics of Inuit/Iberian Names in Southern Labrador in the Historic Past," *Newfoundland and Labrador Studies* 33, no. 1 (2018): 94.

52 Mitchell and Marguirault, "The Onomastics of Inuit/Iberian Names in Southern Labrador," 100–101.

53 Tasha Hubbard, "Buffalo Genocide in Nineteenth-Century North America: 'Kill, Skin, and Sell,'" in *Colonial Genocide in Indigenous North America*, eds. Andrew Woolford, Jeff Benvenuto, and Alexander Laban Hinton (Durham, NC: Duke University Press, 2014), 292–93.

54 Hubbard, "Buffalo Genocide in Nineteenth-Century North America," in Woolford et al., eds., *Colonial Genocide in Indigenous North America*, 294–96.

55 Cited in Hubbard, "Buffalo Genocide in Nineteenth-Century North America," in Woolford et al., eds., *Colonial Genocide in Indigenous North America*, 297.

56 For more on the importance of buffalo, and their disappearance, refer to Jack W. Brink, *Imagining Head-Smashed-In: Aboriginal Buffalo Hunting on the Northern Plains* (Edmonton: Athabasca University Press, 2008).

57 BC Geographical Names Database, https://apps.gov.bc.ca/pub/bcgnws/names/3313.html. Accessed February 2022.

58 George H. Shirk, *Oklahoma Place Names* (Norman: University of Oklahoma Press, 1965), 156.

59 Two excellent examples include Philip J. Deloria, *Playing Indian* (New Haven, CT: Yale University Press, 1998) and Circe Sturm in *Becoming*

Indian: The Struggle over Cherokee Identity in the Twenty-First Century (Santa Fe, NM: School for Advanced Research Press, 2011).

60 Little critical scholarship on heraldry and race exists, particularly in Canada. For a comprehensive, if somewhat dated, overview of heraldry in Canada, refer to Conrad Swan, *Canada: Symbols of Sovereignty* (Toronto: University of Toronto Press, 1977).

61 "Wetaskiwin Coat of Arms," City of Wetaskiwin, https://www.wetaskiwin.ca/360/City-Logo-Crest. Accessed February 2022.

62 The Latin text is "Munit haec et altera vincit."

63 The Canadian Heraldic Authority's description of Edmonton's coat of arms, https://reg.gg.ca/heraldry/pub-reg/project-pic.asp?lang=e&ProjectID=626&ProjectElementID=2216. Accessed February 2022.

64 Thunder Bay's coat of arms, https://www.thunderbay.ca/en/city-hall/thunder-bay-coat-of-arms.aspx. Accessed February 2022.

65 Royal Heraldry Society of Canada, https://www.heraldry.ca/content/arms_badges_prov.php#NewBrunswick. Accessed February 2022.

66 The Latin text is "Gloriosus et liber."

67 Coat of arms of Nunavut, https://assembly.nu.ca/about-legislative-assembly/coat-arms-nunavut. Accessed February 2022.

68 The Canadian Heraldic Authority's description of Sault Ste. Marie's coat of arms, https://reg.gg.ca/heraldry/pub-reg/project.asp?lang=e&ProjectID=2724&ShowAll=1. Accessed February 2022.

69 Dania Igdoura, "An Examination of Settler Colonialism in Canada's Legal Institutions: 1492 Land Back Lane," *Aletheia* 1, no. 2 (2021): 39–40.

70 Igdoura, "An Examination of Settler Colonialism in Canada's Legal Institutions," 43–44.

71 Jorge Barrera, "Beyond the Barricades," *CBCNews*, 25 November 2020.

CHAPTER FIVE

1 Bertrand Bickersteth, *The Response of Weeds: A Misplacement of Black Poetry on the Prairies* (Alberta: NeWest Press, 2020), 14. My thanks to Karina Vernon for bringing this poem to my attention.

2 My thanks to Des Kappel, provincial toponymist of Manitoba, for this information.

3 While coined in the context of Indigenous identity, the term has broader application beyond the settler–Indigenous racial continuum in Canada. Refer to Circe Sturm, *Becoming Indian: The Struggle over Cherokee Identity in the Twenty-First Century* (Santa Fe, NM: School for Advanced Research Press, 2011).

4 Michael Buzzelli, "From Little Britain to Little Italy: An Urban Ethnic Landscape Study in Toronto," *Journal of Historical Geography* 27, no. 4 (2001): 573–87.

5 Buzzelli, "From Little Britain to Little Italy," 578. Refer also to the essays in Franca Iacovetta, Roberto Perin, and Angelo Principe, eds., *Enemies Within: Italian and Other Internees in Canada and Abroad* (Toronto: University of Toronto Press, 2000).

6 Anastasia N. Panagakos, "Mapping Greektown: Identity and the Making of 'Place' in Suburban Calgary," in *Claiming Space: Racialization in Canadian Cities*, ed. Cheryl Teelucksingh (Waterloo: Wilfrid Laurier University Press, 2006), 65–82.

7 Joel Dickau, Jeffrey M. Pilcher, and Samantha K. Young, "If You Wanted Garlic, You Had to Go to Kensington: Culinary Infrastructure and Immigrant Entrepreneurship in Toronto's Food Markets before Official Multiculturalism," *Food, Culture and Society* 24, no. 1 (2021): 41.

8 Watson Kirkconnell, *Canadian Toponymy and the Cultural Stratification of Canada* (Winnipeg: Ukrainian Free Academy of Sciences, 1954), 8–10.

9 John C. Lehr and Brian McGregor, "Did Your Mother Go to Bimbo School? Naming Schools, Power, and Politics in Canada's Prairie West," *Canadian Ethnic Studies* 47, no. 4/5 (2015): 114.

10 Chris W. Post and Derek H. Alderman, "'Wiping New Berlin off the Map': Political Economy and the De-Germanisation of the Toponymic Landscape in First World War USA," *Area* 46, no. 1 (2014): 83–91.

11 Jason F. Kovacs, "War Remembrance in a Sacralized Space of Memory: The Origins and Evolution of *Volkstrauertag* in Kitchener, Ontario, Canada," *Memory Studies* 9, no. 2 (2016): 222.

12 Stephanie Lewthwaite, *Race, Place, and Reform in Mexican Los Angeles: A Transnational Perspective, 1890–1940* (Tucson: University of Arizona Press, 2009), 2.

13 Deena Rymhs, *Roads, Mobility, and Violence in Indigenous Literature and Art from North America* (New York: Routledge, 2019), 83.

14 BC Geographical Names Database, http://apps.gov.bc.ca/pub/bcgnws/names/5879.html. Accessed February 2021.

15 BC Geographical Names Database, https://apps.gov.bc.ca/pub/bcgnws/names/54957.html. Accessed February 2022.

16 Lily Chow, "The Chinese Canners in Port Essington," *British Columbia Historical News* 34, no. 2 (2001): 6.

17 Andrew D. Nelson and Michael Kennedy, "Fraser River Gold Mines and Their Place Names," *BC Studies* 172 (2011–2012): 105–25.

18 BC Geographical Names Database, https://apps.gov.bc.ca/pub/bcgnws/names/48298.html. Accessed February 2022.

19 BC Geographical Names Database, https://apps.gov.bc.ca/pub/bcgnws/names/5887.html. Accessed February 2022.

20 Frank Nuessel, "Ethnophaulic Toponyms in the United States," in *Onomastics between Sacred and Profane*, ed. Oliviu Felecan (Wilmington, DE: Vernon Press, 2019), 188.

21 The Oxford English Dictionary speculates about the term's origin, being a possible borrowing from a Chinese word or some reference to the shape of Chinese people's eyes. In any event, it first appears in use in the late nineteenth century.

22 BC Geographical Names Database, https://apps.gov.bc.ca/pub/bcgnws/names/39178.html. Accessed February 2022.

23 Statistics Canada, "Diversity of the Black Population in Canada: An Overview," 2019, https://www150.statcan.gc.ca/n1/pub/89-657-x/89-657-x2019002-eng.htm. Accessed February 2022.

24 The list of terms provided by Michael D. Harris expands our understanding of what might comprise a racialized place signifier beyond the most commonly known two or three, while acknowledging that his list remains incomplete: "black, noir, Negro, darkie, Sambo, nigger, mammy, coon, colored, and so on." Michael D. Harris, *Colored Pictures: Race and Visual Representation* (Chapel Hill: University of North Carolina Press, 2003), 3.

25 Harris, *Colored Pictures*, 8–9.

26 Donald H. Clairmont and Dennis William Magill, *Africville: The Life and Death of a Canadian Black Community*, 3rd ed. (Toronto: Canadian Scholars' Press, 1999), 38.

27 Clairmont and Magill, *Africville*, 38.

28 Although published before the apology issued in 2010, a great history of this settlement can be found in Clairmont and Magill, *Africville*.

29 Clairmont and Magill, *Africville*, 195.

30 See William Hamilton's exploration of the name's history in *Place Names of Atlantic Canada* (Toronto: University of Toronto Press, 1996), 281–82.

31 District 21, British Columbia, near Telegraph Creek. Refer to Library and Archives Canada, RG 31, Statistics Canada, 1921 Census, 4645776, 3.

32 BC Geographical Names Database, http://apps.gov.bc.ca/pub/bcgnws/names/13476.html. Accessed February 2022.

33 BC Geographical Names Database, http://apps.gov.bc.ca/pub/bcgnws/names/38687.html. Accessed February 2022.

34 BC Geographical Names Database, http://apps.gov.bc.ca/pub/bcgnws/names/10081.html. Accessed February 2022.

35 BC Geographical Names Database, http://apps.gov.bc.ca/pub/bcgnws/names/40607.html. Accessed February 2022.

36 Ted Bower, "What of the Name Carved into Western Memory?" *The Globe and Mail*, 20 May 1961, A6.

37 Karina Vernon, "Writing a Home for Prairie Blackness: Addena Sumter Freitag's *Stay Black and Die* and Cheryl Foggo's *Pourin' Down Rain*," *Canadian Literature* 182 (2004): 67.

38 Bower, "What of the Name Carved into Western Memory?"

39 Such a controversial perspective was taken by anthropologist Richard Slobodin, who questioned how terms deemed offensive today were received without issues in earlier decades. Refer to "Follow the Drinking Gourd," *The Northern Review* 6 (1990): 52–53.

40 Ontario Official Geographic Names Database, https://www.lioapplications.lrc.gov.on.ca/Geonames/index.html?viewer=Geographic_Names.Geographic_Names&locale=en-ca. Accessed February 2022.

41 Wheeler would have been his enslaver's name. Historians unfortunately do not know his place of origin or whether this name was given to him in his home country or in the United States (which may have been his home country).

42 GeoNB is a useful tool for seeing the province divided up into lots and it reflects the most recent toponymy. While Negro Lake appears west of

Grand-Bay Westfield near Route 7, neither it nor Corankapone Lake appear in the search results. http://geonb.snb.ca/geonb/. Accessed February 2022.

43 BC Geographical Names Database, http://apps.gov.bc.ca/pub/bcgnws/names/2122.html. Accessed February 2022.

44 Search "Cape Negro" in the province's provincial toponym database: https://nsgi.novascotia.ca/geonames/. Accessed February 2022.

45 International and national media coverage leading up to the referendum on the name change was extensive in 2020. Refer to, for instance, David Cox, "Why the Canadian Town of Asbestos Wants a New Name," BBC.com, 12 October 2020, https://www.bbc.com/worklife/article/20201008-why-the-canadian-town-of-asbestos-wants-a-new-name. Accessed February 2022.

46 Geoffrey Reaume, "The Place of Mad People and Disabled People in Canadian Historiography: Surveys, Biographies, and Specialized Fields," *Journal of the Canadian Historical Association* 28, no. 1 (2017): 280.

47 Reaume, "The Place of Mad People," 294.

48 Refer to, for example, Christopher Dummitt, *Unbuttoned: A History of Mackenzie King's Secret Life* (Montreal: McGill-Queen's University Press, 2017) and compare his approach to mental illness to earlier works, such as Denis Smith, *Rogue Tory: The Life and Legend of John G. Diefenbaker* (Toronto: Macfarlane Walter & Ross, 1995).

49 Reaume, "The Place of Mad People," 292–93.

50 BC Geographical Names Database, http://apps.gov.bc.ca/pub/bcgnws/names/4826.html. Accessed February 2022.

51 Duncan Light, "Tourism and Toponymy: Commodifying and Consuming Place Names," *Tourism Geographies* 16, no. 1 (2014): 142. Refer also to Laura Kostanski, "Toponymic Dependence Research and Its Possible Contribution to the Field of Place Branding," *Place Branding and Diplomacy* 7, no. 1 (2011): 9–22.

52 Nick Clarke, "Town Twinning in Cold-War Britain: (Dis)continuities in Twentieth-Century Municipal Internationalism," *Contemporary British History* 24, no. 2 (2010): 173–91.

53 Rolf. D. Cremer, Anne De Bruin, and Ann Dupuis, "International Sister-Cities: Bridging the Global-Local Divide," *American Journal of*

Economics and Sociology 60, no. 1 (2001): 377–401. For another branding example, look no further than Vulcan, Alberta. Refer to Heather Mair, "Searching for a New Enterprise: Themed Tourism and the Re-Making of One Small Canadian Community," *Tourism Geographies* 11, no. 4 (2009): 462–83.

CHAPTER SIX

1 Robin A. Kearns and Lawrence D. Berg, "Proclaiming Place: Towards a Geography of Place Name Pronunciation," *Social and Cultural Geography* 3, no. 3 (2002): 283–302.
2 Laura Glowacki, "Queen's University to Remove Sir John A. Macdonald's Name from Law School Building," *CBCNews*, 19 October 2020.
3 Tyler Dawson, "Queen's University Strips Sir John A. Macdonald Name from Law School Building after Two Month Study of Issue," *National Post*, 19 October 2020.
4 *Final Report of the Building Name Consultation Advisory Committee* (Kingston: Queen's University, 2020), 7.
5 *Final Report of the Building Name Consultation Advisory Committee*, 17.
6 See the university's senate-approved "Naming Policy," https://www.queensu.ca/secretariat/policies/senate/naming-policy#11. Accessed February 2022.
7 Michelle McQuigge, "Student Union, Indigenous Group Want to See Ryerson University Change Its Name," *The Canadian Press*, 5 July 2017.
8 Amy Luft, "Meet the Redbirds: McGill University Announces Name Change for Men's Varsity Athletics Teams," *CTVNews*, 17 November 2020.
9 For an overview of name changes of this nature, see Alex Cyr, "What's in a Name Change?" *The Ryersonian*, 8 October 2020.
10 Brian Morton, "Enrolment Numbers Higher after Malaspina Changes Name," *Vancouver Sun*, 16 September 2008.
11 Calgary Aboriginal Urban Affairs Committee, *White Goose Flying: A Report to Calgary City Council on the Indian Residential School Truth and Reconciliation Calls to Action 2016* (Calgary: The City of Calgary, 2016).
12 Drew Anderson, "Langevin Bridge Is Now Called Reconciliation Bridge after Council Vote," *CBCNews*, 23 January 2017.

13 Notice of Motion, City of Calgary, https://pub-calgary.escribemeetings. com/filestream.ashx?DocumentId=15394. Accessed February 2022.

14 City of Calgary, https://www.calgary.ca/csps/cns/first-nations-metis-and-inuit-peoples/reconciliation-bridge-renaming.html. Accessed February 2022.

15 Refer to Schedule 2 of the policy, "Requirements for Municipal Naming of City Assets (Other than Communities and Roadways)," https://www.calgary.ca/CA/city-clerks/Documents/Council-policy-library/ CP2016-01-Municipal-Naming-Sponsorship-and-Naming-Rights.pdf. Accessed February 2022.

16 Refer to Section 5 of the policy: https://www.calgary.ca/CA/city-clerks/ Documents/Council-policy-library/CP2016-01-Municipal-Naming-Sponsorship-and-Naming-Rights.pdf. Accessed February 2022.

17 Refer to Schedule 1 of the policy, "Requirements for Municipal Naming of Communities and Roadways," https://www.calgary.ca/CA/city-clerks/ Documents/Council-policy-library/CP2016-01-Municipal-Naming-Sponsorship-and-Naming-Rights.pdf. Accessed February 2022.

18 Called the Recognition Review, its recommendations are presently before the city's council for consideration, https://www.toronto.ca/community-people/get-involved/community/recognition-review/. Accessed February 2022.

19 Editorial board, "Farewell to 'Dundas Street.' Now Make Sure Renaming Promotes Unity, not Division," *The Star*, 29 June 2021.

20 *Draft Guiding Principles for Commemoration in the Public Realm* (Toronto: City of Toronto, 2021), 4.

21 *Principles and Procedures for Geographical Naming* (Ottawa: Natural Resources Canada, 2011).

22 Banque de noms de lieux du Québec, https://toponymie.gouv.qc.ca/ct/ normes-procedures/regles-ecriture/traduire-toponymes.html. Accessed February 2022.

23 On this topic, refer to Lynn Peplinski, "Accommodating the Inuit Majority: Traditional Placenames in Nunavut Today," in *Indigenous and Minority Placenames: Australian and International Perspectives*, eds. Ian D. Clark et al. (Canberra: ANU Press, 2014), 365–80.

Notes to pages 178–82   233

24 Banque de noms de lieux du Québec, https://toponymie.gouv.qc.ca/ct/ToposWeb/Fiche.aspx?no_seq=441990. Accessed February 2022.

25 David Cox, "Why the Canadian Town of Asbestos Wants a New Name," *BBC*, 12 October 2020.

26 Maureen O'Hare, "Canadian Town of Asbestos Chooses New Name," *CNN*, 20 October 2020.

27 Laurel Wamsley, "The Town of Asbestos, Quebec, Chooses a New, Less Hazardous Name," *NPR*, 20 October 2020.

28 *Principles and Procedures for Geographical Naming*, 5.

29 *Principles and Procedures for Geographical Naming*, 8.

30 *Principles and Procedures for Geographical Naming*, 9.

31 *Principles and Procedures for Geographical Naming*, 6.

32 Refer to, for example, BC Geographical Names Office, *Geographical Naming Principles, Policy and Procedures* (Victoria, BC: Ministry of Forests, Lands, Natural Resource Operations and Rural Development, Heritage Branch, 2017).

33 Refer to the *Charter of the French Language*, available in both English and French, particularly section 22 (1977).

34 Banque de noms de lieux du Québec, https://toponymie.gouv.qc.ca/ct/ToposWeb/Fiche.aspx?no_seq=444528. Accessed February 2022.

35 "Sauvage sera remplacé peu à peu par Indien, Autochtone, puis par Amérindien, qui sont des désignations plus neutres. De nos jours, l'appellation Sauvage est sortie de l'usage courant et ne conserve qu'une dimension historique au Québec," Banque de noms de lieux du Québec, https://toponymie.gouv.qc.ca/ct/ToposWeb/Fiche.aspx?no_seq=58549. Accessed February 2022.

36 *Local Governance Act*, SNB 2017, c. 18, ss. 59–62.

37 Northwest Territories Cultural Places Program, *Community Name Change Process* (Yellowknife: Government of Northwest Territories, 2017). Also refer to Nunavut's *Cities, Towns and Villages Act*, RSNWT (Nu) 1988, c. C-8, s. 5.

38 NB Toponymy Services, *Place or Feature Name Proposal Form* (Fredericton: Department of Tourism, Heritage, and Culture, Heritage Branch, n/d).

39 *Principles and Procedures for Geographical Naming*, 18.

40 *Principles and Procedures for Geographical Naming*, 18.

41 In British Columbia, names can be changed by the Lieutenant Governor in Council after receiving a recommendation to do so as per the province's *Local Government Act*, RSBC 2015, c. 1, s. 41(4).

42 Refer to the vocabulary resource on FirstVoices.com, https://www.firstvoices.com/explore/FV/sections/Data/Athabascan/Dakelh/Nak%E2%80%99azdli%20Dakelh/learn. Accessed February 2022.

43 Some scholarship on this subject, albeit in non-Canadian contexts, can be found in the essays included in Harold Koch and Luise Hercus, eds., *Aboriginal Placenames: Naming and Re-Naming the Australian Landscape* (Canberra: ANU Press, 2009); Ian D. Clark, Luise Hercus, and Laura Kostanski, eds., *Indigenous and Minority Placenames: Australian and International Perspectives* (Canberra: ANU Press, 2014); and Laura Kostanski and Guy Puzey, eds., *Names and Naming: People, Places, Perceptions and Power* (Blue Ridge Summit, PA: Multilingual Matters, 2016).

44 Canadian Press, "What's in a Name? For Alberta First Nations Seeking Heritage Recognition, Plenty," *CBCNews*, 13 November 2017.

45 Quoted in the town council's minutes for 18 August 2020. https://canmore.ca/documents/4093-2020-08-18-council-agenda-regular. Accessed February 2022.

46 Jill Croteau, "Mountain Loses Racist and Misogynistic Name, Returns to Former Title," *Global News*, 29 September 2020. My thanks to the Alberta toponymist, Ron Kelland, for confirming the name's status.

47 *Alberta Municipal Government Act*, RSA 2000, c. M-26, s. 98.

48 See *Ontario's Municipal Act*, 2001, SO 2001, c. 25, s. 187.

49 Alberta Geographical Names Program, *Geographical Names Manual* (Edmonton: Alberta Culture and Community Services, Historic Resources Management, 2012).

50 Evan Cleave et al., "Just Because You Could, Doesn't Mean You Should: Exploring If (And When) Cities Should Brand through a Case Study of the City of London, Ontario," *Canadian Journal of Urban Research* 26, no. 2 (2017): 1–14.

51 Refer to "Vancouver City Councillor Wants City Signage to Reflect Region's Diversity," *CBCNews*, 28 March 2017. The motion has been archived by the council on its website, https://council.vancouver.ca/20170328/documents/motionb2.pdf. Accessed February 2022.

52 On this topic, see Patricia M. Barkaskas, "Decolonizing the 'Contemporary Left'?: An Indigenous Reflection on Justice in the New World Order," in *Spectres of Fascism: Historical, Theoretical and International Perspectives*, ed. Samir Gandesha (London: Pluto Press, 2020), 191–206.

53 "Lack of Consultation Over Red Indian Lake Renaming Stirs Anger in Central Newfoundland," *CBCNews*, 26 April 2021.

54 This and similar comments were posted on a Change.org petition against the name change. Change.org, https://www.change.org/p/government-of-newfoundland-and-labrador-keep-the-current-name-of-red-indian-lake. Accessed February 2022.

55 The city's coat of arms represents the treaty through the inclusion of a British officer carrying the scroll upon which the treaty was written and a Mississaugan man holding the four quills with which his people signed the treaty. Darin Wybenga, "Historical Tidbit: The City of Mississauga, Origin of Name and Coat of Arms," *Mississaugas of the Credit First Nation*, August 2020. Other considerations of Indigenous-led place-name changes that are useful in the context of this study can be found in Brian Tucker and Rueben Rose-Redwood, "Decolonizing the Map? Toponymic Politics and the Rescaling of the Salish Sea," *The Canadian Geographer* 59 (2015): 194–206, and Reuben Rose-Redwood, "Reclaim, Rename, Reoccupy: Decolonizing Place and Reclaiming of PKOLS," *ACME: An International Journal for Critical Geographies* 15, no. 1 (2016): 187–206.

INDEX

Italics indicate illustrations or images

150+ Place Naming Project, Vancouver, 193

1492 Land Back Lane, Caledonia, Ontario, 107–8, 138, 139, 175, 177

ableist attitudes, 160, 161, 164

Acadia, 87, 124–25

Africville, Nova Scotia, 154–55

age, in place names, 95–96

Alberta: Japanese tourism in, 167–68; renaming places in, 189–90

Alberta, place names, 156–57; bodies of water in, 91; bridges, 178; Canmore, 190; geographic features, 32–35, 91, 189–91; municipalities in, 95, 127, 133, 145, 160, 167–68. *See also* Calgary; Edmonton

Alberta, World Heritage Site, 132

Alberta Municipal Government Act, 190

Algonquian people: history of name, 66; language family, 41; places

referencing, 126, 132–33; treaties with settler-colonists, 109–10

Algonquin Park, 94

Alice in Wonderland, 166

Anishinaabe people, 7, 110, 112–13

Anû kathâ Îpa (Bald Eagle Peak), Alberta, 190–91

appropriation of Indigenous names. *See* Indigenous naming practices: European translation, misunderstanding

Arctic Ocean, 68

Asbestos, Quebec, aka Val-des-Sources, 161, 182–85

Assiginack, Jean-Baptiste (1768–1866), 112

atlas, development of, 62–63

Atwood, Margaret, 47, 75

authority, to determine place names; governmental bodies, 11–12, 188, 190–91, 193–97, 202; and gender, 104–5; historical sources, 10–11, 121,

126; in Indigenous cultures, 85–86; provincial, 113–14, 151, 185–86

Bahamas Islands, 49, 51
Banque de noms de lieux du Québec, 13
Barry, Patricia Steepee, 33–34
Barthes, Roland, 58
Basso, Keith (anthropologist), 23
Bateman, Tom, 91
BC Geographic Names Database. *See* British Columbia Geographic Names Information System (BC)
Before the White Man Came (Leman), 101
Beothuk people, 195–96
Berneau, Claude (c. 1638–1716), 86–87, *88–89*
Bickersteth, Bertrand (poet), 141–42
bilingualism, names in French and English, 85, 181–82, 185–88
binary gender/non-binary gender approaches, 105
Binnema, Theodore, 10–11
bison hunting, 31–32
Blackfoot people, 18, 31–35, 91; naming practices, 31–35
Black Loyalist Brook, New Brunswick, 158
Black people: demographics in Canada, 153, 159; description of, 153; history in Canada, 153, 154–58, 180–81; racial slurs against (*see* derogatory naming, of Black people)
Black studies, 10

blindness, reference to in names, 162–63
blood quantum, 115
Brant, Joseph, aka Thayendanegea (1743–1807), 113
Brébeuf, Jean de (1593–1649), 82–85
British Columbia: Black presence in, 155–56; Chinese immigration in, 150–53; coat of arms, 98
British Columbia, place names in: bodies of water, 26–28, 95, 102, 113–14, 132, 151, 152, 153, 155–56, 159, 162, 165; mountains, 92–93, 159; municipalities, 70, 72; province name, 80; statues, 87; universities, 176–77
British Columbia Geographic Names Information System (BC), 13, 92, 155–56
British naming practices, 68, 72, 80–81, 82, 87, 91, 142, 186
British Union Jack, 17
buffalo: on coat of arms, 136; extermination of, 130–31; places named after, 130–31

Cabot, John (c. 1450–c. 1500), 8, 52; voyages, 52
Calgary, Alberta, 144, 178–80, 189, 191; naming policy, 179–80
Canada: coat of arms, *71*, 71–72; history of country name, 50, 121–23; national identity (*see* national identity, Canadian, and place names); Upper and Lower, 69

238 *Index*

Canada Post Corporation, 12
Canada–Turtle Island, 5, 119, 191
Canada's Wonderland, 166
Canadian Geographical Names
  Database, 12–13, 116, 189, 197
Canadian Heraldic Authority, 133, 135
cancel culture, 4, 173, 181
Cape Breton University, 177
capitalization, practices used in book,
  20–21
caribou hunting, 29–30
*Carte geographique de la Nouvelle
  Franse* (1613), 59, *60–61*
Carte de l'Amerique septentrionale (c.
  1681), *88–89*
Cartier, Jacques (1492–1557), 16, 56,
  121–22; naming of places, 56–57, 79
cartography: early modern practices,
  63–64; for colonial purposes,
  49, 52, 58; long eighteenth-
  century practices, 67; modern
  discipline, 8–9, 57–58; projection
  techniques, 58
Catholic place names, 79
Catholic symbols, on Quebec
  emblems, 17
Cayuga. *See* Haudenosaunee
Champlain, Samuel de (c. 1567–1635),
  16–17, 56, 59, 62–65, 79, 80, 86, 126;
  map-making practices, 63–65
Chinatowns, 144, 148–49, 154, 169
Chinese immigrants in Canada, 148,
  150–51
Chipewyan (Dene), 18; naming
  practices, 28–31

Chow, Lily, 150
Christianity as justification for
  colonialization, 52–53
Christian names and patriarchy, 81–82
Churchill River/descok, 30
Chuzghun, aka Tezzeron Lake, British
  Columbia, 26–28
Clark, William (1770–1838), 73
Clement VII, Pope (1478–1534), 52
climate change, 9, 44, 195
coat of arms, 7, 15, *70, 71, 99, 100,
  134, 135, 137,* 197–99; animals and
  meaning, 98–99, 133–34, 136–37; of
  Canada, 71–72, *71*; and colonialism,
  16–18, 99, 133, 136; digital use, 198;
  gendered representation in, 98–100;
  and Hudson's Bay Company,
  69–70, *70*; Indigenous cultural
  symbols, use of, 133–37, *134, 135,
  137,* 236n55; Indigenous language
  on, 137, *137*; mottos, 70, 71; Nova
  Scotia, 134–35; Nunavut, 136–37,
  137, 198; Quebec, 98, *99*; United
  Kingdom, provincial references to,
  15, 70–71, 98–99; universities, 176
collective identity, 5, 14, 101, 139, 178,
  191–92
collective memory, Indigenous place
  knowledge, 25, 26
colonial period of British and French
  North America (c. 1498–1867), 15
colonial standards, 15
colonists. *See* settler-colonists
Columbus, Christopher (c. 1451–1506),
  48–51; diary-style naming, use of,

Index 239

57–58, 59, 62, 214n4; map-making practices, 49; naming practices, 49–51, 73, 79, 204; places named after him, 80; report of arrival, 55–56

commemorative naming: alternatives to, 178–80, 193, 202; by explorers for patrons, 50, 62, 79, 204; and gender, 96–98, 163, 174, 185–86; of Indigenous peoples, 78, 126, 172, 185–86; men, recently deceased, 146, 161, 164; policies for, 179–81; re-evaluation over time, 7, 10, 157, 172–73, 177–78, 180–81, 201–2, 204–5; of treaties, 113–14; use by settler-colonists, 79–81, 86–87, 90; Western methodology, 94, 130, 172–74

commemorative signs and symbols. *See* coat of arms; flags

commemorative statues. *See* monuments

Common and Contested Ground (2001, Binnema), 10

compendia projects, 62–64, 65, 74–75

Confederation of Canada (1867), 6, 115, 126

Coppermine (now Kugluktuk), 68–69

Coronkapoon, Richard, aka Wheeler, Richard (born c. 1746), 157–58, 230n41

Cornwallis, Edward (1713–76), 87

Covenant Chain, 109–11

cows in Alberta, 132

Crayke Creek, British Columbia, 155–56

creation myths, Indigenous. *See* Indigenous creation myths

Cree, 29–31, 33, 68–69, 93, 120, 121, 133, 154, 189; and Chipewan, 30–31; naming practices, 68–69, 121, 133

creeks, names of, 95, 102, 113–14, 132, 151, 152, 153, 155–56, 157, 159. *See also* rivers, names of

cripple, use in place names, 161–62

critical toponymy, 9–10; influences, 10–11

cross: of St. Andrew, 15, 134; of St. George, 15, 136

Crown–Indigenous Relations and Northern Affairs Canada, Department of (INAC), 12, 116, 118

Danforth, Asa, Jr. (1768–c. 1821), 144

Danforth, The, Toronto, 144–45

databases for toponymy, 11–13, 81, 197, 209n17, 220n11. *See also* Banque de noms de lieux du Québec; British Columbia Geographic Names Information System; Canadian Geographical Names Database; GeoNB

dates, use in book, 11–12

deafness, in place names, 162

de Bry, Theodore (1528–98), 63

Dee, John (1527–c. 1609), 53

democratic, political system, 40

demonym, definition, 128

derogatory naming, 66–67, 84; of Asian peoples, 150–52, 229n21; based on female anatomy, 91, 93–94, 189–90; of Black people, 151,

240   *Index*

155–60; explanations for, 94–95; of Indigenous peoples, 185–86; of people with disabilities, 161–62, 165

Description du pais des Hurons (c. 1631–1651), 82–84, *83*

dictionaries, 56, 65–67, 74, 216n20

dictionary, Dog Rib–English, 72–73

dictionary, written by Sagard, 66–67

Diefenbaker, John (1885–1979), 164

diminutive, use of in place names, 123

disabilities, people with, 20; of celebrated men, 163–65; definition over time, 163; naming after, 160–65

disclaimer, 21

discovery, European understanding of, 5, 52–57, 143

diseases, places named after, 160–61, 168

Dodge, Richard Irving, Colonel (1827–1895), 131

Dog Rib–English dictionary project, 72–73

Dolly Varden trout, 26

Donnacona, Chief, 122, 128

Dugas, Jean-Yves, 82

Dundas, Henry (1742–1811), 180–81

Dundas Street (Toronto), name change, 180–81, 196

Eades, Gwilym Lucas, 11

econym, 11

ecumene, use of term, 5–6

Edmonton, Alberta: coat of arms, 135–36; sports team, 177

Elizabeth II, Queen, 101

Elsipogtog, aka Big Cove, aka Richibucto Reserve 15, 116–17, 129, 194

emblems: history of colonialization, 14–15; of places, 14–15 (*see also* coat of arms, flags, seals); and text, 15

encyclopedias, compendia, 62

endangered species, preservation, and conservation of, 123–24

equality, diversity, and inclusion naming policies, 17–18, 103, 181, 192–93, 203

eskers, 28–30

ethnic neighbourhoods. *See* Chinatowns; Greektown; Little Italy

ethnophaulisms, definition of, 150. *See also* derogatory naming

etymology: in place name studies as lexicography, 7–8; of Indigenous place names lost in European translations, 65–67, 91, 120–21

eurocentrism, 5, 134

European naming practices, 79–81, 85 (*see also* commemorative naming); versus Indigenous practices, 84

European settlers (Euro-settlers). *See* settler-colonialism

exonyms, definition of, 79

false toponymies: of Asian communities, 152–53; of Indigenous names, 66, 74, 84

Fidler, Peter (1769–1822), 73, 121

firsting, historical approach, 54–55, 56

Index 241

First World War. *See* World War I

fisheries and Oceans Canada, 12

Five Nations. *See* Haudenosaunee

flags: colonial symbolism, 14–18, 70–71, 91, 133, 136; colours, meaning of, 15, 17, 71, 98; Indigenous cultural symbols, use of, 136–37; Quebec, 14, 16–17; scholarly attention, 14

fleur-de-lis, 16–17

forced removal of Indigenous peoples, 115, 123–24, 125, 132. *See also* Indian Act (1876)

forest as metaphor for navigating landscape, 23–24, 43

Fornel, Louis (1698–1745), 129–30

Forte, Maximilian C., 128–29

Fox, Terry (1958–81), 161, 165

Foxgate Developments v. Doe et al., 138–39

Francis I of France (1494–1547), 52

French exploration of North America, 52–53, 56–57, 63, 66–68, 86

French names and gender, 96

French naming practices, 50, 52, 53, 56–57, 63–67, 68, 84, 86, 145, 186–87

fur trade, 70

Fuson, Robert, 10

Gandhi, Mohandas Karamchand (1869–1948), 152

gaze, western, of settler-colonist, 8, 10, 49, 53, 54, 74, 78, 120, 149, 155

Gazette officiele du Quebec, 160–61, 184

gender, and place names, 94–96

generics, translation of, 188–89

Geographical Names Board of Canada (GNBC), 74, 149; authority, 193–94; French language naming, 181–82; gender and, 103–4; generic names, advice on, 188–89; history of, 12–13; Indigenous reservations, 116, 129; naming principles, 183–84, 185, 187, 188

GeoNB (New Brunswick), 158, 230n42

German Mennonites in Canada, 145–46

German place names in Canada, 145–47

ghettoization, 143–44, 153

Gilbert, Humphrey (c. 1539–89), 53

GNBC. *See* Geographic Names Board of Canada

GNBC database. *See* Canadian Geographical Names Database

González Holguín, Diego (c. 1560–c. 1620), 65

Google Maps, 51, 144, 158, 189, 190–91

Great Lakes, 65–66, 74, 86–87, 109, 122, 125–26

Greek immigrants in Canada, 144–45

Greektown, 143, 144–45

Greenpeace Canada, 183

Gros Ventres, 33–35

Guelph, Ontario, coat of arms, 99, *100*

Gužauskytė, Evelina, 50

hagiotoponyms, 79, 82, 85

Hakluyt, Richard (1553–1616), 53

Haldimand Proclamation of 1784, 107, 138–39, 146

Haldimand Tract, protests around, 138–39

Halifax, Nova Scotia, 87, 152, 154–55, 157, 163, 165, 177

Harris, Michael D., 153

Haudenosaunee: Confederacy, 39–40, 42, 109, 111; naming practices, 18, 39–43, 107, 111, 132–33; people, 57, 77; place names appropriated by settler-colonists, 121–22, 126; treaties, 108–12, *112*, 138

Haultain River/ena'ikwazeni'I, 31

HBC. *See* Hudson's Bay Company

Head-Smashed-In Buffalo Jump, Alberta, 132

Hearne, Samuel (1745–92), 68–69, 72

heraldry. *See* coat of arms

heteronormative masculinity, 11

Hiawatha, places named after him, 126

Hiawatha Belt, 41–43, *42,* 108–9, 214n51

High Arctic Relocation of 1953–55, 123

hills, breast-shaped, 92–93

Hodges, Frederick (1918–99), 158

Hubbard, Tasha, 130

Hudson's Bay Company, 69, *70,* 72, 91, 148, 182; cataloguing Indigenous toponymy, 119; coat of arms, 69–70; mapping, 119–21; trading posts, 72

hunting, places named after, 24–25, 27–28, 29, 31–32, 35, 37, 95

Hurons/Huronia, as insulting name, 66–67, 84. *See also* Wendat

Hurst, Rachel, 70

identity: and place names, 18, 74, 77–79, 203–4; shared, 5, 21, 125, 167, 181

Igdoura, Dania, 138–39

Igloolik, 37

immigration, in Canada, 142; European minorities, 142–47

INAC. *See* Crown–Indigenous Relations and Northern Affairs Canada, Department of

independence of colonies, 16, 17, 69, 122

Indian, adjective, as relating to Indigenous peoples, 148

Indians, from India, immigrants, 148; place names, 152

Indian Act (1876), 87, 115–16, 118, 129, 138, 148

Indian Residential School system, 87, 107, 178

Indigenous figures and symbols on flags and coats of arms, 133–37, *134, 135, 137*

Indigenous identity, false, 127, 128–29, *128*

Indigenous masculinity, erasure from maps, 85–86

Indigenous mythology: cosmology, 23–25, 31–32, 36, 39–40, 66; creation myths, 32, 38, 40; used for place names, 28, 35, 38–39, 31–35, 44, 84–85; written by settler-colonial scholars, 120–21

Indigenous naming practices: European translation,

Index 243

misunderstanding, 49–50, 66, 84, 127; narrative use, 31, 32, 34–35; settler-colonial activities, description of, 120. *See also* individual groups, Blackfoot, Haudenosaunee, Chipewyan (Dene), Cree, Inuit, Stony Nakoda Nation, Tl'azt'en, Wendat

Indigenous people, specific, commemorated, 172

Indigenous peoples. *See* individual groups

Indigenous place knowledge, 5–6, 18, 19–20, 25, 26, 43–45, 107–8, 172–73, 189, 193–95, 202; stories, 25, 26, 31–32, 34–35, 43–45, 84–85, 125

Indigenous trauma and genocide, from disease and loss of food, 131–32

Innu: names, 185–86; people, 57

Inuit, 18, 93, 213n36; migration across Arctic, 36; mythology, 38; naming practices, 36–39, 123–24; peoples, 129–30

inuksuk, 36–37, 136, *137*

Inuksugait, construction, 37

Iroquois Confederacy. *See* Haudenosaunee

Iroquois, as misnamed Indigenous peoples, 121–22

Irwin, Lee, 92

Italy, immigration to Canada, 144

Japanese tourism, in Alberta, 167–68

Jesuit missionaries, 8, 65, 82–84, 125

Johnson, William (1715–74), 110–11, *112*

Jones, Cyril Meredith, 127

Kana:ta Village (Brantford, Ontario), 122

Kimmerer, Robin Wall, 24

King, William Lyon Mackenzie (1874–1950), 164

kinship, 24

Kitchener, Herbert (1850–1916), 146

Kitchener, Ontario, 139, 146–47, 160

Kouchibouguac National Park of Canada, New Brunswick, 124–25

Kublu, Alexina (translator), 38

Kugluktuk, aka Coppermine, 68–69

Labrador, place names in, 129–30

Lady Liberty, 18

Lake, John Neilson (1834–1925), 127

lakes, names of, 26–28, 30, 39, 66, 86–87, 92, 93–94, 95, 96, 102, 127, 143, 150, 151, 152, 154, 155–56, 157–58, 161–62, 165, 181, 188, 195–96

Langevin, Hector-Louis (1826–1906), 178

language: and place identity, 149, 186; of place names, 20–21; non-Romanized alphabets, 149; of scholarship, 8

Larry Brander Bridge, Northport, Nova Scotia, 164

Laurie, John (1899–1959), 192

Laurie, Mount, 189, 192

lasting, as historical approach, 54, 55. *See also* firsting

legends, in place names. *See* Indigenous mythology, used for place names

legends, maps, 59–62, *60–61*

Leman, John, 101
Lescarbot, Marc (c. 1570–1641), 63, 64
Lewis and Clark expedition, 73, 91, 121
Lewis, Meriwether (1774–1809), 73
Lewthwaite, Stephanie, 147
lexicographical studies. *See* place name studies
lifespans, human and plants, 24
lists, of place names, 51, 59, 64, 65, 215n7
Little Italy, Toronto, 144
livingness of all things, 5–6, 24
local history, as discipline, 8
Longboat, Thomas, aka Cogwagee (1887–1949), 77, 78
long eighteenth century (1660–1830), 67, 218n32
longhouse, as cosmological metaphor for land, 39–40. *See also* Haudenosaunee
Los Angeles, California, 147
Lyell, Charles (1797–1875), 130–31

Macdonald, John A. (1815–1891), 87; alcoholism, 163; de-commemoration, 172–73
Mafeking, Manitoba, 159–60
Magellan, Strait of, 68
Malaspina, Alessandro (1754–1810), 176
Malaspina University-College. *See* Vancouver Island University
Manitoba: bodies of water in, 143, 150, 151; coat of arms, 136; geographic features, 32–36; municipalities in, 145, 159; naming policies, 187
maple leaf, 71–72

map-making. *See* cartography
marginalized groups, participation in naming, 20, 202–3
mascots, sports teams, 5, 177–78
masculinity, 4, 10–11, 77–81, 85–87, 90, 98, 102, 141, 163–64, 184
Matless, David, 53
McGill University, 175
McKenzie, Nathanial Murdoch William John (1857–1943), 120
Medusa, as place name, 97–98
memorials for veterans of World Wars, 146–47, 160
mental illness in public/scholarly discourse, 164–65
Mercator, Gerardus (1512–94), 57, 62
Métis peoples, 125, 135, 178, 213n36
Micmac. *See* Mi'kmaq
Mignolo, Walter D., 77–78
Mi'kmaq, 57, 110; spelling of name, 117
mining. *See* resource extraction
minority groups and place names, 20, 202–3
missionaries, 8, 65, 66, 68, 84, 113
Mississauga, Ontario, 128, 202, 236n55
misunderstanding of Indigenous names by Europeans, 49–50, 66, 84
misuse of Indigenous names, 119–26
Mitchell, Greg, 129
modern-colonial matrix of power, 77–78
modernity, 55, 77–78, 216n16. *See also* firsting
Mohawk. *See* Haudenosaunee
Monckton, Robert (1726–82), 87
Monmonnier, Mark, 90–91

Index   245

Montreal, Quebec, 152

Monture-Angus, Patricia (1958–2010), 172

monuments, 14, 91, 107, 147, 160, 181; for German prisoners-of-war, 146–47; for veterans, 101; of women, 101

Monument, Famous Five (Ottawa), 101

moral economy, 110

Morito, Bruce, 110

Mount Allison University, 200

Mount Desert Island, Maine, 62, 65

mountains: named after nipples, 91–93; names of, 27–28, 32–33, 39, 92–93, 152, 155, 156, 159, 189, 192; shape of, relation to body, 92

multiple names for places, 23, 116, 188–93

mythological sources for place names, European, 92, 97–98. *See also* Indigenous mythology, used for place names

Nakoda Nation naming practices, 189

naming practices, colonial, 49

narrative place names, 31, 32, 34–35

narwhal, on coat of arms, 137, *137*

national identity, Canadian, and place names, 3–5, 14, 69, 73, 74–75, 81, 120, 141–42

National Defence, Department of, Canada, 12

National Park system, Canada, 123, 124–25, 138

Native American and Indigenous studies (NAIS), 10

Natural Resources Canada, 12

negro, use in place names, 153, 155–57, 159, 168, 204, 229n24

New Brunswick: coat of arms, 136; database of place names, 13; naming policies, 187–88; place names, 116, 126, 157–58, 186–88, 193–94, 196

Newfoundland and Labrador: coat of arms, 98; place names, 92, 95, 97, 129–30, 161, 162, 195–96

New France, 17, 59–62, *60–61, 86,* 126. *See also* Acadia; Quebec

New Zealand, aka Aotearoa, 119, 200

Niagara Falls, Ontario, 166

"noble savage" motif, and Canadian identity, 17

normalizing practices, for patriarchy and colonialism, 81

Northwest Territories, place names, 24–25, 29, 72, 121, 187

nostalgia, as obstacle for renaming, 157, 175, 187

Nouvelle France. *See* New France

Nova Scotia: bodies of water in, 62, 92, 126; bridges in, 164; buildings in, 117, 177; coat of arms, 134–35, *135;* database of place names, 13, 159; geographical features, 95, 163, 159, 165; Negro Point, 155, 157, 168, 204; place names in, 154, 168; streets in, 144. *See also* Halifax, Nova Scotia

Nunavut, coat of arms, 136–37, 138, 198; places in, 12–13, 38–39, 96, 123

246   *Index*

O'Brien, Jean, 55
obstacles to renaming. *See* renaming, obstacles to
Oetelaar, Gerald A. (anthropologist), 33, 35
Oklahoma, 132
Oneida. *See* Haudenosaunee
Onondaga. *See* Haudenosaunee
onomastics, history of in Canada, 7–8
Ontario Geographic Names Board, 94
Ontario: bodies of water, 66, 91, 93–94, 95, 98, 143, 152, 157, 161, 162, 182, 188; Brantford, 77, 122, 139; buildings, 77, 172, 174; coats of arms, 99, 100, 136; database of place names, 157; geographic features, 91, 93; history of province name, 69, 125–26, 182, 188; London, 6–7; Mississauga, 128, 202, 236n55; monuments, 101, 146–47, 160; municipalities, 6, 90, 137, 146, 167; policies on name changes, 190; tourist attractions, 122, 166–67; universities, 174, 175–76; Windsor, 90. *See also* 1492 Land Back Lane; Caledonia; Guelph; Kitchener; Toronto
Ontario, Lake, 66, 182, 188
orient, term, use in place names, 152–53
Oromocto, New Brunswick, 193–94, 196
Ortelius, Abraham (1527–98), 57, 62
orthography; practices used in the book, 20–21; rules, 65–66, 194

paintings, 100–1, 113, *114*
Parks Canada, 12, 123–25
parks, national and provincial, 123–25, 138, 157, 159, 166; urban, 152, 155
paternalism, toward Indigenous nations, 49, 115
patriarchy, 6, 81
Peace and Friendship Treaty, 109, 116
pizzle, 98–100, 102, 198
place knowledge, 5, 23–24, 44–45; availability of, 197; commercial, 190–91; and settler-colonial authority, 63
place knowledge, Indigenous. *See* Indigenous place knowledge
place names, as collective Canadian identity. *See* national identity, Canadian, and place names
place-name science, 5–6, 19, 74
place-name studies, critical: history, 7–13, 73–74; language-based studies, 7–9; lexicography, early modern, 64–65; overlooked aspects, 7, 13–14; scholars, not Indigenous, 8; use of knowledge from other disciplines, 9
place onomastics, 7, 9, 11, 13, 74, 163, 181
place stories, 9, 25, 26, 31, 43. *See also* Indigenous place stories
Pokiak, Frank (Inuvialuit harvester), 24–25
politics, influence on name changes, 9–10, 100–1, 117–18, 119, 146, 207n2. *See also* authority, to determine place names

Index   247

Pompey, use of name, 130
province names, origin stories,
125–26
pseudo-Indigenous names, 118, 127–33
public buildings, 101, 105, 134–35,
173–74, 177

Qausuittuq National Park of Canada,
Nunavut, 123
quarantine, naming, 160–61
Queen's University, 172–74, 176,
196–97
Quebec City, 121, 160, 182
Quebec, 154, 160, 162–63, 185–86;
changing place-names, 183, 197;
coat of arms, 98–99, *99*; database
of place names, 160–61, 184;·
Francophone mandate, 185–86;
history, 69, 125–26; nationalism,
16–17; prohibition on religious
symbols, 17
Quebec, place names, 84, 87, 97, 143,
Asbestos, aka Val-des-Sources, 161,
182–85; bodies of water, 92, 93, 94,
96, 123, 152; geographic features,
160–61; municipalities, 121–23, 160,
161, 182–83
Qulliq (stone lamp), 136, *137*

race-shifting, 143
racism, 7, 139, 172–73, 175, 179, 182. *See
also* derogatory naming
railway system, 72, 127, 133, 148, 155,
185
Raper, Peter E., 118

reciprocity, between human and non-
human worlds, 32, 34
Reconciliation Bridge, aka Langevin
Bridge, Calgary, Alberta, 178–80
red, as racial slur, 175
Red Indian Lake, Newfoundland,
195–96
reductive naming practices, 62, 65
"Reincarnation of Captain Cook, The"
(Atwood), 47–48
religious naming practices, 67, 79,
81–84, 94, 201
relocation, of Indigenous peoples.
See forced removal, of Indigenous
peoples. *See also* Indian Act (1876)
renaming: costs of, 168, 184–85;
of French names by British,
82, 90; and gender, 90, 97;
intergenerational support for,
174, 183, 187; obstacles to, 103–5,
149, 157, 174–77, 183, 187, 197, 203;
policies and process, 20, 178–81,
187–88, 190, 196, 199–203; response
to racial slurs, 152, 155–56, 168, 175,
177–79, 195–96, 202; by settler-
colonists, 151, 168; universities (*see*
university, renaming). *See also*
Asbestos, Quebec
re-racializing, of white people, 133–34,
142–43
reservation system, 115–16, 129, 138,
148. *See* the Indian Act (1876)
resource extraction, 72–73, 151, 159
resource extraction, companies:
naming by, 72–73; Hudson's Bay

248   *Index*

Company, 119–20; naming based on, 68, 69, 85, 90, 94, 120; women's bodies as metaphor for, 93

Riel, Louis (1844–85), 163

Rio Tinto, 72

rivers, names of, 68–69, 72, 79, 80, 86, 91–92, 95, 116, 121–22, 127, 148, 150, 162–63, 189. *See also* creeks, names of

Rocky Mountains, 33

Roman Empire, place names descended from, 16, 79–80, 130

Roosevelt, Franklin Delano (1882–1945), 163–64, 165

Rotinonshonni. *See* Haudenosaunee

Royal Proclamation of 1763, 109, 126, 222n4

Ryerson, Egerton (1803–82), 107, 174–75; statue of, headless, 107, 175, 204

Ryerson University, aka Toronto Metropolitan University, renaming of, 174–76, 177, 204

Sagard, Gabriel (1590–1640), 66

Saskatchewan: history of name, 121–22; place names, 28–31, 100–1, 127

saskatoon berries, 127, 212n25

scale, in cartography, 57–58

Schneider, Joseph (1772–1843), 146

Schreyer, Christine, 119

Scotland, coat of arms, 134

Second World War. *See* World War II

Seneca. *See* Haudenosaunee

settler-colonists, 207n1; Indigenous place knowledge, use and misuse of, 19, 68–69, 73, 84, 119–26, 137, 193–95; Indigenous peoples, interaction with, 10–11 (*see also* treaties; between Indigenous peoples and settler-colonists); place name practices, 11, 18 (*see also* British; French; and Spanish naming practices); romanticized past, 16–17; use of European place names, 16, 69, 90, 145, 167

sexism, 7, 97

Six Nations, 39, 41, 77, 107–8, 111, 122, 138–39, 146. *See* Haudenosaunee

Sheridan, Philip (1831–88), 131

sister cities, or twin cities, 167–68, 201

Sockbeson, Rebecca, 127

somatoponymy, 92

South Africa, 160, 207n2

Spadina Avenue, Toronto, 148–49

Spanish, as false denominator, 143

Spanish naming practices, 50–52, 55, 56, 65–66, 68

Spencer, Herbert (1820–1903), 130–31

sponsored names, 179

sports teams, mascots, 177–78

squaw, use of offensive term, 93, 102, 127, 185, 189

Stanley, George (1907–2002), 200

Stanley, Ruth (1922–2017), 200

St. Lawrence region, European reconnoitering of, 56, 79

St. Lawrence River, 56, 79, 121–22, 123, 126, 160, 215n9

St. Pierre and Miquelon, 210n26
Stony Nakoda Nation, 117, 189–90;
  naming practices, 189
street names, 94, 117, 126, 159,
  181; street names, in ethnic
  neighbourhoods, 144, 146, 148–49.
  See also Dundas Street; Spadina
  Avenue
Sun Dance grounds, 34
Sweetgrass Hills, 32–35
sweet pine, 33, 212n25

Taino, 49, 50
Tejonihokarawa, Hendrick, aka King
  Hendrick (1660–c. 1735), 113, *114*
terra nullius, 53, 54, 57, 80
Teton, etymology, Tintonha, 91
Thayendanegea, aka Joseph Brant
  (1743–1807), 113
Thirteen Colonies, aka United States
  of America, 69
Thunder Bay, Ontario, coat of arms,
  136
Tl'azt'en (Dakelhne), naming
  practices, 18, 26–28
toponymy: critical, 7, 9–10;
  perpetuating social ills/inequality,
  11; recent history of discipline, 11;
  versus onomastics, 9
Toronto, Ontario, 125, 143–45, 148,
  166, 180–81, 196; Dundas Street,
  180–81, 196; renaming policy,
  180–81, 192, 196; Spadina Avenue,
  148–49

Toronto Metropolitan University. *See*
  Ryerson University, renaming of
Toronto Temperance Colonization
  Society, 127
tourists, appeal to, 161, 165–68, 192,
  201
tourist attractions, 122, 166
tourist trinkets. *See* emblems
Traditional Ecological Knowledge,
  210n4
Trail of Tears, aka the Great Removal,
  132. *See also* forced removal, of
  Indigenous peoples
travel accounts; basis for maps, 57–58;
  of explorers, 52, 55, 56, 57
treaties: between Indigenous peoples
  and settler-colonists, 109–16, 116,
  138, 202, 222n1, 222n4; places
  named after, 113–14
Treaty, Peace and Friendship, 109, 116
Treaty of Paris (1763), 108
Treaty of Tordesillas, 52–53, 54
Treaty of Utrecht (1713), 108
Truth and Reconciliation Commission
  of Canada, 173
trigger warning, 21
Tuktoyaktuk, Northwest Territories,
  25
Turtle Island, history of name for
  North America, 5, 48, 84–85, 119;
  use instead of Canada, 191
Tuscarora. *See* Haudenosaunee
Two-Row Wampum Belt, 109, 110
typography, 20–21

unicorns, in coat of arms, 71, *71,* 99, 134, *135,* 136

United Nations' Commission on Geographic Names, 81, 118

United Nations' Declaration of the Rights of Indigenous Peoples (UNDRIP), 19–20, 108, 118–19, 139, 194

university, colours of, 176

university, renaming, 105, 107, 172–78, 196, 200; difficulties with, 176–77

University of Western Ontario. *See* Western University

Val-des-Sources, Quebec. *See* Asbestos, Quebec

Vancouver, city of, 120, 150, 193

Vancouver, George (1757–98), 177

Vancouver Island University, 176–77

vanity place naming, 86–87. *See also* commemorative naming

Vautour, Jackie (c. 1928–2021), 124–25, 138

Vernon, Karina, 157

veterans, 101, 160

Victoria, Queen (1819–1901), 80, 101

Vintners Quality Alliance (VQA), 166–67

vista/viewshed, 23

visual descriptions of places, 11, 13

visualizations of places. *See* coat of arms, emblems, flags

Vowel, Chelsea, 116–17

Walsh, Catherine E., 77–78

Walters, Mark D., 112–13

Wampum belts, 40–43, 108–11, 113, 114, *114,* 223n7

Wampum Baking Powder, 127

Ware, John (c. 1845–1905), 156–57

Wars of Religion, 67

wayfinding: digital tools and, 51, 158; Indigenous place knowledge and, 18, 26, 30, 36–37, 119, 158, signs and, 166, 175, 200

we, use of collective noun, 3–4

Wendake, Wendat name for their land, 66, 84–86

Wendat, peoples, aka Hurons, 7, 8, 109, 121; name in French, 66; naming practices, 66, 83–85, 125; naming Lake Ontario, 125, 188

Western University, renaming of, 175–76, 177

Wetaskiwin, Alberta, 133–34, *134*

white patriarchy and supremacy, 6, 11, 75, 78, 163, 173, 204

Windsor, place name, 12–13

wine, locales, 166–67

Winnipeg, 127

Wolastoqiyik people, 186–87

Wolostoq (friendship collars), 136

women: bodies and landscape, 90–92, 93; derogatory naming (*see* derogatory naming, about female anatomy); as symbols, 98–102

World War I, 143, 145, 146, 160

World War II, 144, 146, 152, 160, 167

Index   251